What Else But Love?

What Else But Love?

The Ordeal of Race in
Faulkner and Morrison

Philip M. Weinstein

Columbia University Press
New York

Columbia University Press
Publishers Since 1893
New York   Chichester, West Sussex
Copyright © 1996 Columbia University Press

Library of Congress Cataloging-in-Publication Data
Weinstein, Philip M.
    What else but love? : the ordeal of race in Faulkner and Morrison
/ Philip M. Weinstein.
        p.   cm.
    Includes bibliographical references (p. 221) and index.
    ISBN 0–231–10276–3 (cloth). — ISBN 0–231–10275–5 (pbk.)
    1. Faulkner, William, 1897–1962—Political and social views.
2. Literature and society—United States—History—20th century.
3. Women and literature—United States—History—20th century.
4. American fiction—20th century—History and criticism.
5. Morrison, Toni—Political and social views.   6. Race relations in
literature.   7. Afro-Americans in literature.   8. Authorship—Sex
differences.   9. Race in literature.   I. Title.
PS3511.A86Z98553   1996   96–17153

∞

Casebound editions of Columbia University Press books are printed on permanent
and durable acid-free paper.

Printed in the United States of America
c 10 9 8 7 6 5 4 3 2 1
p 10 9 8 7 6 5 4 3 2 1

For Mother and in memory of Vannie

"What good is a man's life if he can't even choose what to die for? . . . It *is* about love. What else but love? Can't I love what I criticize?"

—Toni Morrison, *Song of Solomon*

That was why it did not matter to either of them which one did the talking, since it was not the talking alone which did it, performed and accomplished the overpassing, but some happy marriage of speaking and hearing wherein each before the demand, the requirement, forgave condoned and forgot the faulting of the other . . . in order to overpass to love, where there might be paradox and inconsistency but nothing fault nor false.

—William Faulkner, *Absalom, Absalom!*

To *understand* . . . a man must *stand under.*

—*The Autobiography of Frederick Douglass*

Contents

Acknowledgments

Since this book enacts, in a number of ways, my return home, I begin with my unpayable debt to the two women from the South who helped me grow up: Rose Weinstein and Van Price. Their gift to me, like other gifts that matter most, was made unself-consciously and day by day—a sustained act of generosity I have been drawing on for the better part of a lifetime.

With respect to professional acknowledgments, the Faulkner portion of chapter 2 appeared in separate form in the *Faulkner Journal*, 10.2 (1995): 36–69. In addition, a different version of " 'Mister': The Drama of Black Manhood in Faulkner and Morrison" was delivered at the Faulkner and Yoknapatawpha Conference of 1994.

I am grateful to Random House and to Curtis Brown, London, for permission to quote from *Light in August* (copyright 1932 and renewed 1959 by William Faulkner), *Absalom, Absalom!* (copyright 1936 and renewed 1964 by Estelle Faulkner and Jill Faulkner Summers), *The Unvanquished* (copyright 1934, 1935, 1936, 1938 by William Faulkner, renewed 1961, 1962 by William Faulkner, renewed 1964, 1965 by Estelle Faulkner and Jill Faulkner Summers), and *Go Down, Moses* (copyright 1942 by William Faulkner). I am grateful as well to Toni Morrison and to International Creative Management for permission to quote from *The Bluest Eye* (copyright 1970 by Toni Morrison), *Sula* (copyright 1973 by Toni Morrison), *Song of Solomon* (copyright 1977 by Toni Morrison), *Tar Baby* (copyright 1981 by Toni Morrison), *Beloved* (copyright 1987 by Toni Morrison), and *Jazz* (copyright 1992 by Toni Morrison).

Swarthmore College attracts every year the students whose intellectual energies keep the questions of this book alive, contentious, in process. More specifically, the George Becker Fellowship awarded by the college in

1994–1995 allowed me to develop, refine, and complete this study. I am increasingly aware that few home institutions foster the growth of its faculty as mine does.

I am grateful to Ellen Pifer for inviting me to lecture on Faulkner and Morrison at the University of Maryland in the spring of 1994. Donald Kartiganer and Ann Abadie of the University of Mississippi encouraged my work by inviting me to deliver the essay on "Mister" and the drama of black manhood at the Faulkner and Yoknapatawpha Conference in August 1994. The University of California at Berkeley Department of English kindly offered me, as a visiting research scholar, university library privileges during the fall of 1994. To Carolyn Porter and Charles Altieri I am especially indebted for the opportunity at that time to rehearse in a number of forums — an American Literature Association panel at Cabo San Lucas, a Berkeley lecture, an ongoing series of lively discussions — the germinal ideas of this book. The following spring, Pierre-Yves Petillon at the Ecole Normale Supérieure in Paris and Robert Rehder at the University of Fribourg in Switzerland aided my project by inviting me to lecture on Faulkner and Morrison.

I have been lucky in the quality of attention that different readers have bestowed on my work-in-progress. Carl Bradley and John McIntosh — neither a professional critic, both passionate readers — gave hours of their time to test my argument and to think about the understanding of race that it proposes. Professional colleagues were no less generous: Karla Holloway, Cheryl Lester, John Matthews, and Warwick Wadlington scrutinized my text page by page, entering into its premises and proposing a wealth of critical and sympathetic suggestions. And Minrose Gwin, in a full and judicious reading of the manuscript, Patricia Yaeger, in an invaluable thirty-minute phone call, and the anonymous black reader for Columbia University Press, in an endorsement of this project that nevertheless identified its vulnerability, all helped me to deepen my understanding by revisiting my assumptions and thus to move from draft to book.

The move from draft to book is hedged with other hazards as well, and here, too, I have had good fortune. Jennifer Crewe, of Columbia University Press, was unwavering in her support of this project long before it became a book. In addition, the sympathetic and expert advice I received from Columbia's copyeditor, Jan McInroy, transformed the chore of mere correction into the drama of genuine reseeing. Further, I am grateful to Kathy Vanderhook, Swarthmore College Class of 1997, for taking on much of the work involved in preparing the book's index.

My twin brother, Arnold, shares with me a commitment to these two writers and (in every sense) a kindred experience of growing up in the South. Without his "rememories" and his meditation on them, I could not have reconstructed the autobiographical materials in the first chapter. Likewise, Rose Weinstein's enduring love for Van Price enabled her to recall pertinent details about Vannie's employment as well as to put me in touch with Vannie's family who live outside of Memphis. Hattie Mae Bond, Van (Nelson) Price's sister, was kindness itself when (in late 1994) I met her in Somerville, Tennessee, twenty-three years after Vannie's death; she provided indispensable information about three generations of the Nelson family.

Finally, my wife, Penny, has accommodated the genesis and midwived the delivery of each of my books in ways that exceed telling. As Morrison's Sixo puts it in a different context, "She is a friend of my mind. The pieces I am, she gather them and give them back to me in the right order." She is an animating presence in whatever order these pieces may possess.

Note on Texts and Abbreviations

In this study, citations from Faulkner's texts refer, where possible, to the Library of America Edition (New York, 1985–). Thus far, three Faulkner volumes—the novels from 1930 to 1935, the novels from 1936 to 1940, and the novels from 1942 to 1954—have been published. Citations from *The Sound and the Fury* refer to the Norton Revised Critical Edition (1994).

Citations from Morrison's texts refer to the following editions:

Beloved, 1987 (New York: NAL Penguin, Plume, 1988)
The Bluest Eye, 1970 (New York: Penguin, Plume, 1994)
Jazz, 1992 (New York: Penguin, Plume, 1993)
Playing in the Dark, 1992 (New York: Random House, 1993)
Song of Solomon, 1977 (New York: Penguin, Plume, 1987)
Sula, 1973 (New York: NAL Penguin, Plume, 1982)
Tar Baby, 1981 (New York: Penguin, Plume, 1982)

For reasons of practicality, I use throughout the study the following abbreviations:

AA	*Absalom, Absalom!*
AILD	*As I Lay Dying*
CS	*Collected Stories*
FU	*Faulkner in the University*
GDM	*Go Down, Moses and Other Stories*
ID	*Intruder in the Dust*
LA	*Light in August*
RN	*Requiem for a Nun*

SF   *The Sound and the Fury*
U   *The Unvanquished*

B   *Beloved*
J   *Jazz*
PD   *Playing in the Dark*
S   *Sula*
SS   *Song of Solomon*
TB   *Tar Baby*
TBE   *The Bluest Eye*
TM   *Toni Morrison: Critical Perspectives*

Introduction

"What else but love?" Guitar makes this answer to Milkman (in Morrison's *Song of Solomon*), when he identifies the emotion that fuels the most deliberate action he is capable of : racial revenge. "What good is a man's life if he can't even choose what to die for?" (223). Later in the same novel, watching a captured and killed bobcat undergo rhythmic evisceration in a scene almost unbearably devoted to the rehearsal of death, Milkman replays in his mind that same phrase seven times—a phrase that seems to identify a fundamental racial dynamic that he has come to understand. As title of my book, it touches down upon a bedrock dimension of race relations, and I want the reader to hear it in a number of senses.

First, there is the immediate context of love under pressure. How can love guide a politics of racial violence, Milkman asks his friend, and the answer comes back that it must: what else could justify that violence, give it a human shape? We hear in the phrase the counterreality of racial grief and retaliation, of love cohabiting with murder and hate. "The Ordeal of Race" is a necessary subtitle of my book. Centuries of racial turmoil in this country make any focus on love, perforce, more than half ironic. So much else than love shapes the ways in which black and white Americans experience their own and others' racial identity. Race is not mainly lived as an ordeal—the most cursory reading of Morrison's *Sula* makes this clear—but there is no good in denying the larger national failure embodied in black-white relations. Slavery and its aftermath remain the disaster coiled at the core of American history. Faulkner and Morrison are among our greatest writers for understanding this disaster.

Among our greatest not least because they register the mix of love and hate that seethes through the American experience of race relations. White abuse, prejudice, and guilt; black suffering, humiliation, and dereliction—these realities course through the pages of both writers, and however splendidly they may be overcome, they are rarely forgotten. Both writers acknowledge the full spectrum of racial damage—*Absalom, Absalom!* and *Beloved* are perhaps our two most compelling tragedies of race—yet they do so, I want to argue, out of love. Not that love is all-comprehending. No love is without its blindness, and the love that moves across the membrane of race is one that sees much by missing more. Love balked or limited, love imagined, love misguided or made impossible: love emerges in their work as the most precious resource wasted, the only resource finally useful, in the confronting and telling of American race relations.

Finally, I draw on the phrase to acknowledge a personal blindness. Born and bred in the South, liberal ever since I was old enough to understand the term, I seek to register in this book a bit of my own racial innocence lived through and later decoded. Despite my efforts, decoding does not serenely mean discarding. I accept, in advance, that a margin (maybe a large one) of innocence—which is not an innocent term in this book—continues to operate in these pages and will be as blatant to some readers as it remains invisible to me. On some issues it is impossible to be right, and race in America is one of them. But silence would be more wrong than speech. I have a debt to acknowledge that outweighs rectitude. Although this is a book essentially about Faulkner and Morrison, I have tried, occasionally, to make pertinent my own investment in their representation of race.

My own investment: but there will be readers for whom my positioning as white and male partially or entirely discredits this project. "I believe we must concede that a white critic is differently invested in Afro-American texts than a black critic," Michael Awkward writes in "Negotiations of Power" (583), basing his claim on the white critic's lack of experience of racial oppression. I might qualify Awkward's implication that the black experience of oppression is somehow uniformly shared, but I assent to his claim of difference and indeed base my own work upon it. This book is, without question but not unquestioningly, a white male's reflection upon Morrison. At the heart of my project is a desire to recognize the role played by race and gender positioning in the making and receiving of literature, and that role is considerable.[1] "Eurocentric literary critics—more versed in Faulkner than Black folk culture, in New Criticism than cultural criticism": thus Gay Wilentz (white herself) describes white scholars in "Civilizations Underneath" (62), and though we've never met, she is talking about me. I come to this project as a former New Critic, a participant in the theory-laden practice of the past two decades, and a continuing Faulknerian—orientations that leave their trace, for better and worse, on how I go about the activity of reading. Without that investment in Faulkner I would have lacked my angle of entry into Morrison's work; without a subsequent investment in Morrison I would have lacked a new understanding of Faulkner.

What besides my interest in both of them justifies this pairing? There is a willfulness in any yoking of writers, not to speak of the host of binary temptations that attach to the consideration of a *pair*. It is hard not to oppose them. Since my aim is to argue both for and against differences in their practice that are shaped by racial positioning, oppositional claims are at once necessary and dangerous. I have preferred to press a difference too far rather than let it remain unnoticed, but I will have failed altogether if a reader comes away from these pages with his or her prejudices reinforced.

An immediate reason for pairing them (which risks sounding vulgar) is that each is a widely celebrated American writer. Both have won the Nobel Prize (Faulkner in 1949, Morrison in 1993). Neither is "easy" (as many readers have discovered to their discomfort), yet the texts of both have found their way into innumerable American households and libraries. For a study that seeks to reach more than a professional audience, it is useful to deal with figures that many have heard of—and often have read—if I am to succeed in persuading my reader to reconsider each writer's practice and, more broadly, to rethink the meanings of race and gender.

Second, and more significant, they are both major novelists of racial turmoil. Faulkner's predilection was from the beginning for tragedy, but only in his race-infused narratives does the tragic impulse attain its furthest implication. Morrison has less opportunity than Faulkner to avoid the materials of racial impasse, and in any event her greatest talents are released by the possibilities of this topic. In part 3 I pursue a couple of her specific encounters with earlier Faulknerian texts, but I am not concerned with questions of influence. Rather, I choose these two novelists because each is extraordinarily invested in imagining American racial dynamics, and—equally important—because each is a supreme writer. Their texts sing, refusing conventional novelistic paths and instead overwhelming the reader with formal experiment, with sequences that range from the flight of lyricism to the gravity of tragic insight—in a word, with writerly authority. What they sing is the drama of the subject in culture: the ways in which individuals live out their passional and reflective lives in relation (both enabling and deforming) to cultural norms.[2]

The subject in culture is, in the pages of this book, the individual marked by both race and gender. These are not the only ways in which culture proposes the materials out of which identity is made, but they are major ways. We become who we are through our unpredictable negotiation with our society's racial and gender norms. This is a truth applicable to writers, characters, and readers, and I seek throughout to make the most of it. Faulkner as white male, Morrison as black female: how do these dimensions of their writerly identity position them differently, disposing them toward their characteristic novelistic moves? Each chapter of my book stages an encounter of the two writers' fictional practice designed to highlight differences attributable to this positioning. My project is to identify ways in which race and gender "speak" in Faulkner and Morrison without reducing or deforming the specificity of their achievement.[3]

If addressed acutely enough, the practice of Faulkner and Morrison sheds light on the remarkable range of resources available for understanding the other, and on the stunning biases that limit that understanding. All seeing is perspectival; no one sees all. Indeed, Morrison's *Playing in the Dark* explores acutely the ways in which, "in the wholly racialized society that is the United States" (*PD*, xii), white writers unknowingly project upon blackness their own disowned fears and desires: "The subject of the dream is the dreamer" (17). Yet Morrison knows as well that, for the novelist, entry into the other is mandatory: "Imagining is not merely looking or looking at . . . It is, for the purposes of the work, *becoming*" (4).

We might open up this tension between "projecting" and "becoming" by turning to a widespread current term for white-projected constructions of the other: Edward Said's *Orientalism*. *Orientalism* says little about Orientals and much about the elaborate nineteenth- and twentieth-century Eurocentric discourse used to conceptualize the Orient. Said's argument about Orientalism—"in which each particle of the Orient told of its Orientalness, so much so that the attribute of being Oriental overrode any countervailing instance" (231)—seems to be in the background of Morrison's exploration of white-projected "Africanism." "I am using the term 'Africanism,'" she writes, "not to suggest the larger body of knowledge on Africa . . . nor to suggest the varieties and complexities of African people and their descendants who have inhabited this country. Rather I use it as a term for the denotative and connotative blackness that African people have come to signify, as well as the entire range of views, assumptions, readings, and misreadings that accompany Eurocentric learning about these people" (PD, 6–7). Morrison succeeds in disclosing a set of essentializing alien tropes for figuring blackness—for defining and manipulating it in the service of producing (as its counterpart) whiteness—through a number of white American texts. More, this critical stance allows her to reveal the shadowy, inertial presence of blackness even in those texts where its presence is denied.

Although *Playing in the Dark* oscillates, in theory, between "projecting" and "becoming," it leaves unexplored the latter dynamic. I seek in this book to make good on that omission, by examining the ways in which writings that cross the membrane of race may be simultaneously projective and identificatory. Faulkner and Morrison, I argue, access the realm of the racial other between the extreme poles of self-projection and becoming the other, an activity fraught with danger and possibility. A major aim of this study is to generate sympathy for the richness of such seeing (what I later call "relational seeing") in the work of both writers.

If positioned seeing is precious, it is also intrinsically problematic, and I am not here interested in the hagiography that might attach to the fantasy of a writer's perfected vision. The point is worth making because two pitfalls immediately appear on the horizon, both of them disabling. One might (quaintly) seek to show how Morrison tries but cannot quite match Faulkner's achievement. Or one might (shrewdly) seek to show how Morrison writes her way out of (sees her way beyond) the impasses of race and gender within which we now find Faulkner's work constantly embattled. I am old enough to find the first pitfall attractive and young enough to find the second one even more so. I can only trust that my exposure to the first keeps me from succumbing excessively to the second.

It is necessary to proceed with utmost caution when talking about race and gender. I begin by assenting to two polar claims by contemporary black scholars. The first is from Henry Louis Gates, in "Dis and Dat": "No poet, ultimately, knows more than 'race.' " The second is from Kwame Anthony Appiah's *In My Father's House*: "The truth is that there are no races" (45).[4] How can these claims accommodate each other? The answer is, only by an understanding of race as a culturally constructed position—premised on no significant biological base—yet one that, however contingent, shapes the indi vidual's life experience in a number of ideological ways. Gates is arguing that to grow up black does not foreclose the kind of identity one will take on—note that *race* is put in quotes—but it does determine that that identity will be black-inflected and that one's subsequent knowledge will register, however indirectly, the pressure of that inflection. Only the most willful insistence on our sovereign right to become whoever we wish—a fantasy (usually white and male) of the first order—could have obscured from us the fact that the conditions into which we are born must be, not our fate, but surely (at the risk of being tautological) our *conditions*.

Appiah, drawing on late-twentieth-century biological research, claims that the genetic significance of race as a determinant of temperament, belief, or intention, is virtually nonexistent. He argues, after a scrutiny of the scientific data, that "the chances . . . that two people taken at random from the human population will have the same [gene-based] characteristic at a random locus are about 85.2%, while the chances for two (white) people taken from the population of England are about 85.7%" (36). A pair from the most homogeneous population and a pair from the most random one: the probable genetic differential between these two pairs comes to no more than 0.5 percent, hardly enough to support a racist argument:

> In a sense, trying to classify people into a few races is like trying to classify books in a library: you may use a single property—size, say—but you will get a useless classification, or you may use a more complex system of interconnected criteria, and then you will get a good deal of arbitrariness. No one—not even the most compulsive librarian!—thinks that book classifications reflect deep facts about books. . . . And nobody thinks that a library classification can settle which books we should value.   (39)

Appiah concludes: "The truth is that there are no races: there is nothing in the world that can do all we ask race to do for us" (45).

Race as unreal, race as primary reality: this makes sense not as biology but as culture. Identity formation is inseparable from the absorption, refusal, and reaccenting of the subject roles that make up our culture's repertory for ways of being. We are engaged (on a scale moving from conscious choice to all-but-unconscious coercion) in drawing from this repertory and in treating such roles as mirrors in which to recognize ourselves, as we go about the never innocent business of negotiating identity, becoming white and black, men and women. With this background I now reach the point where the greatest care of all is required. *The ways in which we take on race and gender identity are radically unforeclosed.* We express these socially proposed components of ourselves with such individual accenting that no prejudging—no prejudice—can account for us on these bases. From this precious truth flows, in recoil, the entire argument of transcendent individualism: no group orientation can possibly predict us. The purpose of this book is to go in the other direction: to return to the shaping power of racial and gender positioning, without falling into reductive clichés about a writer's/character's/reader's racial or gender identity.[5] These impersonal alignments, I shall argue, bring both resource and limitation to the lineaments of individual identity. They enable and delimit, as culture more largely enables and delimits. I seek throughout this study to understand the roles of race and gender as neither the pernicious other of some mythically pure individuality nor the true social core of an illusory individuality that we ought therefore simply to dismantle.

The opposition between individual and group identity that I just characterized has exerted a considerable hold in the humanities. An entire aesthetics (based often on Kant and flourishing in the New Criticism of the mid-twentieth century) has fetishized the work of art as supremely achieved, individual, and disinterested. Such a work of art was said to appeal universally (it was undeformed by group biases) and to enact the artist's heroic individuality. While this aesthetic model may vaguely operate in the general public's notion of masterpieces, it ceased some time ago to command assent within the academy itself. University scholars are at greater risk of going altogether in the opposite direction: of dissolving individuality within the group orientations from which it arises. Faulkner disappears into his white maleness, Morrison into her black femaleness. Since all texts are interested and speak both from and to the orientations of race and gender that enable them, the argument runs, no text possesses transcendent value or universal appeal. This is, in a word, the entry of identity politics into the literary field, and if it didn't circulate around a germ of insight it would be less disturbing. Group orientations *do* contribute indispensably to artistic identity and expression—but not in such a way as to dissolve individuality or to reduce the value of a writer's utterance to the groups with which the writer affiliates.

This is a study devoted, then, to the individual power of Faulkner's and Morrison's practice and at the same time to disengaging the major role that race and gender play in shaping that practice: race and gender as neither biologically given nor settled once and for all, but as differential social positions that entail differential experiences and from which significantly divergent insights and procedures become available. In other words, I attend to race and gender as cultural resources (repertories of normative stances) that individuals draw on in their struggle for coherent identity—not that this process is always benign, but it is equally fruitless to regard it as always disabling. Out of what materials would we stitch the thoughts and feelings that we grow to recognize (reflexively) as the lineaments of selfhood, if not the materials provided by our cultural inheritance? The value of a writer's work, I wish to argue in these pages, inheres in the imaginative and contestatory ways in which he or she formally exploits this inheritance, not in some godlike transcendence of it. Imaginative and contestatory: the formal energy of great texts seeks both to make the most of, and to see around, the framework of the writer's own orientations—reaching toward the other in ways that reveal not merely the one who sees, and not certainly the one who is seen, but (most powerfully) a true *relation* between the one and the other, the seer and the seen.

It is time to speak more specifically of the analyses conducted here. I discovered, more than halfway through the writing of the book, that I was engaged in a developmental study in several senses. From the beginning I was committed to understanding the development of each writer's corpus, to charting the genetic history of their imaginations as this may be inferred from text to text. This mapping may be done in many ways, however, and I realized while writing that I kept attending to the same way: focusing on how Faulkner and Morrison represent the drama of human development itself. In their works, what do black and white, male and female children inherit from their parents? How do both writers understand mothering and fathering, as these activities are (and are not) race-inflected? Given the inheritances available to them, how do Faulkner's and Morrison's black and white boys and girls become men and women of their respective races? To pursue these questions, I have devoted separate chapters to the dramas of mothering, fathering, and inheriting. In working through this material, I have come gradually to believe that these dramas in Faulkner circulate around the failure of a (white, male) patriarchal model of cultural descent, whereas in Morrison's work they involve an increasingly decisive refusal of that model. Finally, though, and deeper perhaps than these differences, the fundamental human drama of development itself underwrites the black and white versions explored in these pages. I seek, in unfolding this drama, to avoid the pieties of a universalizing blindness (in which cultural difference disappears), but I seek equally to reveal an underlying set of conflicts and challenges that convey something of the dignity of human struggle within and across racial divides.

Two other developmental histories emerged as I continued to explore my writers. One might be called the history of race relations in America, which I have abbreviated to three major stages: slavery, segregation, and the civil rights activity of the 1950s and 1960s. I refrain from attending to more recent history, but it seemed important to recognize the differences of thought, feeling, and behavior that attach to these earlier periods. Finally, I began to see the pertinence of where I myself came in—the period of segregation in the midSouth of the 1940s—and I realized that I had to begin this study not with slavery but with its sequel, segregation. This is the period into which both Faulkner and Morrison were born as well. It serves as the beginning from which, in time, they learn to recognize and understand the beginning further back, the germinal nightmare of American slavery.

This book is organized, then, as follows. Part 1 explores beginnings, and it understands these in terms both personal and historical. I open with a study of mammies, maids, and mothers in both writers' work (in my own life and Faulkner's life as well), and I then turn to the historical beginning that is slavery. How do Faulkner and Morrison imagine this institution as their careers continue to unfold? What different stories of modern America are they implicitly writing as they find narrative form for this historical disaster? Part 2 moves to the realm of the male—the territory traditionally associated with culture—in two related ways. It first inquires into the ordeal of black manhood as this must be negotiated within a society that denied to black men the perquisites on which (white, male) American identity has been constructed: the inheritances of property, propriety, and a sense of the proper. Thereafter the analysis considers the phenomenon of fathering itself—white and black—in both writers. What is a father? What does he bequeath to his offspring? These questions receive different answers according to the racial positioning of the subjects represented and of the writer doing the representing, answers that—taken together—bring into focus the crisis of the larger patriarchal drama enacted in the institution of fathering. Faulkner stages the failure—and Morrison the race and gender exclusiveness—of the patriarchal pact: the dysfunction at the heart of the passage from (white) father to (white) son of those legacies meant to keep the social structure of power and propriety intact.

The chapters of part 1 and part 2 attempt synoptic readings as they move from text to text in pursuit of an oeuvre's emerging stance toward the issues identified above. Part 3 proceeds in a different manner, intent upon specific and "slow-motion" comparisons. What has Morrison taken from Faulkner, and in the taking made her own? I pursue this question in two pairings—Go

Down, Moses and *Song of Solomon,* followed by *Absalom, Absalom!* and *Jazz*—and again I seek to disengage, from minute verbal practices, the role played by each writer's racial and gender positioning. Part 3 then concludes with the most sustained comparison in this book: the different ways in which *Light in August* and *Beloved* deliver their writers' characteristic understanding of racial turmoil in America.

Who is this book for? This question points in several directions and has vexed me no end. At one level it asks, Is my study written for white and black, male and female readers? My first answer is yes, all of the above, for my deepest aim is—by acknowledging some of the differences in artistic practice occasioned by race and gender positioning—to participate in the work of bridging (not erasing) those differences, helping the races and genders to speak to each other across them. Yet even as I write toward female and black readers, I write from a white male orientation—one that I seek to make as accommodating and self-aware as possible.

At another level the question asks, What preparation and interests does this study assume in its audience? Here, too, the answer is not simple, inasmuch as my academic training disposes me toward one readership while my predilection proposes another. Following a theory-laden study of Faulkner meant to be savored best by experts, this study of race and gender in the work of two major writers neither abandons that audience nor is willing to forgo another, larger audience. I would like (perhaps impossibly) to make sense to professional colleagues and to literate friends. There are thousands of readers of these two novelists, thousands more interested in race and gender as they emerge in literature. These concerns—the ways in which two remarkable writers (white male and black female) represent self and other, the kinds of story they tell when they imagine self and other—matter to more than a professional audience.

The issue of audience, however far-reaching the intellectual stakes, poses some immediate questions of practical procedure. Does one assume that one's reader has read Faulkner's and Morrison's oeuvre more than once, along with a good deal of theoretically informed scholarship (the professional audience of experts in one's field, alert to the current discourse on these writers, an audience for whom certain questions are pressing, others outmoded)? Or that one's reader has read a fair number of Faulkner's and Morrison's novels once and has a modest familiarity with the critical literature (the larger university audience of colleagues in literature or cognate fields, of enterprising students—graduate and undergraduate—coming to grips with their texts)? Or that one's reader has read perhaps a work or two of both writers, has little familiarity with secondary materials, but is interested in the representation of race and gender in American culture (the largest public of sophisticated general readers, often university-trained but not members of the academy and not especially committed to either Faulkner or Morrison)?

I have sought continuously to make sense to that larger second audience, yet kept the questions and orientations of the first audience in my mind throughout. I have tried, as well—and this has been the hard part—to reach some of that amorphous third audience.[6] This means keeping jargon to a minimum and not assuming automatically that my reader has read the book I am discussing (let alone current commentary on that book). But it also means that, however broad the questions raised about race and gender, I am always talking about the practice of two difficult writers. A reader uninterested in their novels—in the ways in which race and gender become textualized, take on narrative forms—is not going to find this book rewarding.

The critical model propelling the more than two hundred pages of argument that make up this book surfaces recurrently throughout the study, most saliently in the last chapter. But I owe a prospective reader an abbreviated description of the core convictions motivating my work. First, then, this is a book committed to the drama of identity formation. I understand this drama to be suffused in the ideological resources that a culture makes available to its subjects in process of becoming themselves. *Ideology* (as I use the term) does not mean false consciousness or error; it is not a set of weightless illusions. Rather, it refers to the set of normative beliefs and practices that a culture (and groups within a culture) make available for individuals to draw on as they strive to achieve interior coherence. Selfhood is enacted through engagement with socially proffered materials. We are, as the Marxist philosopher Althusser puts it, *interpellated*—summoned, called—by social roles, pressed to recognize ourselves *as* ourselves in the mirror provided by such roles.

It is less a question of seeing these alignments as false than of noting that the ones we draw on (whenever they function smoothly for us) tend to appear to be naturally, inclusively true. (Ideology reserves its own name for its other, never for itself.) Yet the truths of an ideological alignment are exclusive, dependent on a certain group's practices and interests, resistant toward other groups' kindred practices and interests. Issues of dominance and marginality saturate the field of ideological alignments, each group drawing on its own power (even when that power is limited, hedged in by greater power) to propose truth and norm. In this study, the group paradigms in question are those by which whites and blacks, men and women, secure racial and gender identity.

The activating of group orientations to achieve selfhood occurs within authors, characters, and readers. Rather than godlike creators disinterestedly in possession of their materials, writers are enmeshed in ideology, even as those we think of as great exceed ideological predictability, often inviting (and always permitting) their ideological alignments to come under scrutiny. They are, however creative, also creatures of their own race and gender identities, a creatureliness that operates as both resource and limitation. This study understands the impress of Faulkner's and Morrison's race and gender identities upon their practice as, precisely, both resource and limitation.

I return to the idea of interpellation. Human inventiveness arises from the fact that we, alone among the members of the animal kingdom, wear our identities provisionally. They are open to further interpellation. The other animals so swiftly become what they are that they never wonder—as all humans do sometimes and some humans do all the time—who they are. We lack the instinctual component that would impose identity once and for all. This is why Freud calls the human being "das kranke Tier"—the sick animal, the one in search of him/herself. Literature is one of the resources we draw on in that search. For this reason I have so focused on the strategies (not always conscious) that a specific text employs for reaching and shaping its reader. This interactive commerce is why reading matters, why these two writers' ways of representing race and gender can enlarge our own repertory of roles for understanding race and gender as precious, unstable, and alterable dimensions of identity itself.

I would close this introduction on two notes. The first has to do with candor. As Dominick LaCapra admits in *The Bounds of Race*, "It is at present virtually impossible to write or say anything on the topic of race that is not in some way objectionable or embarrassing" (2). This is so because to speak openly of race is to speak, too vulnerably for comfort (whatever the attempt at detachment), about a part of one's own and one's audience's selfhood. More, as I increasingly realize, whenever one speaks of race one is not only in ideology—a normal phenomenon—but one *knows* one is in ideology: an objectionable and embarrassing one. This is the rub: our awareness that we are speaking (at the same time) our apparently unmediated selfhood and our obviously mediated acculturation into that selfhood. Yet what value can this book have without candor? I have tried not to ignore others' differences, and I hope I have learned something about the appalling extent of (white, male) innocence, its artful capacity to remain unaware of its own privilege. But correctness would surely be more damaging.

This book aims—through literary criticism—to contribute to the ways in which blacks and whites, women and men, may understand each other. What sorts of narrative do two writers differing in race and gender assign to the telling of race and gender? What value attaches to these imaginings of the other? Faulkner and Morrison are my writers, and though I do not wish to draft them to support arguments alien to the tendencies of their own work, I do want to use their practice to probe the larger culture's capacity for racial and gender understanding. Such an inquiry implicates the writer probing as well as the writers being probed. To consider the literary event as involving the several histories of character, writer, reader, and the cultures producing each—to envisage a theater in which we are both actors and acted upon, in which public and private are necessarily faces of each other—is to justify, I believe, beginning this book on Faulkner and Morrison with a segment of my own history.

The final note, then, has to do with Vannie. I was, in large measure, brought up by a black woman named Van Price. I have never ceased to love her, but it is only in the last few years—thanks to the grace and pain of inter-pellation, our capacity to revisit our lives through other lenses and see other things—that I have come to understand something of the complexity of that love—more precisely, have come to learn how much I did not understand during the years I (thought I) knew her. My decision to write about Vannie commits me to territory unamenable to secure knowledge. In pursuing it I court not only the charge of self-indulgence but a renewed misunderstanding of the very person I would understand better. As the black reader for Columbia University Press generously put it, "How much more difficult it is to read the narrative of one's life than any text one can hold in one's hands." Nowhere is the peril of white reading black and reading it wrong greater than in this brief attempt to revisit a formative experience I lived through many years ago. "Had I not been obligated to continue reading, I am not sure I would have," that Columbia reader candidly wrote. I have benefited from her candor by rethinking that childhood relation again and yet again. My need to map it remains unavoidable: without Van Price there would have been no interracial love to acknowledge, no book to write. What else but love could be at once so perceptive in its blindness, so blind in its perception?

PART 1

Beginnings

Two kinds of beginnings are here under consideration. The first opens as an exploration of personal histories, my own and then Faulkner's, before attending to Faulkner's and Morrison's fiction. The second seeks to understand two writers' ways of representing a formative historical institution, American slavery. In neither discussion do I pretend to access a pure beginning, but both involve foundational periods from which significant consequences proceeded, still proceed. Each beginning yields a map in which the pressure of race (and, secondarily, gender) upon Faulkner's and Morrison's fiction can be made salient. The two chapters in this section carry out this analysis quite differently, serving as opposing weights to each other.

Chapter 1 begins in the mid-twentieth century, discussing a period between 1940 and 1958; slavery had ended almost a century earlier. During that period, as most informed Americans know, whites continued daily to impose upon blacks a systemic injustice, effected by an entire network of segregated institutions "justified" by the 1896 *Plessy v. Ferguson* doctrine of "separate but equal rights."[1] This is the time of my own Memphis beginnings, and though I was not explicitly informed about segregation, I lived its repercussions nevertheless. So I open this book on my childhood experience of white/black relations, an experience steeped in innocence, unaware of (though no less engaged in) my Southern culture's ideological arrangements. It is important to recapture something of the texture of that innocence, to sift through it rather than merely indict it (to see that ideology proposes ways of living, not merely ways of being right or wrong), though I can access this period of my life only through the critical prisms that came after.[2] After speculating on what two Southern whites (myself and Faulkner) could know of blacks during a time of white supremacy—and how Faulkner could represent them—I go on to consider how a black woman writer thirty-four years younger than Faulkner and nine years older than me, Toni Morrison, revisits many of the same racial topics. The chapter turns, accordingly, from the role of the mammy in Faulkner to the relation (in both writers' work) between black maids and mothers white and black.

In chapter 2 I move back in time to historical beginnings, past the personal experience of any of us (Faulkner, Morrison, me, my readers), and seek to assess how these two writers have chosen to represent—have come to imaginative terms with, found an acceptable story for—the institutional reality and repercussions of slavery. But I wish to postpone critical analysis of that earlier period until I have first set the stage for my own—and, I argue, Faulkner's—dawning awareness of its significance.

How did whites in the early twentieth-century South first encounter the realities of race and gender? For many white middle-class children, those realities were twinned—the inseparable experience of the black mammy and the white mother—and together they served as crucial determinants of early subjectivity itself. I begin, then, by exploring the initial encounter with race and gender in the separate domains of my own life and Faulkner's, as this encounter may have affected both his representational practices and my response to them. Finally, in turning to Morrison's richly contrastive treatment of these figures outside the lens of a Southern white male imaginary, my aim is not to propose Morrison's work as a triumphant address to Faulkner's racial and gender problematics. I want to respect the different positions enabling each writer's work, within an argument that makes its claims outside the registers of praise or blame.

Literary criticism usually deals with represented mothers and mammies more detachedly, as impersonal figures upon a writer's canvas. But the beginnings I am charting go beyond the representation of characters. Assessing the ways these writers critically and uncritically inhabit a culture—the stances and resources they draw on in the act of creation—has provoked a reflection upon how I myself (a white Southerner born in Memphis in 1940) learned to inhabit my culture. I seek to draw on my history in ways that are personal without being indulgent—to understand my own subjective trajectory as simultaneously an engagement with my culture's ideological norms of race and gender. "Simultaneously" because the shaping of personal identity is incomprehensible apart from an accepting, reaccenting, and refusing of various subject roles made available by the culture. Nothing could have seemed more private than Vannie's formative role in my personal becoming; in reality nothing could have been more socially proposed.

1

Personal Beginnings
Mammies and Mothers

> He seemed to kind of dissolve and a part of him turn and rush back
> through the two years they had lived there like when you pass
> through a room fast and look at all the objects in it and you turn and
> go back through the room again and look at all the objects from the
> other side and you find out you had never seen them before, rush-
> ing back through those two years and seeing a dozen things that had
> happened and he hadn't even seen them before . . .
>
> — Faulkner, *Absalom, Absalom!*

Vannie

In the beginning there was Vannie. Like other beginnings, this one took on its
resonance only after it was long past. Van Price was the black woman who
raised me and my two brothers from our earliest childhood on, until our
departure for college in the Northeast. We grew up in Memphis, where black
maids were common — even for families with moderate means, though not for
the poor — and their capacities, however appreciated, were pretty much taken
for granted within a spectrum of responses that never called the practice itself
into question. Since I have been trying recently to take such capacities less for
granted, this book begins with Vannie. It does so because my own mix of racial
ignorance and knowledge, confusion and affection, begins there.

All we knew at first was that she was present (eight or nine hours a day, six
days out of seven, and — it seemed — unfailingly when needed) and that she
cared for us physically and emotionally and unsentimentally, like a mother.
She watched, bathed, dressed, fed, advised, comforted, and scolded us. She
would move through the entire house, though her favorite room was the
kitchen. There she ironed in the afternoons, singing if alone, chatting with us
(while she worked) after we came home from school. (The clothes she ironed
she had washed earlier that morning, then taken out in a huge straw basket to
hang on the clothesline in the backyard to dry, gathering them up in the same

basket several hours later.) In the late afternoon, having got the house into the state she wanted, she would prepare dinner and set the table, usually leaving for her own home in the early evening, before we sat down to enjoy her meal.

We knew she went home each evening to a world of other people, but my images of her are of her alone—such as her putting on several layers of old family clothes (and a beat-up fraternity jacket that belonged to my older brother) before braving the cold weather to make the trip to the backyard clothesline. (In Memphis it could be as cold in April as on that Easter morning when Dilsey emerges from her cabin, dressed in motley pieces of once-elegant Compson hand-me-downs, heading across the yard for the white family's kitchen.) Vannie had a husband named Jim, but we rarely saw him. (He came now and then to pick her up, always remaining inside his car in our driveway. I don't remember his ever entering our house.) My images of her remain of her alone because, fueled by my affection and dependence, they leave room for only the two of us: Vannie the capacious object seen and me the needy subject seeing.

At times, though, my twin brother finds his way into this picture, making it a threesome. He and I had a hard time adjusting to the first grade, and when we would return from the school bus at three in the afternoon, dropped off just a block from our house, Vannie would be coming down the road to meet us, sometimes to pick one of us up in her arms. She picked us up often, to take us out of the tub once she had scrubbed us clean, but also to separate us when we fought. I especially remember her coming into our screaming bedroom one afternoon and silently picking us both up, one on each arm (she was a big woman): that effectively broke up the fight. This image stays in my mind because we had reached an age (six? seven?) when our mother was picking us up less often.

She gave us advice from the earliest days on—about respecting our parents (especially our father), about being kinder to each other, about seeing less of some friends and more of others, about not telling lies (she would wash our mouths out with soap if she caught us doing this). Five years older than my mother, she was also more determined in her views, so we often heard her "pronounce" on ethical (but never on racial) issues. Her wit was irrepressible, though (about a drunken black man who once bartended at a family party and claimed not to have touched a drop, she declared: "He sho do stagger sober"—a phrase that has taken on family immortality). As soon as we were old enough to drive our parents' car, we would regularly take Vannie to the bus stop on Highland around 6 P.M. If we arrived late and that bus had already come, we would take her all the way to Jackson (another couple of miles), where she would catch the second bus that she normally transferred to from Highland. We felt virtuous doing this but never said so.

Memphis in the 1940s and most of the 1950s was a peacefully segregated city. No blacks were visible in our neighborhood or present in our public school (though they made up 40 percent of that larger neighborhood's population). But *Brown v. Board of Education* had occurred in 1954, and during my high school years the teachers were full of racial anxiety. A chemistry teacher co-opted a full class period in order to correlate urban violence with black character. When my brother and I demurred, he asked us if we were nigger-lovers. With such encounters accumulating, it was easy in 1958 to decide (for other reasons as well) to go to the Northeast to college, and in effect neither my twin nor I has ever returned to the South.

Vannie died in April 1971. I was living in Cambridge, Massachusetts, at the time, but my twin brother had gone home for a visit, with his wife and one-month-old baby. She was taking care of the baby, putting on his tiny shoes, when my brother heard the recurrent sound of something being dropped and then dropped again. Vannie was unable to put the shoes on, unable to let this task go, unable to speak clearly. It soon became evident that she was experiencing a tremendous internal upheaval (it was later diagnosed as a cerebral hemorrhage). She went in and out of consciousness for the next fifteen minutes, and the last words she said, as the ambulance arrived, were "Put on my red shoes." She eventually lost all consciousness and died later that day in the hospital.[1]

I have been writing on Faulkner for the past twenty years (I think of Vannie every time I encounter *The Sound and the Fury*'s Dilsey), but only recently have I realized how much my way of knowing and not knowing Vannie shapes my optic not just upon Dilsey but upon Faulkner's work more generally and indeed upon the realities of race itself during the middle of the twentieth century in the South. This book comes into focus, then, as an enlarged meditation upon Vannie, for what I knew about her—however deep my attachment to her—has all along, and not accidentally, remained shrouded in a deeper ignorance. A few years ago I started to try to undo that ignorance. As I return to my opening portrait of Vannie, I see its lineaments differently, for the return recasts all the lights and shadows.

What seemed the most natural and intimate phenomenon imaginable— Vannie's continuous presence in our house—I now see as a social and public arrangement.[2] Serving as housemaids in white households was the dominant form of work that Southern black women were able to find for almost a century after the war that was supposed to liberate them had ended. Such work could be peculiarly galling for at least two reasons. First, it often repeated, within a framework slightly altered, the fate of enslaved black women. One was once again installed in the "big house," there to take on the most onerous chores. Second, one was providing not an expertise that might be charged for by the hour and that permitted a margin of independence but a presence that could be drawn on as needed, by a mistress who might be as understanding as my mother but might also be as tyrannical as she wished. It was the physical *person* that was being hired, not that person's skills. Black women had virtually no opportunity for higher education (Vannie had finished the eighth grade), and all they could often offer, within market terms, was the unskilled labor of their bodies.

Such labor was poorly paid. In 1936, the year Vannie came to work for us, we paid her three dollars a week, an amount that must have been normative at the time. She worked five and a half days a week, eventually (some twenty years later) cutting back to five days. Her wages increased to ten dollars per week in the 1940s, and at the time of her death (1971) she was being paid forty dollars per week. It is hard to see how she could have lived on this, but so long as her husband was alive he supported her with his garage business. Years later I learned that she sent almost all of her wages to her younger sister, who still lived in Somerville (where Vannie had grown up) and whose children (Vannie had none herself) those wages helped to support.

The layered clothes and fraternity jacket move me now in complex ways. On the one hand, Vannie scrupulously protected her own finer clothes (and she had stylish tastes) from the routine work of our household—a protection that has a psychic as well as a material dimension. On the other hand, she lived her life with us in a makeshift uniform that, however it might have "professionalized" her, also signaled something close to servitude; the borrowed clothes and fraternity jacket bespeak a certain alienation. These motley combinations radiated her "inscription" within our hierarchical system of clothing. She would not have been caught dead (I mean this literally) wearing such things in her own world. More, the house that seemed unconstrainedly hers was itself subdivided racially in ways that I only later understood—the kitchen her "favorite" room in the sense that the greatest amount of work to be done took place there. (Trudier Harris speaks, in *From Mammies to Militants*, of the kitchen as "the one room in the house where the white woman can give up spatial ownership without compromising herself" [15].) The meals she cooked in that room were for us alone. During the eighteen years I spent at home I never saw her eat a meal, never saw her sit down anywhere else than in the kitchen. Her husband's casual absence from our house now reads as the motivated enactment of an unstated racial code; and the fact of our driving her first to one bus stop and then (if needed) to another testifies eloquently, now, to the racial map that ensured the segregated neighborhoods of midcentury Memphis. For, as C. Vann Woodward noted in *The Strange Career of Jim Crow*, the proliferation of Jim Crow laws throughout the South underwrote (ever since the 1890s) a racial barrier extending "to virtually all forms of public transportation, to sports and recreations, to hospitals, orphanages, prisons, and asylums, and ultimately to funeral homes, morgues, and cemeteries" (8): from cradle to grave.

As Vannie's daily presence in our house made her other (her entire routine conveying her difference from us), it simultaneously made us normal.[3] Like countless middle-class white families in the urban South of the 1940s and 1950s, we demonstrated our middle-classness, in part, through our ability to hire Vannie. Indeed, the entire economy of white families with black housemaids descends, relatively undisguised, from the antebellum South, advertising, even, a tiny measure of race-based aristocratic ease almost a century after the Lost Cause was lost. With a black woman working in our house, we became (automatically, like our neighbors) members of the leisure class. And since my own family's origins were Jewish, not Christian (our nineteenth-century history was Eastern European, not American), this veneer of traditional Southern practice served us effectively. (All the more effectively for being unconscious.)

What Vannie did for me—taking care of me physically, washing and dressing and attending to me—I now see no longer as a care destined for me alone, but as a (beautifully carried out) part of her larger socially proposed and accepted role: to take care of a white family's (luckily, my family's) extended physical enterprise—our bodies, our food, our clothes, our rugs, rooms, furniture. "Having got the house into the state she wanted," I wrote above, but this was not her house, nor was the chore of cleaning it her chosen project. I shall return later in this chapter to the gratitude that Faulkner felt and expressed for his black mammy's care of himself and his household, but I can at least gesture now toward the different meaning that this arduous association with a white family's dirt might hold within the mind of a black maid herself. When Ondine (in Morrison's *Tar Baby*) finally can no longer restrain herself, she faces her dysfunctional white family, looks the helpless Margaret in the eye, and says: "I am the one who should have more respect. I'm the one who cleans up her shit!" (*TB*, 178). The work Vannie did for us for thirty-five years involved infinitely more than cleaning up our shit, but at the same time it rarely involved less.

In late 1994 my wife and I drove from Memphis to Somerville (less than an hour away) and finally met Vannie's younger sister, Hattie Mae Bond. ("I've been waiting for this visit for twenty-three years," she told us, in a tone located somewhere between anticipation and gentle upbraiding.) There, in the presence of a sibling who uncannily resembled Vannie herself, I saw the photographs of her extended family—all the images absent from my childhood sense of her. I learned that she was one of eleven children (eight of whom survived and went to the Somerville school through at least the eighth grade), that she had lived in St. Louis a number of years before coming to us in Memphis, and that she had helped to pay for the college education of Hattie Mae's four children—who had become teachers and doctors. I suddenly brought together two ideas scrupulously kept apart during my own childhood: black people and higher education.[4]

Two further vignettes remain, both resonant beyond my capacity to unpack them. "Put on my red shoes," Vannie commanded just before being taken in the ambulance to the hospital. When her brother-in-law, Reverend Brewster, asked my family about the events of Vannie's last hours, my brother supplied that detail. A couple of days later it came back amplified unforgettably, for Reverend Brewster had woven it into his funeral sermon and had inserted it into the overwhelming gospel music that the gathered group of family and friends sang in memory of Vannie. Now the red shoes were transformed into the sign of her entry into heaven, by the side of Jesus, her triumphant negotiation of this life she had endured below. I was to discover, more than twenty years after Vannie's death, that the motif of transcendent shoes figures in traditional black spirituals, and that Reverend Brewster drew on the resources of a still-living culture to make this local detail shine with prophecy. ("What kind o' shoes is dem-a you wear? . . . Dat you can walk upon de air?" the slaves had asked in an early spiritual, and the answer came loud and clear: "Dem shoes I wear am de gospel shoes . . . An' you can wear dem ef-a you choose.")[5] It took me twenty years to see that these red shoes might harbor a resonance not just personal but cultural, because up to that time I had remained more or less unaware of the extent to which blacks *had* an enabling culture.

Finally, Hattie Mae Bond showed us the photograph she had been saving for last, the one of her mother and father, Evelyn Taylor Nelson and Thomas

Nelson. Evelyn Nelson had a strong, dignified, unsmiling face; she wore a simple saronglike dress and looked about thirty-five. Thomas Nelson, some fifteen or twenty years older, was white. I stared at this photograph, too stunned to speak, and my wife turned to Hattie Mae and said, "But your father was white?" "Yes," she answered, with a smile hovering about her lips, knowing she had furnished us information we had never guessed on our own. We asked a few timid questions that tiptoed around the issue of segregation, and Hattie Mae responded that none of her family had especially suffered from it. They had lived together on a large Somerville farm, and her father had conducted his professional life as an administrator in the local school system. On the way home I replayed in my mind a number of scenes from the past, and I read within a new perspective Vannie's light-colored skin and her ability to hold her own in any encounter (without ever venturing outside her "assigned" territory, however). Hattie Mae's daughter had left the room when this photograph was unveiled, perhaps because the mixed blood that could be a complex source of pride in one generation had become a distinctly more troubled inheritance in the next one, perhaps not for this reason at all. Most suggestive is the way in which this capital fact remained unknown to us during Vannie's lifetime: doubtless affecting her daily way of accessing her own subjectivity yet unspeakable to us, the white family who hired her but who loved her too.

I want to close this impressionistic report on the note of love. All of us loved her, and I believe that, despite everything, she loved us in return. At least I want to believe this. The structural constraints that I have sought to identify, the impersonal racial pressures ensuring that this relationship remain one between unequals, shrouded in an impenetrable ignorance—these constraints need not invalidate an affection that was precious. But they do rewrite it as a racial pact, enabled and disfigured by larger social norms and opening into mystery. When does a more or less forced labor (she had to work, to accept our meager wage) turn into love? To what extent is what I took for a gift of self better understood as the best of a necessary bargain? What can you know of someone when you never meet that person's family, never even consider broaching the unspoken barriers that construct the contact itself? How can my knowledge of her count as valid when it lacks virtually every element of the knowledge of her that her own friends and family possessed?

Yet the feeling we shared was real, in part (perhaps) because the differences between us were not just white and black but childhood and maturity. I needed to love and be loved; so did she. In many houses throughout the South up to the mid-twentieth century, such black women must have responded to

the call of needy white children—this despite the inequality of the arrangement. (In many more houses, doubtless, it did not happen.) The solicited generosity of spirit that passes across the membrane of race is not illusory, even
though it is steeped (for the white child) in illusion, maintained (for the black
woman) by economic constraints. Something precious was given and received. Still, the imbalance of it all never ceased to intervene. We did not both
need to love in the same way, nor was our love of the same kind. In fact, at this
distance of almost forty years, it is hard not to wonder whether my continued
insistence on this bond does not participate (at least in part) in a larger
Southern white myth of black understanding and forgiveness of white privilege. Is this lingering fantasy of intact innocence one of the reasons I keep
returning to her image?

I come away with mystery. What she thought of me in her heart, how she
silently negotiated the differences between the constraint of mandated labor
and the flow of free feeling, I shall never know. I need to remember that I do
not know this, that "what else but love?" is an unanswered question as well as
a compelling response. All I do know is that what I took to be ours alone—my
reciprocated love for Vannie—was at the same time my culture's way of keeping the races unequal in the very act of putting them so intimately together.
This precious and disturbing double truth underwrites the pages that follow.

Faulkner: Dilsey/Callie/Vannie

Vannie has everything to do with me, but what can she have to do with Faulkner's novels? I want to address this question by exploring the autobiographical
relation (always debatable) between personal experience and artistic creation.
In Faulknerian terms, this means that we turn from Vannie and me to the relation between Faulkner's knowledge of Mammy Callie (the black woman who
brought him up and later lived on his land until her death) and his artistic creation of black mammies: Dilsey of *The Sound and the Fury*, Molly of *Go
Down, Moses*, and Nancy of "That Evening Sun" and *Requiem for a Nun*.
Thereafter, I shall pursue the more impersonal imbrication of white-in-
black/black-in-white that occurs upon the novelistic canvas itself—the ways in
which, following Morrison's suggestions in *Playing in the Dark*, we can see
blackness functioning implicitly in the writer's imagination of whiteness. This
latter illuminates the role of the mother in Faulkner's work, for the mother
and the mammy operate often as antithetical versions of each other. We begin
with the autobiographical.

What personal experience does Faulkner draw on to create Dilsey? It is certainly normal to read Dilsey only within the context framed by the novel itself, as untold readers have done, yet autobiographical information is pertinent. For Faulkner to arrive at Dilsey, another black woman may be said to play an enabling role (and for me to follow him there, a second black woman plays an equivalent role). Both of them—the real Callie for the writer and the real Vannie for this reader—serve as conduits toward the fictional Dilsey. Faulkner found his way to this first overwhelming black portrait (published in 1929) through the formative detour of Mammy Callie (Caroline Barr). Born a slave, the middle-aged Mammy Callie joined the elder Faulkners' family when they moved to Oxford in 1902, and she remained as a house servant with the younger Faulkners' family until her death in 1940.[6] Her early role in bringing up the children was second only to Faulkner's mother's: "Mother trusted her profoundly," Faulkner's brother John writes in *My Brother Bill*, "and we soon learned to mind one of them the same as we would the other" (48). William Faulkner was five at the time of her arrival, his two younger brothers were three and one, and his tomboy cousin, Sallie Murry, was likewise three. The structural resemblance to the Compson family: three boys, one girl, and a black mammy/maid is hardly accidental.

Callie enters Faulkner's work decisively only twice—in *The Sound and the Fury* (1929) through the figure of Dilsey Gibson and in *Go Down, Moses* (1942) through the figure of Molly Beauchamp. The latter portrait is suffused in elegiac feelings—Callie had died in 1940 and the bereaved Faulkner spoke her funeral address—whereas the earlier Dilsey is a quite different order of being. First and foremost, she is physically impressive (whereas Callie—like Molly—was small, as small as Faulkner's own mother, Maud). Second, she is unfailingly capable. Molly of *Go Down, Moses* is granted alterability in time—she can be recalled in her childbearing years as well as presented in her grandmotherly role—but Dilsey is locked into an inalterable older age and commanding body. If we think about the dramatic situation that occupies the background of this novel—four children in the care of a capacious black mammy who has replaced their defective white mother—we see why her temporal frame is inalterable. Only in the appendix to *The Sound and the Fury*, written in 1945 (after *Go Down, Moses*, and after Callie's death), is Dilsey permitted to be not just attacked but subdued by time. In the novel proper she has the size required by a child's fixed memory, as though her body registered physically and responsively to the need projected by those four white children. Fictional Dilsey shares with autobiographical Callie a crucial maternal role in nurturing a needy white child. Both black women are bodily present for the child—picking him up and setting him down, washing and soothing and protecting his body—in ways that the more delicate white mother has been trained not to do.

Dilsey differs significantly from Callie as well. She has a husband (Roskus) and her own offspring, whereas Callie had different male partners from time to time but no husband. More, Dilsey serves centrally as Compson cook, a role that furthers her function as bodily caretaker, whereas Callie never performed that chore for Faulkner's family, serving instead as their all-purpose housemaid. Finally, unlike Dilsey, who has (so to speak) no pre-Compson memories, Mammy Callie was one of the young Faulkner's rare firsthand sources of Civil War tales.

About Callie Faulkner actually wrote very little, though his behavior—scrupulously caring for her and her family's needs until the time of her death—spoke a great deal. Presiding over her funeral, Faulkner emphasized Callie's "half century of fidelity and devotion," and he went on to identify her as one of his "earliest recollections, not only as a person, but as a fount of authority over my conduct and of security for my physical welfare, and of active and constant affection and love."[7] On her tombstone he had these words engraved: "Her white children bless her." It detracts nothing from the sincerity of this engraving for us to note, at the same time, that the white Faulkner had taken over the roles of both wounded subject and grateful offspring, organizer of her funeral and spokesman of the grief her death caused others. In none of this do we register the reality of her own black culture, the friends and relatives who likewise (and surely with equal intensity) suffered her loss. Like my childhood images of Vannie, there is room here only for the thankful white subject and the generous black object. What case can be made for the effect of this black servant upon the subjectivity of her young white master, in ways that shape the fictional portrait of Dilsey?

I've already touched on Dilsey's being locked into a fixed time period, denied memory, seen forever through the lens of a grateful white child. (Seven years later, when Faulkner wrote *Absalom, Absalom!* and reinserted Dilsey's grandchild, Luster, into the narrative, he made a temporal error that may be related to this point. Luster is still a fourteen-year-old boy, though the *Absalom* chronology of a hunting scene sometime before 1909 [some twenty years earlier than *The Sound and the Fury* chronology of 1928] would predate his birth and make his appearance impossible. I have long noted this error but only recently come to understand it. Luster, like his grandmother Dilsey, is locked permanently in a single time frame, the same age regardless of the novel Faulkner inserts him in.) With Dilsey's maturity comes her maternity; she supplies unstintingly the missing breast that these needy white children require. An entire representational schema follows from this childhood orientation.[8] The Compson blacks are, so to speak, always already there, the capacious old ones serving as fixed backdrop for the needy young Compsons. Permanently adult, they draw on a wisdom that remains intact, however unavailable to their white charges now grown confusedly adult.

As should be clear, the autobiographical source brings with it limitations as well as opportunities. The light cast by a white boy's unchanging gratitude toward his black mammy is a light that makes her other. Consider just a sentence from the extraordinary description that opens the final chapter of *The Sound and the Fury*: "She had been a big woman once but now her skeleton rose, draped loosely in unpadded skin that tightened again upon a paunch almost dropsical, as though muscle and tissue had been courage or fortitude which the days or the years had consumed until only the indomitable skeleton was left rising like a ruin or a landmark above the somnolent and impervious guts" (*SF*, 165). Landmark indeed: no white person in this novel could possibly sustain the symbolism of such a description. Dilsey's otherness registers in the form of an awe and admiration inconceivable for a white person "like us."[9]

This takes me to my final point about the Callie/Dilsey connection. Mammy Callie introduces this little white Faulkner boy to the twin mysteries of blackness and maternal care. Her stark black color and unreconstructed linguistic patterns make her indelibly not-him—the Faulkner children's written recollections dilate (with unconscious condescension) on her fracturing the English language—yet her maternal generosity, her intimacy with the needs of his body (an intimacy forsworn by his own mother), her wise aphorisms: all this tells him that this black woman who is other is also same, inside him as well as outside. In other words, through Mammy Callie the child William Faulkner first encounters the deepest fault line of his culture's way of construing race relations. She may live in his family's yard and spend untold hours in his presence, yet she can never register like a white Faulkner. Because she lives in his family's yard and spends untold hours in his presence, she can never be dismissed as a "nigger." Personally enabling yet irremediably foreign, same and other, Mammy Callie introduces William Faulkner to his culture's central neurosis. In so doing, she crucially affects the lineaments of his own emergent racial identity, his soon-to-be permanently painful way of being white.

I return to Vannie, aware, of course, that a reader who knew neither Vannie nor Callie (and this accounts for all but the tiniest portion of Faulkner's readers!) need not miss anything in the portrait of Dilsey. The pertinent point is that I cannot access the fictional Dilsey except by making a moving detour through Vannie, just as (I argue) Faulkner wouldn't have created Dilsey as he did, without the prior and moving detour of Mammy Callie. The elements these black women share—their ways of being both intimate and alien, of having everything and nothing to do with their grateful white charges—are already tolerably clear. My own sense of Vannie's preciousness, in any event, turned that word *nigger* into an unbearable offense; and I left the South in 1958, in part, to escape hearing it.

Vannie is instrumental both in my departure and in the form of return that I am attempting through this book. Like Faulkner (and how fatuous in other connections it would be to sound this phrase), I grew up with an overpowering sense of racial debt and racial difference. My investment in his work is inseparable from his capacity to dramatize both the debt and the difference, and his anguish over both. I read Dilsey through Vannie, and this is such a rooted and comfortable reading for me that it takes a disturbance to realize how culturally angled that reading is. Increasingly, at Swarthmore where I teach, I get that disturbance: my students resist Faulkner's portrait of Dilsey. They chafe at her absent anger and absent desire. They are uneasy in the presence of her accepted and therefore empowering servitude within a white economy. I urge them to look more thoughtfully into the portrait and to consider whether, under such conditions as the segregated South of the 1920s, it is possible that a black maid as Faulkner represented her might be fully human. They usually remain unpersuaded.

Several years ago, teaching at Rhodes College in Memphis for a semester, I think I found out why. This time I had made the reverse argument about Dilsey, emphasizing her absent anger and absent desire (as opposed to the plentiful supply of these emotions among the white Compsons), and I ran into a stone wall. My well-bred students at Rhodes spoke as one in resistance to this non-Southern claim that Faulkner—despite, and indeed because of, his special love for her—had othered Dilsey, had produced her through a representational strategy commanded by racial difference. I glimpsed, in their resistance, that they were pleading with me to grant currency to white gratitude as a generous and fully human lens (read: one unbiased by race) upon black lives. And I glimpsed as well the cultural construction of my own lens, fluttering homeless somewhere between Southern piety and non-Southern critique. This autobiographical lens gives me no special insight, and certainly no innocent pleasure. But insofar as it is partly constitutive of how I see at all, it is time to start taking into account the lens as well, to acknowledge that my own cultural orientation affects what I see by shaping how I see it. As best as I can construe it, this is how Faulkner and I found and find our way into Dilsey, a portrait as compelling (for me) in what it misses as in what it sees.

Faulkner: *The Sound and the Fury*

I turn now from the genesis of the text to its functioning: to the ways in which, within the novel itself, the black female in the kitchen and the white one outside it mutually shape each other—how Faulkner knows the one woman through the other. Mrs. Compson is Faulkner's most unforgivingly represented mother.[10] She talks nonstop (her suicidal son's head aches with her pronouncements). Incapable of caring for her children, she indicts them for not caring for her. Her denied breast (denied because for her the breast is a salacious organ) orphans her offspring at the moment of birthing them. "If I could say Mother," Quentin's refrain (*SF*, 60), bespeaks a maternal dysfunction that devastates all of her children save Jason. The aftershocks of this dysfunction fill Faulkner's narrative, never more so than in her repeated role of "keeper of the rooms." Unwilling to use the kitchen (or perhaps, because there was always a black woman to carry out this function, simply untrained: "En who gwine eat yo messin?" Dilsey wearily reminds Mrs. Compson [*SF*, 169]), she patrols the stairs, locks the bedrooms, is soonest awake and last asleep. When her granddaughter Quentin finally bolts from this suffocating regime, Mrs. Compson and Jason struggle for almost a page over the huge chain of rusty keys she carries, Jason desperate to locate his fleeing niece, Mrs. Compson elaborately shielding those keys in her protected midsection, as though they are elements in touch with her womb and must never be exposed to the light of day. "The dungeon was Mother herself" (*SF*, 109), Quentin muses—nothing in her womb fully emerges—for Faulkner has figured Mrs. Compson as simultaneously the jail (the mother who refuses to succor her children so as to enable their release into the world), the jailer (the patroller of their desires, reprimander of their feelings), and finally the inmate (she herself the most complete victim of her gendered identity, unable to understand her womb as anything other than a source of shame).

Dilsey registers as the novel's sustained maternal counterpart to Mrs. Compson the failed mother. (The servant Dilsey rather than the daughter

Caddy, for in Caddy's poignant rebellion against the mother we witness an inability—given Caddy's fatal inscription as aristocratic white—to find other gendered terms that might accommodate her conflicting sexual and maternal drives.) Spared Caddy's internal warfare, Dilsey remains intact and narratively available for the most damning maternal contrasts. If Mrs. Compson functions to turn a home into a house, then Dilsey turns that house into a home. She unlocks the domestic spaces her mistress closes up, makes the meals her mistress would mismanage, brings warmth and human dimension into a space dehumanized by Mrs. Compson. She caretakes the white bodies abandoned by their white mother.

Unlike the white women in this text, Dilsey (because black) is represented as at ease with her gendered identity, yet this ease entails certain abbreviations. The portrait is deeply selective. Her breast, unlike Mrs. Compson's, is available, but Faulkner is concerned to offer it mainly to her "white children." And it is always on offer, a resource the needy Compson infants draw on tirelessly. What else Dilsey's racial and gendered identity might mean to her, how she registers the vicissitudes of feeling outside the realm of maternal care, remains unrepresentable within Faulkner's narrative strategy. She is so busy mothering her "white children"—occupied with feeding or washing or scolding Benjy or Caddy or Jason—that we have no sense of her other female resources or requirements.

We see so little of her relation to her own children that we don't know for sure which are her own children. Versh, T.P., and Frony are the candidates, but it may be that only two of them descend from her and the third has married into her family.[11] Her relationship with her grandchild, Luster, does, however, command Faulkner's more generous attention, and this pairing reinforces her representation as an *old* woman. Old, perhaps, but given no memories that solicit with the reminder of other, lovelier, departed options. She is not permitted to reminisce in such a way as to let us into her own past. Her conversations with Roskus are pressed undeviatingly into service as perspectives upon white Composonhood. We are never reminded with her—as we are with Mrs. Compson—that the passage from puberty through marriage and into old age has its own tensions. (Not that Faulkner treats Mrs. Compson's tensions with the tenderness that he bestows upon those of her offspring.)

Lacking internal tension means that Dilsey is denied doubt; this omission operates to unify her at every level. No queries arise as to the metaphysical sanction—the risen Christ—that oversees and rewards her travail in this household. Time is for her a true and trustworthy arc. In place of Mrs.

Compson's anxious insistence that God *must* be a gentleman, and of Quentin's feverish denial of Him who "not for me died not" (*SF*, 111), Dilsey holds steadily to her conviction that she is on God's eternal roster. When she is called for, "All I got to say is Ise here" (*SF*, 38). Such certainty focuses her subjectivity, protects her against the interior ravages inflicted by space and time and unwanted thought and feeling, fuels the knowing conservatism of her comments throughout the text. Faulkner's admiration for her is simultaneously his limited vision of her. This novel, perhaps the most brilliant of our century to convey the subjective experience of radical self-division, is therefore forced to "do" Dilsey in terms that, however impressive, remain external and conventional, compared to the tortured rhetoric Faulkner has invented to do justice to Compson pain. Only one black woman in his entire oeuvre suffers with Compson-like intensity, and only as represented in one story. I leave *The Sound and the Fury* and turn to Nancy in "That Evening Sun."

Faulkner: Nancy

If Dilsey's first counterpart is Mrs. Compson (the two of them conveying the race-commanded polar possibilities of maternal identity), then her second counterpart is Nancy (the two of them conveying the polar possibilities of black sexual identity). Dilsey's postmenopausal dignity is silhouetted against Nancy's indescribable sexual exposure. It is as though Faulkner's affection for Dilsey requires a representational focus upon the breast, while his fascination with Nancy fixes upon the womb. It is one thing for the breast to nourish offspring white and black, it is quite another for the vagina to be penetrated by organs white and black. Nancy in "That Evening Sun" is an almost purely transgressive figure, and the story powerfully conveys the failure of traditional forms to contain her. Her eyes, her mouth, and her heart can be represented only incoherently: seeing becomes not-seeing, moaning becomes not-human noise, and motive becomes an unspeakable mix of fear, love, jealousy, and anger.[12]

Faulkner (through the narrative focus of Quentin) cannot keep his eyes off her, and in her presence a host of norm-sustaining distinctions start to dissolve. The white children's innocence is menaced by this black woman's uncensorable speech and actions. The elaborate spatial geography designed to maintain their innocence—the separations between kitchen and bedroom, between rooms for child's play and rooms for sexual innuendo, between lockable white house and unlockable black house, between street and ditch—

begins to lose its mooring. Nothing is more resonant than Faulkner's refusal to conceptualize this unmooring, for it is, precisely, beyond conceiving within the social norms of his culture.

Quentin's innocence survives this encounter (he never understands what he is seeing), yet simultaneously reveals a shattering of racial norms that we as readers are invited to decipher. Through his eyes we witness the collapse of a culture's strategies for organizing racial segregation. The protection coded in Dilsey turns into the exposure coded in Nancy, the innocence that Mr. Compson is meant to assure ("Why don't you do something about it?" [CS, 299] his wife complains) escapes his patrolling as the children wander from white house to black one, and Jesus in the ditch doubles intolerably with Mr. Stovall in the street. Inflecting all of these collapses is the opening image of the story—the black women of Jefferson in the good old days, carrying huge laundry baskets precariously balanced upon their heads: black women engaged in the time-honored task of cleaning up white dirt. Here, more than anywhere else in his fiction, Faulkner reveals how extensive, unmanageable, and reciprocal that dirt is.

To turn from "That Evening Sun" to *Requiem for a Nun* is to encounter, some twenty years later, a completely different authorial stance. The story's focus on an unsayable Nancy has been replaced by the novel's focal/vocal concern with Temple. "Nancy Manigault is not even concerned in this" (*RN*, 562), the ever-garrulous Gavin announces, and he is correct. Nancy's black body is taken hold of—she will be executed—as a symbol of the price to be exacted by Temple's vicious behavior many years earlier, and the text addresses such manipulation only as part of Temple's subjective trajectory: "Because all this was not for the sake of her [Nancy's] soul because her soul doesn't need it, but for mine" (*RN*, 604). This Nancy is so imperturbable— she has become psychically resolved, "Dilseyfied"—and removed from the dramatic agon of this text ("her soul doesn't need it") that she talks less to Temple or Gowan than to herself and the Lord: "I tried everything I knowed. You can see that. . . . Yes, Lord, I done it" (*RN*, 602–3).

Subjective black anguish that Faulkner's text had earlier gestured toward yet left unanalyzed is replaced by white anguish requiring no gestures and open to inexhaustible analysis. Nancy here finds her "place," all but disappearing into the racial stereotype of transcendent black mammy. No one in the text (including, most tellingly, Nancy herself) wonders for a moment about the morality of her murdering Temple's baby to "save" the child from Temple's coming abandonment. As to the question of her paying with her own life for this salvational murder, we soon learn that the white authorities wouldn't dream of taking from her this one chance for significance. Says the governor: "Who am I, to have the brazen temerity and hardihood to set the puny appanage of my office in the balance against that simple undeviable aim? Who am I, to render null and abrogate the purchase she made with that poor crazed lost and worthless life?" (*RN*, 614). *Temerity, appanage, abrogate*: his lofty Latinate vocabulary speaks eloquently the cultural/discursive gap between university-trained white men and "nigger dope-fiend whores." (The heavy irony of this last phrase is oddly complicated by its obsessive recurrence in the text, as though Nancy has no available racial role between the two extremes of living whoredom and martyred sainthood.) In any event, she accepts her immolation without demur ("not looking at anything, motionless, almost bemused, her face sad, brooding and inscrutable" [*RN*, 594]). What such sacrifice might actually feel like beneath that "inscrutable" demeanor, what it would mean for the child you must destroy to be your own rather than the white one you caretake, what might be at stake if the originating damage springs from the institution of slavery itself rather than from a white woman's illicit intercourse and adultery—for this we will have to go to the most powerful requiem for a nun written in our century: *Beloved*. I turn now from Faulkner to Morrison.

Morrison: *The Bluest Eye*

In Morrison we find not black mammies but black maids, and the drama changes accordingly. There is no Dilsey (or Vannie) in Morrison's world. It takes the optic of white indebtedness to envisage the deep but narrow pathos of this figure (in texts, but also in life). From the beginning, Morrison accesses black maids in white houses as paid servants whose subjective life is lived on other terms than their caring for white charges. If they are also mothers, the children Morrison concerns herself with are black. Her focus is diagnostic, eschewing the rhetoric of white gratitude in order to explore, first, the interior dysfunction that attaches to black mothers who double as mammies for white families and, later, the intricate economy (simultaneously psychological and monetary) of racial oppression operating within a family frame. I begin with Pauline in *The Bluest Eye*, as preparation for a fuller discussion of racial dynamics and domestic pathology in *Tar Baby*.

> Hereisthehouseitisgreenandwhiteithasareddooritisveryprettyhereisthe-familymotherfatherdickandjaneliveinthegreenandwhitehousetheyarevery-happy. (*TBE*, 4)

Every reader of this text remembers the orthographic games Morrison plays with the Dick and Jane narrative, opening each chapter with a passage from that innocent white narrative gone berserk. ("Father is a drunk and Mother is a maid; Dick runs away from home, Jane inadvertently poisons the dog, and the cat is almost killed," Harris writes in *From Mammies to Militants* [60].) Morrison's refusal of typographical convention flaunts what Faulkner's textual deployment of the mammy works to deny—that the black woman doesn't belong in the white house. That house's operative norms (two parents, two children, family pets, nice furniture, owned and cared-for house) only selectively make sense (it is a white paradigm), and Morrison exposes these norms as constructed *texts* and therefore alterable (rather than as immovable stand-ins for the real).[13] Black women who take on this domestic model risk disfigurement. Often they cannot afford to own their houses, and they have trouble making a neatly shared life work with husband, children, and pets. The shabby domestic items they do manage to possess testify eloquently to their economic failure.

Pauline Breedlove is a beaten figure, a black mother inconceivable within the Faulknerian field of vision. Inconceivable because she is sexually repressed rather than sexually at ease (Faulknerian white women occupy the former territory exclusively), because she is all but paralyzed by the contrast between her youthful memories and her present miseries (Faulknerian black women labor under few memories), and because her way of being a mammy in a white house ensures her failure as mother in her own (black mothers in Faulkner care for offspring: failed mothers are obligatorily white). Pauline enters the Fishers' Dick and Jane house, puts on her spotless white uniform, changes her name to Polly, and tries to forget her own flesh-and-blood family.[14] She becomes other; it is better than the movies. Morrison has considerable sympathy for the black maid's suffering (which registers in Pauline's hauntingly vernacular musings), but once the writer exits from Pauline's interior voice and attends to her maternal behavior, she reveals a fatal dysfunction. It may be Pauline's husband, Cholly, who rapes their daughter, Pecola, and hastens her descent into insanity, yet Pauline's part in the destruction of their child is equal to his. Cherishing the little "girl in pink" in the Fishers' immaculate white house helps Pauline achieve something like a daily lobotomy. She becomes mammy to cease being mother; her success in this enterprise is eventually complete.

Morrison never repeats herself, but she likewise never abandons an earlier problematic. Cholly will reappear in dozens of black men on the run in her later novels, and Pecola will reemerge as the sacrificed child (usually but not always black) that recurs throughout her texts: Chicken Little, Hagar, Michael, Beloved, Dorcas. But perhaps the most disturbing role engaged in *The Bluest Eye* is that of the defective black mother. This seems to be the problematic that *Sula* addresses head-on, simply bursting with the maneuvers of unconventional mothers. *Beloved* eventually conducts Morrison's supreme testing of the mother, but first we must turn to her sustained exploration of maids and maternity in *Tar Baby*.

Morrison: *Tar Baby*

Within the kitchen of Valerian and Margaret Street's sumptuous island home in the Caribbean the married house servants, Sidney and Ondine, are engaged in the following discussion:

> "What's the Principal Beauty hollering about?"
> "Turkey."
> Ondine looked at her husband over her shoulder. "Don't fool with me this morning."
> "And apple pie."
> "You'd better get me a plane ticket out of here." She straightened.
> "Calm down, girl."
> "She want it, she can come in here and cook it. After she swim on back up to New York and get the ingredients. Where she think she is?"
> "It's for the boy."
> "God help us."
> "She wants an old-fashioned Christmas."
> "Then she can bring her old-fashioned butt in here and cook it up."
> (*Tar Baby*, 34)

Mrs. Compson may be as inept a homemaker as Margaret Street (and an equally damaging mother), but one cannot imagine Dilsey and Roskus represented as talking about her thus. Shrewd though that latter pair be, their portraiture is ringed round with silences, one of which contains the censored perspective of domestic blacks upon the whites they work for. Faulkner permits himself to represent Mrs. Compson with as much brilliant malice as he wishes, but her black retainers may not. They talk instead of Roskus's rheumatism and his reading of the "signs," of Dilsey's conviction that the abandoned Quentin should be free to speak of her departed mother. Their own work situation with white Compsons is naturalized by a discursive silence. We are to believe ourselves in the presence of bonds rooted at a level deeper than dollars.

Sidney and Ondine, however involved they may become with the Streets' neuroses, never forget the fragile, contractual nature of their role in that house. Infuriated by Valerian's capricious acceptance of the unwashed Son into the house, the fine-grained Sidney fumes about their possibly having to leave. Ondine replies: "We have a future here, as well as a past, and I tell you I can't pick up and move in with some strange new white folks at my age. I can't do it." As Sidney continues to indulge in outrage toward Son, she faces him and says: "Drop [that bone] before it chokes you. You know your work. Just do what you're supposed to do. Here. Take him [Valerian] his potato. Finish the rest of the mail later. Just give Mr. Street his. He likes to read it while he eats, if you call that eating" (TB, 101–3). When both of them confront their potential departure later in the novel, Ondine reflects: "And I'm grateful [toward Valerian]. You know I am. I've never had no problem with him. He's a nuisance but he stood by us when we needed him to" (TB, 193). "Her old-fashioned butt," "some strange new white folks," "if you call that eating," "a nuisance": Ondine reads her employers with colloquial and unforgiving accuracy, registering at every moment the inner accommodations, the fragile options, she has had to accept to live with the dominance of this unaware, dysfunctional white couple.

Whites in Tar Baby specialize in knowing nothing of their black help. Valerian addresses Gideon instrumentally as Yardman, not humanly as Gideon, and all his laundry maids are Marys, despite the present one's name being Thérèse.[15] Indeed, when "Yardman" is commanded to let "Mary" go, he just brings Thérèse back and tells "them it's a brand-new woman." "They don't know?" "Not yet. They don't pay her any attention" (TB, 153). Quentin realized that "black" was only a form of behavior toward whites, a constructed surface and not a natural depth, but The Sound and the Fury could do little with this knowledge since it showed no interest in black depths.[16] Tar Baby's blacks, by contrast, delight in the repertory of black stereotypes expected of them and wielded by them when useful. When Son needs to "sound black" to Valerian, he provides the following: "Yes, sir. I uh thought I smelled oyster stew out back yesterday. And it got dark early, the fog I mean. They done left the kitchen and I thought I'd try to get me some" (TB, 147). This is the same man who, instead of being actuated by the brute (and "black") need of mere food, would stare for hours at the unconscious Jadine, seeking to inform her sleeping dreams with his waking ones; but Valerian will never be privy to such complexity. Between themselves, Jadine and Son put on accents at will (Porgy and Bess are always good for a laugh), but with whites Jadine is careful to follow a few simple rules: "She needed only to be stunning, and to convince them she was not as smart as they were. Say the obvious, ask stupid questions, laugh with abandon, look interested, and light up at any display of their humanity if they showed it" (*TB*, 126–27). This white employment of stereotype goes beyond discourse and extends into behavior as well. Jadine realizes that just because Son "was in her [Margaret's] closet, she [Margaret] thought his sole purpose in life was to seduce her. Naturally her. A white woman no matter how old, no matter how flabby, how totally sexless, believed it" (*TB*, 186). Just how virulent this belief can be, any reader of "Dry September" or *Light in August* can testify. Whereas Faulkner gives us the full pathology that induces such beliefs among whites, Morrison gives us the range of discourses — the artfulness induced by racism, if you like — that blacks summon to become known to each other while remaining unknown to their white masters.[17]

Valerian is a white master unlike any of Faulkner's patriarchs. Morrison emphasizes his mix of helplessness and tyranny, his old age that never achieved the seasoning of maturity, his brutality that is fueled by innocence — an inability to imagine the otherness of others. Mr. Compson is no less ineffectual than Valerian, but Faulkner saturates that portrait in Mr. Compson's provocative platitudes, his tenderness toward his children silhouetted against his wife's alienating rage. There was once Compson money, but now we see manners without substance beneath, a desiccated culture reduced to gesturing rather than shaping realities. Valerian is even more childlike. His emotional life never developed past the devastating death of his father, and the only soothing available to him for enduring this loss came from a drunken laundry woman named Mary. The candy named for Valerian by his candy-manufacturing uncles actually identifies a sweetness both premature and stale within him. We see him obsessively on one of two stages, either at the dining table or in his greenhouse. Both settings radiate a sense of regression and nostalgia. He lives in the former like a spoiled child, hoping to take in through the mouth a sustenance denied in his childhood and unreplaceable since, and he repairs to the latter to suck on memories, to summon ghosts.

Not only does Morrison diagnose the psychopathology of this white master with a corrosive rigor that Faulkner's Compsons and McCaslins usually escape, but she also insists upon his naked pecuniary power. Valerian has the power of the purse, and he uses it. He buys things endlessly (this text is bursting with the useless things Valerian has bought); we register him as a child of capitalism. His heart truncated, his wallet overdeveloped, Valerian lives in a reified world. He has bought every item (including Margaret, Sidney, Ondine) in it, and he addresses these human figures only as sources of his own pleasure or pain. Sidney reads him exactly and warns Son: "White folks play with Negroes. It entertained *him*, that's all, inviting you to dinner. He don't give a damn what it does to anybody else. You think he cares about his wife? That you scared his wife? If it entertained him, he'd *hand* her to you!" (*TB*, 162–63). An arrested child emotionally, Valerian lives in a world presided over by his own appetites and fantasies. When Ondine, Sidney, and Son finally call him to account and he helplessly commands, "Call the harbor!" no one moves: "There was no one to do his bidding. He had played a silly game" (*TB*, 208).

Margaret differs from Valerian in any number of superficial ways (age, gender, class, education, intelligence), but she shares his central trait: terminal immaturity. The "Principal Beauty" grew up ignored, unnurtured. Eventually able to negotiate her world by exploiting her good looks, Margaret conceals the yawning chasm at the center of her being by accumulating (like Valerian) items on its periphery. Perhaps these will persuade her that she exists. It is as though the fundamental duties in Morrison's world—the completed birthing and training of an infant, the passing on of a cultural history that confirms that infant's being and thus permits the development of an identity—were systematically ignored in white society. Valerian and Margaret are "absent" in this text, and Morrison shows that forsaken children who grow up as "absent" adults become parents who "absent" their own offspring. At the heart of the novel is Margaret's motiveless abuse of her child, Michael, an abuse witnessed and loathed by the maternal Ondine.

The revelation of this abuse serves as the fulcrum of *Tar Baby*'s plot, and I shall attend in a moment to the explosion that follows it. But it would be worthwhile to linger briefly on the way Morrison's representation of the damaged child differs from Faulkner's. Morrison's Michael serves merely as a pretext in this novel centered on adults, a figure who collects upon his unrepresented person the various failures of his parents. By contrast, Faulkner's Benjy and Quentin and Joe Christmas are the very motor of the narrative. Their tortured psyches fuel Faulkner's stylistic experiments and take center stage. Elaborately doomed figures, they spell out the larger collapse of human resources within the culture that produced them, whereas Morrison's doomed children spell out the obstacles (not overcome, but not necessarily invincible either) that her struggling adults must encounter. When *Tar Baby* ends, all the lives Morrison has engaged (Son and Jadine, but also Ondine and Sidney, even Margaret and Valerian) are still in process.

The explosion occurs, appropriately, at the dining table. Valerian casually announces his having summarily fired "Yardman" and "Mary" for taking some of his expensively imported apples without asking permission, and Son suddenly glimpses the entire panorama of racial exploitation. The passage is long and in its very anger hypnotic:

> Son's mouth went dry as he watched Valerian chewing a piece of ham . . . approving even of the flavor in his mouth although he had been able to dismiss with a flutter of his fingers the people whose sugar and cocoa had allowed him to grow old in regal comfort; although he had taken the sugar and cocoa and paid for it as though it had no value, as though the cutting of cane and picking of beans was child's play and had no value; but he turned it into candy, the invention of which really was child's play, and sold it to other children and made a fortune in order to move near, but not in the midst of, the jungle where the sugar came from and build a palace with more of their labor and then hire them to do more of the work he was not capable of and pay them again according to some scale of value that would outrage Satan himself and when those people wanted a little of what he wanted, some apples for their Christmas, and took some, he dismissed them with a flutter of the fingers, because they were thieves . . . and he probably thought he was a law-abiding man, they all did . . . because they [whites like Valerian] had not the dignity of wild animals who did not eat where they defecated but they could defecate over a whole people and come there to live and defecate some more by tearing up the land and that is why they loved property so, because they had killed it soiled it defecated on it and they loved more than anything the places where they shit. Would fight and kill to own the cesspools they made, and although they called it architecture it was in fact elaborately built toilets, decorated toilets . . . since waste was the order of the day and the ordering principle of the universe. . . . This was the sole lesson of their world: how to make wasteful products, how to talk waste, how to study waste, how to design waste . . . and how to despise the culture that lived in cloth houses and shit on the ground far away from where they ate.   (*TB*, 202–4)

Here the indictment of white capitalism reaches its acme: a system in which a carefully trained group of people—white—runs roughshod over the various corners of the globe, colonizing other cultures and building toilets that they insist are architecture. This economy of waste—where the time and effort of producing (the dignity of work) disappear into the maw of industrial capitalism, where objects lose their makers' humanizing imprint and become pure symbol of their purchasers' power to possess and even more to discard — simultaneously organizes a map of international racism. The shit that black people clean up in Morrison's texts is produced by more than any single dynastic family's concerted efforts. It comes from a systemic cultural pathology that equates the (white) capacity to consume and discard with human success itself. *Tar Baby* thus organizes its canvas within a colonial frame — even a minor figure like Alma Estée works to clean white toilets — which we are invited to read as American. Here is the manic Thérèse speculating on the denatured marvels of American culture:

> Thérèse said that America was where doctors took the stomachs, eyes, umbilical cords, the backs of the neck where the hair grew, blood, sperm, hearts and fingers of the poor and froze them in plastic packages to be sold later to the rich. Where children as well as grown people slept with dogs in their beds. Where women took their children behind trees in the park and sold them to strangers. Where everybody on the television set was naked and that even the priests were women. Where for a bar of gold a doctor could put you into a machine and, in matter of minutes, would change you from a man to a woman or a woman to a man. Where it was not uncommon or strange to see people with both penises and breasts.   (*TB*, 151)

If the explosion at the dining table shows this to be a novel centered on the economics of race relations, Thérèse's vision tells us it is also a text about the economics of gender (and familial) relations. The organs that cumulatively make up coherent men and women are here envisaged as reified, salable parts, a sale that exploits the poor to benefit the rich. Even children are submitted to the profit motive (Michael disappearing into his father's candy factory), and the furthest reach of such relentless technology is to dissolve the integrity of traditionally gendered identity. Here, I think, we come upon Morrison's nostalgic musing, in the form of a folkloric mythology of pure gender represented as still lurking upon this Caribbean island. Once there were truly distinct black men and women — chevaliers and swamp women. Jadine's test is to discover if her insistent (and constructed) modernity is compatible with her endangered (and natural) womanhood. The magnificent African woman in the yellow dress, the smelly swamp women that hold her inescapably to her biological inheritance, the night women with aggressive breasts that visit her dreams: all of these atavistic figures convey a gender destiny that Jadine is simultaneously seeking and fleeing.

It is suggestive that the text's fluid deployment of *racial* roles—its awareness of a range of stereotyping that substitutes for genuine racial identity—turns rather rigid when it comes to *gender* roles; the text's polarized gender models appear patently incapable of conciliating each other. If the authentic way to be black is exactly what *Tar Baby* brilliantly turns into contestation, the authentic way to be a woman seems for Morrison to be less debatable. "I think there is a serious question about black male and black female relationships in the twentieth century," Morrison said in her interview with Nellie McKay. "I just think that the argument has always turned on something it should not turn on: gender. I think that the conflict of genders is a cultural illness" (*TM*, 404). How to be black emerges as the question: Morrison's phrasing effectively erases "male" and "female" from the issue, as though she were imagining a later time when this "cultural illness" will be behind us and the category of "gender" will no longer operate as a scene of conflict. We shall see an oddly similar imbalance, this time the rigidity racial and the fluidity gendered, when we examine Faulkner's *The Unvanquished*.

Unlike Faulknerian narrative, where the telling lineages are masculine—Compsons, Hightowers, Sutpens, McCaslins—Morrison's text pursues resources not yet drawn on (both promising and threatening) exclusively through the female register. The resolution of Jadine's future—if she has one at all—can be articulated only through a wrestling with those mythic women who inhabit the periphery of the novel. I turn now to the larger bearing of this point, the way in which, throughout Morrison's career, the mother appears in heroic guise, heroic even when murderous. Men may flinch in Morrison (they are shown to have good reason for doing so), but women take it all on, never betraying (whatever else they betray) their definitive "ancient properties."

Morrison: Mothers with Ancient Properties

We have seen the ways in which Faulkner construes the white mother as counterpart to the black mammy. Although his resilient old maids (Rosa Millard, Aunt Jenny, Miss Wortham)—postmenopausally at peace with themselves—remain an affectionate icon of strength unbroken by stress, his white mothers have much to answer for. Typically, they either have forsaken legitimacy in order to express desire or have condemned their desire—and with it their maternal resources—in order to honor legitimacy. Both trajectories keep them imprisoned within patriarchal narratives of womanhood (the intoxicating woman the male has intercourse with but cannot control and does not marry, on the one hand, or the repressed woman who keeps intact his line of descent and denatures herself in the process, on the other). Together, these two narratives ensure the white mother's immolation.[18]

In between these extremes of the white mother's repressive honor and trackless desire, the Faulknerian black mother demonstrates a mysterious resilience. Freed from the rigid demands of patriarchal descent (for the husbands of these women have so little to husband, to pass on), Dilsey and Molly (Faulkner's most sustained black female portraits) are permitted to remain themselves as they negotiate conflicting gender requirements. Their desire itself may escape representation, but we see, on the periphery of such portraits, signs that their female identity is still intact. For Faulkner, as for his larger Southern white culture, black women are envisaged as nearer to the earth itself—more in tune with the demands of the clay they are made of—and therefore not at war with the resources of their own bodies.[19]

This proximity to nature can of course mean a reduction of their human complexity, but it can also mean a more peaceful and dignified self-possession. It is a wholeness that Faulkner dearly prizes, inasmuch as it escapes the self-destructive agon of his white women when under the dual pressures of desire and motherhood. Intact, these black women manage to achieve what few white women in Faulkner's oeuvre accomplish: to negotiate the conflicting demands of sexuality and maternity. Because Dilsey and Molly harbor resources that have become warped or defective within Faulkner's white women, they are drafted to bring up the white children abandoned by their own (sometimes living, often dead, always ineffectual) mothers. In being drafted these black mothers become mammies.

It is not surprising that Faulkner imagines black mothers' fulfillment of this maternal task as sharing something of the affection so gratefully felt by otherwise abandoned white offspring. Not surprising, either—though no less for that revealing of his limitations—that he tends not to question the patriarchal economy that simultaneously damages the white mother and secures in her absence the black substitute. Even where the interracial connection is for the black woman a source of anguish—sexual rather than maternal, as in the acts of miscegenation that fill Faulkner's texts—it is less the white male's entry into the black woman's life (an entry usually not resented in his narratives) than his unceremonial and abusive exit from it that wreaks damage and compels his narrative attention. To put it uncharitably: it is as though, if the white man acknowledged her thereafter, the black woman would not complain. At the least, his fiction is not shaped to register that complaint. With the salient

exception of Nancy in "That Evening Sun," Faulkner's representation of
black women who double as mothers and lovers—Eulalia Bon, perhaps
Molly Beauchamp, Eunice and Thomasina Beauchamp, the unnamed "doe"
figure—focuses more upon the racist exploitation of the white lover than
upon the complex and troubled interior economy of the black woman herself.
The abusive dimensions of his agency overshadow the problematics of hers.
All of these emphases alter when we consider the work of Morrison.

To begin with Morrison's white mothers: they are usually absent, but when
present they are no less incapable than their Faulknerian counterparts. The
neurotic Margaret in *Tar Baby* is followed by the ailing, uninformed, but well-
meaning Mrs. Garner in *Beloved*. As in Faulkner's work, the black maid (or
slave) is often required to take care of not just her mistress's house but her mistress herself (Ondine has been Michael's mammy as well). Here the resemblance ends, though, for Morrison shows how much more these black
women's lives involve than white caretaking. They are never just maids or
mammies (yet I hope to have shown that, for Faulkner, being a mammy is not
"just" a minor role nor is it inevitably stereotyped). When, for example, Janey
(in *Beloved*) says to Denver about the Bodwins, "Oh, yeah. They good. Can't
say they ain't good. I wouldn't trade them for another pair, tell you that" (*B*,
255), we observe a social pact inconceivable in Faulkner: black servitude
wryly accepted, good whitefolks better than bad ones and not to be traded in,
but all this a far cry from family or equality. In Morrison's work, therefore, we
may say that the role of the black mammy reduces to its "proper" dimensions—even Pauline, not to speak of Ondine and Sethe, registers only mar-
ginally as mammy. The central figure in her oeuvre is the black mother.
Indeed, it would be hard to find in all of American literature a more compelling range of black mothers than those Morrison has invented.

A full-scale reading of Morrison's black mothers is outside the scope of this
discussion. My aim is rather to juxtapose Morrison's representation of motherhood against Faulkner's so as to accent the cultural play of the writers' race
and gender positioning in shaping those acts of representation. I begin with
the following, unimaginably Faulknerian, passage from *Song of Solomon*. It
comes from Hagar, musing upon the (for once) daunting figure of Ruth Dead
blocking her path:

> The woman who slept in the same house with him [Milkman], and who
> could call him home and he would come, who knew the mystery of his
> flesh, had memory of him as long as his life. The woman who knew him,
> had watched his teeth appear, stuck her finger in his mouth to soothe his

gums. Cleaned his behind, Vaselined his penis, and caught his vomit in a fresh white diaper. Had fed him from her own nipples, carried him close and warm and safe under her heart, and who had opened her legs far far wider than she herself ever had for him.   (SS, 137)

We are in the presence of mystery, a virtually biblical rite of fleshly acknowl-edgment. The black mother is represented as unbearably bonded somatically with her black offspring, so much so that her replacement (the lover who comes after the mother) can never play more than a secondary role. ("A man ain't nothing but a man," says Baby Suggs, "but a son? Well now, that's *some-body*" [B, 23].) The mother has birthed her son from within her own bodily core. Her subsequent caring for him registers as a reenactment of the engulf-ing that precedes birth, a complete embrace of his body. She enters his ori-fices, re-creates within herself the sense of his intimate parts, dirties herself solemnly with his vomit and his feces. It is pre-Oedipal (before the law) through and through. If the white mother's deepest sin in Faulkner is to dis-own her offspring physically, to withdraw her breast, then the black mother's deepest vocation in Morrison is to know that child's body as an extension of her own—a knowing always on the verge of (once again biblical) taboo.

Morrison does not arrive at this vision of the overpowering and pre-Oedipal mother right away, but it is possible to see *The Bluest Eye* as a text in search of her. Only Claudia's mother (a peripheral figure) is described as one capable of cleaning up infant puke: "green-gray, with flecks of orange. It moves like the insides of an uncooked egg. Stubbornly clinging to its own mass, refusing to break up and be removed" (TBE, 11). This lingered-over, sharply focused filth characterizes by metaphoric implication the helpless infant as well ("an uncooked egg"). A mother is one who must enter that filth, share it: a vocation beyond the reach of *The Bluest Eye*'s central mother, Pauline. Unable to embrace such filth, Pauline orphans her daughter, Pecola, by seeking her own release in other terms (always white): the Fishers' spotless kitchen, the movies' blue-eyed heroines. Morrison keys the repression fueling these substitute releases to Pauline's deeper refusal of elements that make up her own black and embodied core.

Those elements energize (to use one of Morrison's memorable phrases) "the dreadful funkiness of passion" (83), a messiness endemic to bodily func-tion when intense. Morrison never insists upon the acceptance of body propensity as exclusively black, but she does pursue the ways in which black women wounded by white icons see themselves as ugly and seek to repress their own bodily birthright. Intense lovemaking is funky, involving unpredictable motions and producing leaky liquids. These liquids make a "glucking sound . . . when she [the lover] is moist" (84). Morrison will focus upon funky black women in her next novel, *Sula*. Here, the sloppy spillover of bodily release is coded in other activities, as in "the blackish blueberries" (108) that splatter when Pecola overturns her mother's pie, or in the "sweet warm insides," the "red guts" (134) released by a black man's split and spreading watermelon, or in the berries the younger Pauline used to put in her dress pocket that "*mashed up and stained my hips. My whole dress was messed with purple, and it never did wash out. . . . I could feel that purple deep inside me*" (115). Cholly's first lovemaking touched her memories of this "purple deep"—"I feel like I'm laughing between my legs" (131)—but Pauline has long since lost connection with her body's liquid possibilities. Alienated, abused by and abusive toward Cholly now, she abjects her own child as so much filth she can no longer mother, make her own.

Funkiness emerges in *The Bluest Eye* only in isolated activities and socially sealed-off spaces, most notably among the three whores whose casual and uncensored physicality Morrison takes delight in. Here is a description of Maginot Line:

> A mountain of flesh, she lay rather than sat in a rocking chair. She had no shoes on, and each foot was poked between a railing: tiny baby toes at the tip of puffy feet . . . massive legs like tree stumps parted wide at the knees, over which spread two roads of soft flabby inner thigh that kissed each other deep in the shade of her dress and closed. . . . She looked at us down through the porch railings and emitted a low, long belch. Her eyes were clean as rain.   (102)

Eyes like a waterfall, clean as rain, body unencumbered with shoes, thighs kissing each other, mouth delighting in lingered-over belches, Maginot Line (her very name makes her other) is beyond domestication, uninterested in maternity, available to description but not to narrative emplotment. Like Faulkner's Benjy, she lets us measure how far from social convention the writer has had to travel to articulate a measure of unco-opted sentience. But she can do nothing for the doomed Pecola in this family-centered text where the line of generational descent is both denatured and all-determining.

The funkiness unavailable to plot and marginalized in *The Bluest Eye* becomes central and familial in *Sula*'s roster of mothers. This shift transforms the entire dynamic of Morrison's canvas, turning the plot of victimization (the undoing of an unmothered child) into one of possibility (unpredictable continuities of funk). From mother to daughter to daughter, the play of uncensored, embodied energy now fuels a narrative of generational descent. The dysfunctional Cholly/Pauline/Pecola trio turns into the indestructible three-generation Peace family. Writ large, these same resources may be seen to undergird a larger black community that, however exploited, emerges as stubbornly protective of its funky and embodied base. Anomie is replaced by neighborhood, isolated abuse by communal resource. We are witness to the birth of the Bottom.

Morrison accomplishes this transformation without sentimentality. People die in *Sula*—more than in *The Bluest Eye*—but the sententiousness that sometimes vitiates that first book has disappeared. The supreme sign of funk in this second novel may reside in its refusal to moralize, its acceptance and pursuit of incarnate possibilities, however monstrous. As Keith Byerman puts it in *Fingering the Jagged Grain*, in Morrison's first novel "the destructiveness of control rather than the creativity of negation predominates" (185). *The Bluest Eye*'s cast of characters, shaped in a certain measure to sociological import (the story of normative white assumptions disastrously internalized by blacks), has here given way to a cast of characters so unrepressed by white norms that they might do anything: characters approaching mythical potentiality.

This potentiality emerges as virtually a gift unconsciously bequeathed by black mothers to their daughters. As though to underline their unforeclosedness, Morrison ensures that we reach these three generations of Peace women only by passing first through two narrative frames of incapacity: Shadrack's war-inflected craziness, Nel and Helene's class-inflected paralysis. Both of these initial portraits show blacks scarred by white violence—arrested in their own subjective unfolding—and they usher us into Nel's desire for another world: "As for Nel, she preferred Sula's woolly house, where a pot of something was always cooking on the stove; where the mother, Hannah, never scolded or gave directions; where all sorts of people dropped in; where newspapers were stacked in the hallway, and dirty dishes left for hours at a time in the sink, and where a one-legged grandmother named Eva handed you goobers from deep inside her pockets or read you a dream" (S, 29). Unencumbered by white icons, casually messy, free of clock-imposed order, organized as an ongoing oral treat where even the peanuts declare their African origin ("goobers") as they rise from deep inside an unknown recess and where Western logic-chopping has given way to African dream-reading—

this "woolly" house signals a world "where all sorts of [black] people" may drop in and be accommodated. The radical liberty embodied in Maginot Line has been reconceived as the resources of a traditional—yet fantastic—extended black family.

All sorts of people do make their appearance: BoyBoy, Plum, the Deweys, Tar Baby, Hannah, and Sula, for starters.[20] Eva names her world and its creatures, oversees the beginning and the end of life, delivers her son Plum from her womb and then reaches all the way into his ass to unblock him, later dosing him in kerosene (a pickled Plum) in order to set him free from life itself. Abandoned by her husband and down to three beets, she reemerges one-legged, enriched by insurance money, and thereafter unstoppable. The careful psychological detail that gives *The Bluest Eye* its diagnostic gravity transforms here into manic, unexplained and inexplicable actions. Critics argue (will continue to argue) inconclusively over the meaning of Eva's treatment of Plum, Sula's of Chicken Little, Morrison's of Hannah (a burning described lyrically and inhumanly as a dance)—in all of this we see compelling gestures being liberated from normative explanation. Which is to say, a mythical rather than sociological focus: as in a new dispensation beyond white male norms, this mother-centered, three-generational world follows no laws but its own. Yet it does follow its own. *Sula* unfolds not as fairy tale or wish fulfillment, but rather seems to enact the rigor of an indecipherable destiny. It is Morrison's keenest, barest, most lyrical book. Like Faulkner's *As I Lay Dying*, it delineates a world both recognizable and beyond prediction.

If the release of *As I Lay Dying* is premised upon the mother's dying, that of *Sula* is nourished by her law-shattering vitality. On this reading, *Sula* is a sort of paradigm text, preparing us for the prodigious role played by the god-like mother—she who gives life and who takes it away—in *Song of Solomon* and *Beloved*. Pilate and Ruth both center upon the generational act (the text accesses them through their definitive relation to the fathers that beget them, the children they literally and figuratively suckle). However distressed, they do not betray what *Tar Baby* names as their "ancient properties"—their adherence to the bodily givens of smell and swamp as sources of female identity, not shame. In Sethe and Baby Suggs—each in her own way—such adherence to the rights of the body reaches sublime heights:

> She [Baby Suggs] told them that the only grace they could have was the grace they could imagine. That if they could not see it, they would not have it. "Here," she said, "in this place, we flesh; flesh that weeps, laughs; flesh that dances on bare feet in grass. Love it. Love it hard. Yonder they do not

love your flesh. They despise it. . . . This is flesh I'm talking about here.
Flesh that needs to be loved."   (B, 88)

Perhaps it comes together here. An "unchurched [female] preacher" (87)
preaching in an unclaimed space (in the Clearing), Baby Suggs speaks a new
gospel, embodying the authority elsewhere wielded (in Faulkner wielded) by
white males. Eva Peace's new dispensation, her central matriarchal engagement with offspring, reveals now the racial pressure that has never ceased to
operate upon it. Whites do not love black flesh. In the time of slavery they
annihilate black flesh, in its aftermath they humiliate black flesh. Insofar as
blacks internalize this white contempt leveled at their bodily condition, they
absorb this poison and—like Pecola—are driven insane. Survival requires a
different tactic, another sense of one's incarnate history.

That new history is limned in female names. Unlike Faulkner's lineage of
demanding males, his ancestral Compsons and McCaslins and Sartorises and
Sutpens that live in the memory of their offspring white and black, sometimes
enabling and more often suffocating—unlike this Oedipal lineage in which
the son finds his identity by establishing a relation to the law and property of
his father—Morrison's world from *Sula* forward moves in time along female
axes. Even *Song of Solomon's* pursuit of Solomon proceeds by way of Pilate
and Reba and Hagar: biblical names that point to roads not taken (a pilot who
does not follow Christ, a mother whose offspring Ishmael travels outside the
legitimate line). At its core this genealogy cleaves to a line of sounded song
rather than of written law, a line of bodily love ("You just can't fly on off and
leave a body" [SS, 147]) rather than of the spirit's tormented transcendence.
You have to love your flesh, you can't leave a body behind. You nourish offspring rather than test or abandon them. Authority is figured as incarnate and
audible and mother-centered. Even the dead speak, as Baby Suggs reaches
through the veil to pass on sought-after advice to her daughter-in-law and later
her grandchild. *Beloved* reaches its resolution by dramatizing thirty singing
women searching "for the right combination, the key, the code, the sound that
broke the back of words" (B, 261). Not Faulkner's Mrs. Compson, whose
rusted keys show her to be, however victimized, the keeper of her culture's
body-punishing code, but rather the glimpse of a dispensation at once new
and immeasurably old, a world configured by the mother and her descent,
outside the property logic and nay-saying humiliation of Oedipus, acknowledging the calls of the sentient body.

It only adds to Morrison's interest to note, in closing, that *Jazz* marks yet
another way of rendering the mother.[21] Less the giver and taker of life, she fig-

ures here most poignantly in scenes of longing. Dorcas, Violet, and Joe have lost their mothers (through fire, suicide, and mystery). Alice, Violet, and Joe have failed to produce offspring of their own. The enacted maternal bond of the earlier texts is sought after in suggestive substitutions. Indeed, *Jazz* echoes *Absalom, Absalom!* in its imagining of a "might have been" more true than truth, its way of exploring possibilities never realized in life itself. Vicarious projections become rampant, as Violet wonders what plural roles the murdered Dorcas plays in her and Joe's psychic life:

> Just when her [Violet's] breasts were finally flat enough not to need the binders the young women wore to sport the chest of a soft boy, just when her nipples had lost their point, mother-hunger had hit her like a hammer. Knocked her down and out. When she woke up, her husband had shot a girl young enough to be that daughter whose hair she had dressed to kill. Who lay there asleep in that coffin? Who posed there awake in the photograph? The scheming bitch who had not considered Violet's feelings one tiniest bit, who came into a life, took what she wanted and damn the consequences? Or mama's dumpling girl? Was she the woman who took the man, or the daughter who fled her womb? . . . "Another time," she [Violet] said to Alice Manfred, "another time I would have loved her too. Just like you did. Just like Joe." (*J*, 108–9)

Like Bon murdered and motionless in the coffin, like the locket of the octoroon that the living are left with, the dead are available for reconfiguring in this autumnal novel of aftermath. Violet sees in Joe's teenage mistress the lineaments of her own unliving child. Did Joe see her thus as well? Feelings are fluid—lovers, daughters, and mothers interpenetrate—reshapable in this latest novel where the damage (once again like Faulkner) has all been done before the narrative even begins. I shall later juxtapose *Jazz* against *Absalom* more deliberately and diagnostically, but I might conclude this chapter of beginnings—of mammies and mothers—by juxtaposing the two novels' endings. While the Faulknerian drama of old letters and sacrifice (the culturally mandated crucifixion of Charles Bon and its unceasing consequences) ends in unbearable indictment (*"I dont. I dont! I dont hate it! I dont hate it!"* [*AA*, 311]), *Jazz* closes out its story of murderous passion as the song of bodily desire, reaccessed as mounting promise: "If I were able I'd say it. Say make me, remake me. You are free to do it and I am free to let you because look, look. Look where your hands are. Now" (*J*, 229).

2

Historical Beginnings
Slavery

Unsettling as late-twentieth-century liberal Americans may find it, slavery has persisted as a recurrent human arrangement throughout history. Orlando Patterson's magisterial *Slavery and Social Death* finds virtually no part of the globe, nor any time period prior to our century, in which slavery did not flourish (vii–ix). "The peculiar institution" struck Americans as "peculiar" only within an Enlightenment interpretive framework in which freedom was celebrated as the founding and conclusive virtue of the American project itself.[1]

The Atlantic slave trade antedated the landing of the pilgrims at Jamestown in 1607—it began in the Spanish Caribbean a century earlier (159–64)—and, as Joel Williamson notes in *The Crucible of Race* (12), the first black slaves arrived on these shores as early as 1619. By the middle of the eighteenth century slavery was thriving in all thirteen of the colonies. Its incompatibility with the Declaration of Independence was not lost on the Founding Fathers, though. By the end of the century slavery was abolished in the Northern states, and the importation of slaves into the country at large was soon made illegal. To many thinkers of that time (often in the South as well as the North), the institution needed to be abolished.[2] The more stubborn problem the majority population faced was how to accommodate the blacks already here (several million by then). As it turned out, getting rid of the institution nearly destroyed the entire country half a century later. And, despite considerable progress since *Brown v. Board of Education* in 1954, the question of genuine equity for blacks remains unresolved, almost four centuries after the arrival of the first slaves.

What is a slave? Patterson suggests three constituent features of enslavement: a position of impotence maintainable by physical force, a condition of "natal alienation" (5), and the positing of slave identity as essentially dishonorable. "Slavery," he claims, "is the permanent, violent domination of natally alienated and generally dishonored persons" (13). In the pages that follow, in both this chapter and the next, I shall take up the implications of each of these features of enslavement. Suffice it to say here that the legally sanctioned infliction of physical force distinguishes slavery from all voluntary forms of subjection (common to ideological allegiances), that natal alienation means the social erasure of one's ancestry and offspring—producing what Patterson calls a "genealogical isolate" (5)—and that the imputation of dishonor announces a general impotence in which one has no publicly acknowledged worth, no name one can defend. As Thomas Ruffin declared as early as 1829, "With slavery . . . the end is the profit of the master, his security and the public safety; the subject [the black man], one doomed in his person and his posterity, to live without knowledge, and without the capacity to make anything his own, and to toil that another may reap his fruits" (cited in Patterson, 3–4).

Sanctioning this cluster of injustices was the all-compelling notion of race. (Winthrop Jordan, in *White Over Black*, has carefully demonstrated how this was not always the case. Throughout the seventeenth century white servitude and black enslavement were understood as close to interchangeable. As the importation of African slaves increased throughout the next century, however, the need to justify increased with it, leading to a sinister amalgamation of fixed religious, geographic, and racial differences: "to be Christian was to be civilized rather than barbarous, English rather than African, white rather than black" [97].) By the mid-nineteenth century an immovable racial code—the essentializing of human difference into a hierarchical typology of races—had become commonplace, serving throughout Europe, and later in the United States, as ideological support for colonial enterprises. Few thinkers in the West would, before the mid-twentieth century, have known how to respond to Kwame Anthony Appiah's recent conclusion, based upon scrutiny of the claims of current genetic biology: "The truth is that there are no races: there is nothing in the world that can do all we ask race to do for us" (45).

Finally, we might note that the "peculiar" paradox of freedom for American whites and slavery for American blacks strikes an increasing number of commentators (including Morrison in *Playing in the Dark*) as disturbingly characteristic of the modern (i.e., postrevolutionary) period itself. "Before slavery," Patterson writes, "people simply could not have conceived of the thing we call freedom. Men and women in premodern, nonslaveholding societies did not, could not, value the removal of restraint as an ideal. Individuals yearned only

for the security of being positively anchored in a network of power and authority" (340). In America, the exemplary modern country founded on the legitimacy of revolution, on escape from despotic networks of power and authority,
the ideal of freedom is the germinal dream in our national imaginary. Is it possible that the concomitant imposition of slavery is not so much a contradiction
of our goals as the conceptually repressed price this country has been willing
during most of its history to pay in order to pursue this gorgeous chimera?
With this question suspended over the entire discussion here, I turn toward the
fictional practice of Faulkner and Morrison as it encounters, and works into
narrative form, the nightmare of American slavery.

No American writer, of course, is required to take up this material.
Novelists are free, as Henry James memorably declared more than a hundred
years ago, to engage only those topics that speak to them. The critic's task,
James insisted in "The Art of Fiction," is to assess novelists according to their
quality of engagement with their topic, not their choice of the topic itself. This
formalist claim has always struck me as both true and suspect, for the topics a
writer manages to take up do intimate, ultimately, the writer's complex insertion within the larger culture. No novelist writes without risk, but some risks
outweigh others, allow greater failure as well as greater success. Faulkner's
importance, on this argument, remains inseparable from his capacity to
address the meaning and consequences of American slavery. I will argue further (in part 3) that, insofar as novels are valuable in their capacity to dramatize (dramatize—not master) the "circulation of social energy" that nourishes
an endless series of ideological clashes, *Beloved* emerges as Morrison's mag-
num opus.[3] It takes on our national trauma—the human energy fueling both
the normalization of slavery and the resistance mounted against it—and no
small measure of its interest and importance flows from this source.

Topical criteria of literary value are of course not alone sufficient, and they
remain liable to abuse—witness the distortive hold of *Gone with the Wind* on
generations of readers, that book's seductive promise being its capacity to pass
off its ideological stance as the vanished Southern real itself. Yet the fact that,
in fiction, content comes to the reader not as the real but as an ideologically
inflected version of the real seems to me a condition intrinsic to novelistic
practice. This condition ought to be met, on the part of the reader, by a greater
alertness to the ideological bias inseparable from *any* act of representing,
rather than by a wholesale discounting of representation itself as noncognitive
and therefore nonpertinent with respect to literary value. To attempt to escape
the deformations of ideology by way of a foreclosed formalism—a technique

for assessing aesthetic value independently of the art object's complex relation to the social, its capacities as witness—is to bypass the work's own ineluctable place within the social fabric it at once encodes and critiques.

Form does matter, but it is not all that matters. The point is worth insisting on in an interpretive climate where both extremes—the text as formal masterpiece, the text as indistinguishable from any other text in its status as social witness—operate extensively yet refuse to acknowledge each other. We are nonnegotiably free to write about what calls to us, yet we shall be judged by both the dimensions of that call and our ways of responding to it. All this to propose the following: Faulkner's and Morrison's engagement with slavery not only requires commentary in a study devoted to their ways of representing race, but it constitutes as well a major component of their claim to our attention. Their ways of telling the nineteenth-century story of slavery are simultaneously their ways (at once conditioned and free) of writing twentieth-century stories of America.

Faulkner's best-known fellow novelists of the 1920s through the 1940s (all of them—with the exception of Richard Wright—white) seemed to evade this topic successfully, and Faulkner himself only gradually took it on. Not until *Absalom, Absalom!* does he interrogate the institution of slavery itself, and it is instructive to follow him making his way to this commitment. In his opening pair of novels (*Soldiers' Pay* and *Mosquitoes*), at any rate, there is no hint of interest in racial trauma, and the third one—*Flags in the Dust*—deploys blacks as comic or idyllic backdrop (acutely drawn but undeveloped) for the more sustained exploration of dislocated young white men. The next work, *The Sound and the Fury*, produces the magnificent Dilsey mainly as a revealing lens upon the depth of Compson dysfunction. Only in *Light in August*, Faulkner's seventh novel, does race take on an unpacifiable subjective importance. There we see emerge, for the first time, the fully racist significance of the Negro—in James Baldwin's terms, "a form of insanity that overtakes white men" (88)—and Faulkner pursues and diagnoses that insanity with unequaled power. If we take seriously Morrison's claim that black always serves in American culture to define white (and does so most insidiously when least consciously), that black and white are inevitable components of the writer's expressive palette (components that reveal the writer as participant, witting or unwitting, in the culture's larger racial arrangements), then it seems clear that Faulkner had from the beginning written *through* blacks. But in *Light in August* the terms of the racial pact change suddenly. He begins to write *about* them.

He can at first write *about* them in *Light in August* only by imagining himself as, impossibly, nightmarishly, one *of* them. Joe Christmas is in no normative sense a black man; Faulkner demonstrates no subjective grasp of Southern black culture's traditional ways of producing identity. Joe experiences blackness not as cultural resource (a shared dimension of innumerable human beings, out of which they generate life narratives like and unlike everyone else's) but as a white man's intolerable secret. This existential take upon blackness—what would I feel like if, in the South of the early twentieth century, I believed I might have a drop of "nigger blood" in me?—severely limits *Light in August*'s exploration of race, guaranteeing the absence of other blacks from narrative emplotment and thus enforcing the "social death" of Christmas himself.[4] Yet at the same time it allows Faulkner to enter blackness and to discover there not the surface tranquillity that makes more salient the torment of his dislocated whites (the terms of the earlier pact) but instead the unmasterable anguish that race can foment within black and white alike. This discovery of anguish transforms that earlier pact into a compelling perspective. In Morrison's terms, instead of seeing the discrete living details within the fishbowl, "suddenly I saw the bowl [itself], the structure that transparently (and invisibly) permits the ordered life it contains to exist in the larger world" (*PD*, 17). Race is no longer picturesque background or salient detail but an organizing differential structure itself. Once Faulkner has his eye on this structure, he will explore it with increasing diagnostic power, producing in *Absalom, Absalom!* and *Go Down, Moses* his most radiant testimony to the systemic damage inflicted by whites upon blacks. There he reveals the American pursuit of freedom itself to be, unbearably, a drama of racial injustice.

Faulkner: *Light in August*

The experience of slavery coils in the background of *Light in August*, never far from the haunted minds of Gail Hightower and Joanna Burden. Its charge registers less as a national wrong inflicted upon blacks than as a disfiguring inheritance for whites, too heavy for its twentieth-century legatees to sustain. Hightower's melancholy memories circulate around a shadowy pair of parents, an even more distant grandfather, and the latter's faithful black retainers, Pomp and Cinthy, who are denied subjectivity in any form other than abiding loyalty to their Confederate master. Pomp accompanied Marse Gail to the War and later chose, "inconsolable," to immolate himself rather than concede that "the master might be dead: 'No suh,' he would say. 'Not Marse Gail. Not him. Dey wouldn't *dare* to kill a Hightower. Dey wouldn't *dare'* " (*LA*, 751). We are witness here to a white writer imagining slave loyalty as virtually approaching suttee: death is preferable to life without the master. (The point is not that such loyalty never occurred but that Faulkner's text uses such motivation as a way of ignoring other responses—such as flight from enslavement or even defection to the Yankee army—that would be more disturbing to white Southern sensibility.) As for Cinthy, not unpredictably, she "ran the household and . . . was [the infant Hightower's] mother too and nurse" (746). This same Cinthy, like young Faulkner's Mammy Callie, spoke endlessly to the impressionable child about the War and his ancestor's exploits. She had no use for emancipation, refusing to leave her master's house in the wake of the War, and then, years later, reappearing upon the family scene:

> "You're free, now," the son [Hightower's father] told her.
> "Free?" she said. She spoke with still and brooding scorn. "Free? Whut's freedom done except git Marse Gail killed and made a bigger fool outen Pawmp den even de Lawd Hisself could do? Free? Dont talk ter me erbout freedom." (752)

"Dont talk ter me erbout freedom": Faulkner's white culture taught him patiently, through story after story, that its antebellum blacks were on the whole figures of grateful fidelity, distraught and deprived of purpose when separated from their benevolent masters. This convenient myth serves as the narrative that his great work regularly transcends but that—as a sort of default position—it never quite discards. In *Light in August* there is no question of discarding it. The War represents a trauma not for blacks but instead for the whites who have inherited either its unusable poetry, like Hightower, or its alienating racial polemics, like the four generations of Burdens. (I say "the War" rather than "slavery," because these two foci represent dramatically different interests—white and black—in kindred materials, and Faulkner's career manifests a permanent vacillation between them. In my view, his great texts focus on slavery, not the War.)

The sudden narration of Joanna Burden's past represents one of the oddest sequences in *Light in August*. For ten uninterrupted pages, we become immersed in four generations of her history, all of it male, violent, and antislavery. The clottedness of this material (readers have difficulty separating out the different Burdens) testifies to Faulkner's unwillingness to probe its pathology, to see in more patient detail how such past histories affect the present dysfunctional ones. It is as though he wants only to tell a twentieth-century story (already requiring hundreds of pages), yet he can't help noticing that it insists upon nineteenth-century moorings—which he all too briefly provides. No blacks make their appearance during this onslaught, as we move through the first minister Burden (Nathaniel) to his runaway son (Calvin) who "spent much of his time talking politics and in his harsh loud voice cursing slavery and slaveholders" (577), then to his runaway son (Nathaniel again) with his Mexican mistress and their son (Calvin again), the middle two of these four Burdens given to picaresque wandering and outbursts of physical brutality.

The elder Calvin seethes with racist anger even though, when younger, he has killed in behalf of abolition: " 'Damn, lowbuilt black folks: lowbuilt because of the weight of the wrath of God, black because of the sin of human bondage staining their blood and flesh.' His gaze was vague, fanatical, and convinced. 'But we done freed them now' " (581). Apart from the polar difference of ideology, this could be Doc Hines, and there is a sense that the violence infusing Burden racial convictions exceeds any particular stance itself, leading to the murder of both Calvins by Colonel Sartoris some years later, during Reconstruction. This last murder resonates in Faulkner's work, and I shall return to it in my discussion of *The Unvanquished*. Here he leaves its opposed meanings intact: at once an act of brutality (killing "with two shots from the same pistol an old onearmed man and a boy who had never even cast his first vote" [582]) and an act of communal solidarity (Joanna's father being enough "French to respect anybody's love for the land where he and his people were born and to understand that a man [Sartoris] would have to act as the land where he was born had trained him to act" [587]).

Be that as it may, the agents and recipients of violence in this compressed Burden history are uniformly white, leaving the black core of racial injustice to emerge figuratively and only once—but then unforgettably—in Joanna's cemetery vision of a world of crucified blacks:

> But after that I seemed to see them for the first time not as people, but as a thing, a shadow in which I lived, we lived, all white people, all other people. I thought of all the children coming forever and ever into the world, white, with the black shadow already falling upon them before they drew breath. And I seemed to see the black shadow in the shape of a cross. And it seemed like the white babies were struggling, even before they drew breath, to escape from the shadow that was not only upon them but beneath them too. . . . I saw all the little babies that would ever be in the world, the ones not yet even born—a long line of them with their arms spread, on the black crosses.   (585)

I shall return to this haunting passage in part 2, for it radiates Faulkner's deepest imagining of blacks as inescapable embodiments of white guilt and white paralysis. Here we may note that these crucified blacks are figured not as active subjects who have undergone (and summoned forth the courage and wit necessary to survive) over three centuries of slavery but rather as passive objects—crosses—on which all whites will eventually experience their own crucifixion. Even as Joanna speaks these words she suffers their consequences: her race-charged alienation from the white community, her pathological investment in Joe's "black" destiny, her nonrelation to actual blacks. Slavery in *Light in August* is a centuries-old catastrophe that registers in the continuing dysfunction of contemporary whites. For Faulkner's view of how slavery might have affected the nineteenth-century blacks who lived its impositions we must go, not to one of his best novels, but to one of his most revealing.

Faulkner: *The Unvanquished*

First, a caveat. This is, for the most part (and despite a good deal of current critical attention), a racially retrograde text; one explanation for its conventional thinking is genetic. All the stories Faulkner gathers together here except for the last one—"An Odor of Verbena"—appeared earlier (between 1934 and 1936) in popular magazines (five of them in the *Saturday Evening Post*). The revising for book publication that took place in 1937, writes Noel Polk in *Faulkner: Novels 1936–1940*, "reflects the same sort of commercial haste that had gone into their writing" (1110). The point is neither apologetic nor condemnatory. Rather, it directs us to the writer's variable involvement with his culture's discursive practices—the *Post* audience is not the same as the *Absalom* audience—and it prepares us to ask, What story of America, destined for what audience, does Faulkner here make of the national trauma of slavery and the Civil War?

One answer is that he makes—of both the War and the slavery that caused it—child's play, the manageable material of a satisfying read. *The Unvanquished* opens on Ringo and Bayard's pretend battle of Vicksburg, and there is a larger sense that Faulkner's manner of textualizing this cataclysmic war seeks systematically to derealize it: Ringo and Bayard hiding under Granny's skirts when Colonel Dick arrives, John Sartoris's successful pretense of a squadron of men for capturing Union soldiers ("Surround them, boys! Dont let a man escape!" [*U*, 364]) when he is actually all but alone, his masquerade as a simpleton when the Yankees pull up (allowing him to escape on Jupiter out the back). These

Twain-like adventures terminate rhythmically with the boys' successful lies, then having their mouths washed out. Granny's enterprise itself—to recover the horses and silver taken by the Yankees—registers as a game (full of disguised identities, misunderstood speeches) whose aim does not vary: to nullify the opponents' moves and return to square one. A game works only if all the players play by the same rules and if, once it is over, nothing "really" has happened. Faulkner has arranged for the Union army to be remarkably complicit: Colonel Dick who amiably ignores the boys under the skirt, then writes out the orders that will allow their larger gambit to succeed, the other Union officers who in their good-humored fuming somehow never figure it all out in time. Granny-Bayard-Ringo's local gamelike maneuvers—to get back all they have lost—reveal the larger narrative strategy of *The Unvanquished* itself: to rehearse that war in such a way as not to have lost it, to remain unvanquished.

For this strategy to succeed, a common idiom is required, the rhetoric of aristocratic honor spoken by friend and foe alike ("But, Colonel," the frustrated Yankee sergeant remonstrates, "we saw them two kids run in here. All of us saw them—" to which the gentlemanly colonel replies: "Didn't you just hear this lady say there are no children here? Where are your ears, sergeant?" [340]). The telling distinction is not North and South but honor and dishonor—a distinction carried out in part at the rhetorical level of Latinate dignity and elegant manners, on the one hand, versus vernacular crudity and treacherous acts, on the other. Race politics seems to disappear into (more manageable) class politics. Granny and the boys do fine with the Yankees. It is Southern trash that undermines their venture by refusing both the behavioral conventions that sustain it (gentlemen do not harm women and children) and the verbal idiom that communicates it. "Ambuscade," "Riposte in Tertio," "Vendée"—the titles of the stories convey a Latinate/European sense of propriety to which the nearly illiterate Ab Snopes (a traitor from within) remains deaf.

We might linger for a moment on "honor," for, as commentators on the Old South have noted, it served as one of the culture's core values, and its latently reactionary bearing on issues of both race and gender is considerable.[5] First, honor is precisely what the emasculated black slave lacks: honor as that capacity to propose publicly and then make good on one's proposal, honor as the realm (restricted to white males) in which one's good name is at stake. As Bertram Wyatt-Brown puts it in *Southern Honor*, "Honor is first the inner conviction of self-worth. . . . The second aspect of honor is the claim of that self-assessment before the public. . . . The third element is the assessment of the claim by the public, a judgment based upon the behavior of the claimant. In other words, honor is reputation" (14). "The honor of the Southerner," John Hope Franklin writes, "caused him to defend with his life the slightest suggestion of irregularity in his honesty or integrity; and he was fiercely sensitive to any imputation that might cast a shadow on the character of the women in his family" (cited in Patterson, 95). Wyatt-Brown and Franklin let us glimpse that the concept of honor both underwrites the expansive, even extravagant terrain of male self-esteem (there is no length one will not go to to preserve it) and operates, simultaneously, as the imprisoning conceptual frame of female behavior, as so many of Faulkner's straitened women reveal. That the discourse of *The Unvanquished* circulates about the idiom of honor implies the conservative racial and gender values at work here, inflecting, if they do not command, whatever unconventional departures the text might otherwise suggest.

At any rate, the rhetoric of honor shared by Granny and her Northern opponents permits this particular language game to remain intact during the war scenes. The stories must therefore turn, for their necessary betrayals, toward a hinterland of internal intrigue: a class-based drama in which two innocent boys and one honorable old man (Buck McCaslin) track a gang of dishonorable men, for the purpose of revenge. Of course they succeed, just as in the last story ("An Odor of Verbena") a more intricate kind of success is proposed, one that will anneal/transcend the real yet textually marginalized traumas of the past. To see how these traumas are marginalized—how the core issue of slavery is largely erased *as* an issue—we must turn to the representation of blacks in *The Unvanquished*.

"Largely erased": Faulkner's text does recurrently and powerfully signal a racial disturbance it will not directly explore, first through the figure of Loosh. We meet him before we meet John Sartoris—he is the first knowing adult in the novel—and what he knows is that the boys' fantasy Vicksburg is replaced by a real Corinth. The Union army is already there. Inasmuch as he informs the Yankees of Granny's doings, he might well be set up to play the heavy. Yet Faulkner grants him his gnomic, biblical eloquence. Pressured by his black family to shut up, he proclaims: "Ginral Sherman gonter sweep the earth and the Race gonter all be free!" (334). Later, his speech becomes even more oracular:

> "Yes," Loosh said. "I going. I done been freed; God's own angel proclamated me free and gonter general me to Jordan. I dont belong to John Sartoris now; I belongs to me and God."
>
> "But the silver belongs to John Sartoris," Granny said. "Who are you to give it away?"

"You ax me that?" Loosh said. "Where John Sartoris? Whyn't he come and ax me that? Let God ax John Sartoris who the man name that give me to him. Let the man that buried me in the black dark ax that of the man what dug me free."   (369–70)

This is in its way sublime, so much so that one forgets how the novel refuses to show Loosh in his slave relation to John Sartoris. It cannot afford to dramatize a showdown between these two, in which Sartoris would "come and ax me that." In the same way the move toward emancipation is relentlessly nonlocal, displaced beyond the Sartoris plantation, apocalyptic. The river they will cross is the Jordan, outside of immediate secular history. When a half-crazed black woman falls behind the immense herd of moving and chanting blacks and is asked who she belongs to and if she wants to die here on the road, she only responds: "Hit's Jordan we coming to. Jesus gonter see me that far" (376). The effect is of a shorthand language for Armageddon that adroitly replaces any longhand representation of racial turmoil in Mississippi.

Such turmoil is what Faulkner's text systematically eliminates from the domestic sanctuary at its center: Granny's household, made up centrally of herself and Bayard as white, and Joby, Louvinia, Loosh, Eleanora, and Ringo as black. Of these, only Loosh seeks his freedom, and in such an obedient context his ardor feels willful, to the other blacks even disloyal. Louvinia functions as Granny's unthinkingly faithful servant/helpmate ("A black man," Granny says of a figure in her dream, to which Louvinia responds, "A nigger?" [345]). Faulkner relies for his sense of the status quo on Louvinia's inertial devotion to antebellum racial norms. The novel quietly ends with "Louvinia laying the table for supper" (492)—an indication that, regardless of the confusion outside, within this Southern household racial decorum remains intact.[6]

The linchpin of the text's racial argument is Ringo, the black figure whose fraternal equality with Bayard—achieved within the sanctuary of the Southern family and immune to outer stress—must embody the text's defiance of abolitionist propaganda: "because Ringo and I had been born in the same month and had both fed at the same breast and had slept together and eaten together for so long that Ringo called Granny 'Granny' just like I did, until maybe he wasn't a nigger anymore or maybe I wasn't a white boy anymore, the two of us neither" (323). Here we reach the central fantasy of *The Unvanquished*, that within the intimacy of this familial cocoon racial difference ceases to operate. Yet Ringo, whose only difference Bayard will concede is a greater intelligence, is in fact produced through a different narrative strategy. He is given all the good lines (most of the wit in this text belongs to

Ringo), but the price he pays for being a repository of these one-liners is considerable. Ringo is denied the humanity of ongoing and fallible white consciousness; he cannot grow or change or wonder. When he merrily tells Bayard, "I aint a nigger anymore. I done been abolished" (454), the joke is in resonant ways on him. Ostensibly refusing "abolition" (like Cinthy in *Light in August*), he is actually fixed (if not abolished) within a racially determined strategy of representation. And he is likewise all but abolished from the later chapters of this text. When he does make his brief appearance in "An Odor of Verbena," his racial reification is complete. Announced as "Your boy is downstairs . . ." (464)—which Bayard calmly accepts ("A fresh horse for my boy," he requests)—Ringo silently joins his young master in the solemn journey back home to avenge the old master. The drama is indeed one of white mastery: Ringo joining Louvinia and the others as passive decor, all of them waiting for Bayard to sustain the old order and to meet violence with violence. Faulkner cannot permit racial challenge at this point, inasmuch as his strategy for resolving *The Unvanquished* turns upon gender challenge—a challenge that, while both male and female, is insistently white.

Others have commented provocatively on the gender experimentation embodied in both Drusilla's taking on traditional male perquisites and Bayard's deliberately relinquishing them.[7] Rather than add to these readings, I would point to the racial fixity that Faulkner seems to require to pursue his gender explorations. The two enterprises (racial and gender) register as inseparable, for Drusilla's iconoclastic bond with John Sartoris is sealed and ratified on the anvil of the Burden murders. Ambivalent in *Light in August*, the murders are now represented as necessary, with certain details changed accordingly ("I let them fire first [Sartoris says]. You all heard. You boys can swear to my derringer" [460]). Killing those two agents of racial change, refusing thus the new order of Reconstruction that they represent, merges with the birth of the free woman, capable of outraging her culture's standards of behavior. As though to underline the reactionary core supporting this gender "advance," Drusilla and Sartoris are surrounded by the latter's old Confederate band—ushers at the wedding, so to speak. The scene of murder and voting—taking place years later during Reconstruction—concludes with a rebel yell ("Yaaaaaaay, John Sartoris! Yaaaaaaay!"): unvanquished indeed. This murder in behalf of the status quo ante not only launches Drusilla's marriage to Sartoris in an antebellum key (ensuring its sterility, its unavailability for further narrative treatment), it also—and now in the opposite direction—launches Bayard's successful reprisal of Sartoris identity, this time in a postviolent, postbellum key.

Bayard's saying no to revenge has enchanted Faulkner's readers for many decades now (this last story is often separately reprinted), and I may close this inquiry into racial representation in *The Unvanquished* by speculating on the blindnesses wrought into that enchantment.[8] In cleaving to Bayard's maturation, we have worked to turn this text into a coherent narrative of male courage under stress, and we have sought to read this gender progress as a larger cultural one. At the limit, we have read it as the birth of the New (and more law-abiding) South, successfully delivered from the brutalities of the Old South. In so doing we have chosen not to linger on the text's racial conservatism and its refusal to propose a resolution for its female deviations with anything like the authority it brings to Bayard's rebellion. "Dont you see we are working for peace through law and order?" John Sartoris incredibly says after having gunned down the Burdens (460): is this a 1930s glance at the Jim Crow "law and order" that followed Reconstruction and that did indeed hark back to that rebel yell?

As for young Bayard, he becomes "the Sartoris," his heroism all the stronger (and admiringly recognized) for his not firing the gun. He does not relinquish the white male privileging associated with the antebellum honor code (its rigid racial and gender binary that assigns potency to one group and dependency to both others); he merely refines it in a nonviolent key. At the end of *The Unvanquished* he is all that Faulkner wants us see. Yet we may note, on either side of this hero, the other gender challenge and the entire racial struggle that have been removed from representation, inobtrusively vanquished: Drusilla's inconsequential rebellion against gender codes, present now only in the metonymic sprig of verbena on Bayard's pillow, and Ringo, Bayard's boy still at his Sartoris station, silently faithful to the Lost Cause and to the genteel/aristocratic vision of race relations that this 1938 text radiates. It is hard to believe that, during the very years these stories were being written, Faulkner was simultaneously producing an immensely greater novel, *Absalom, Absalom!*, in which this vision receives the racial diagnosis it patently deserves. There we find a South not phantasmally unvanquished but, more complexly, both dead and alive, its sustaining myth uprooted though its stubborn dreams remain intact.

Faulkner: *Absalom, Absalom!*

The first blacks we encounter in *Absalom* are casually othered as foreign-born slaves, seemingly sharing nothing with the whites who surround them. Rosa speaks repeatedly of Sutpen's band of "wild negroes" (*AA*, 16), and the text continues to sound this motif of primitive beings (with their own not-language, their own not-human behavior) as a sort of bass note against which its more complex racial re-imagining will be juxtaposed. Those "wild negroes" build Sutpen's Hundred, hunt his fleeing architect, drive his furious phaeton: in sum, they surround this central white figure and are used by Faulkner to convey (as though osmotically) Sutpen's atavistic and unstoppable power. The emphasis in Rosa's and Mr. Compson's narratives upon these primitive figures sets us up as readers (though unknowingly) for the contrasts that are about to arrive: the extraordinarily different black history wrought into four generations of Bons.

Absalom and *Go Down, Moses* both move through exquisitely contrastive narrative designs, virtually mapping out a readerly education in racial misprision. Our first take of the black/white hunt in "Was"—rendered in the insouciant voice of an innocent nine-year-old boy—alters painfully when we replay the hunt later, recognizing that two white men (Buck and Buddy) are in fact merrily engaged in hunting their own (three-quarters) black brother. As for *Absalom*, those "wild negroes" of the opening scenes seem to reach their acme of wildness in the wrestling scene that concludes the first chapter. There, a whole series of offenses that Rosa has registered (Sutpen's brutal imposing on her family, his lack of a past and of decent bloodlines, his daughter Judith's insistence on the reckless phaeton) reaches culmination: Sutpen entering the ring half-naked with one of these "wild negroes," "fighting not like white men fight, with rules and weapons, but like negroes fight to hurt one another quick and bad" (*AA*, 23). Not only does Rosa narrate the violation of a racial taboo—one does not fight that *intimately* with one's slaves—but she shows it to be staged as a scene of perverse learning: the two children, Judith and Henry, are there watching, being intolerably corrupted. As Joseph Boone and other critics have noted, this encounter goes further yet, serving as a kind of primal scene in which the deepest erotic energies of *Absalom, Absalom!* emerge as homoerotic, a crossing between white and black males, serving to show us (did we know while still in chapter 1 how to read it) that Sutpen's larger dynastic ambition will fail not least through its heterosexual conventionality. Yet, even after we think we have mastered this as a scene of taboo, we learn later to resee it through a class prism rather than a racial one, at which point it suddenly becomes poignantly normative. We discover that the alienated mountain man, Sutpen, can relieve the stress imposed by his slaveholding culture's abstract rules for race relations only through entering the ring with blacks, thus renewing his earlier (no longer applicable) sense of human relations as physical, flesh to flesh: "his only relaxation fighting his wild niggers in the stable" (214). What seemed pure taboo now appears to be nostalgic ceremony.[9]

But this is a ceremony only for the white man: *Absalom* never shows us how this event registers upon the blacks who make it possible. More broadly, the text's way of bringing to bear another cultural lens upon its once-visited materials—a lens that shows chaos to be in fact a different order, as the not-language of the "wild negroes" is really a patois French learned in Haiti: all this reconceiving is for whites only. For example, Mr. Compson reads white sexual norms in antebellum Mississippi with virtually sociological precision: "a young man [Henry] grown up and living in a milieu where the other sex is separated into three sharp divisions, separated (two of them) by a chasm which could be crossed but one time and in but one direction—ladies, women, females—the virgins whom gentlemen someday married, the courtesans to whom they went while on sabbaticals to the cities, the slave girls and women upon whom that first caste rested and to whom in certain cases it doubtless owed the very fact of its virginity" (90). Here is the cultural logic of patriarchy normalizing the young white master's behavior, but what does it feel like to be on the receiving end—to be a "Juno or Missylena or Chlory" (91) whom the master has summoned to him while he "rides on into the trees and dismounts and waits" (91)?

Abuse is what it feels like—an abuse wrought into the entire patriarchal paradigm for assigning racial and gender roles, in which the dignified subject positions are filled by white males and the demeaning object positions by white trash and black slaves male and female alike.[10] Eulalia Bon's anger is fueled inexhaustibly by the exclusions of this patriarchal model, in which Sutpen's orderly behavior explodes upon her as cruelly chaotic. Ceremonies formulated for the white subject alone never applied to blacks: this is Bon's triumphant argument with Henry in New Orleans: "Have you forgot that this woman, this child, are niggers? You, Henry Sutpen of Sutpen's Hundred in Mississippi? You talking of marriage, a wedding, here?" (98). Later, in a tragic key—suicidally against himself—he will play this same logic against Henry's desperate plea ("You are my brother") for ceremonious behavior: "No I'm not. I'm the nigger that's going to sleep with your sister. Unless you stop me, Henry" (294).

Black slaves in *Absalom, Absalom!*, then, are figures denied the ceremonial address (the awareness of a kindred subjectivity requiring treatment in kind) that distinguishes human recognition of species kinship. Blacks are to be slept with in the fields, not to be married and taken into the home. Their offspring are sons and daughters who endure social death, whose status is unacknowledgeable slavehood. In my reading this is the central, unalterable fact of *Absalom*, against which all the imaginative energy of the novel—its profusion of "might-have-beens that are more true than truth"—is gathered to show at what cost this fact perseveres, what human loss it entails. The four-generational career of Bons, as inseparable from Sutpen's unfolding lineage as it is unintegratable within it, reveals not only the pain of those outcast but also the foredoomed collapse of those within. Given the uncontrollable mystery of human feeling, you simply cannot build a dynasty by killing some of your children, without thereby maiming those that remain.

The humanity of Faulkner's diagnosis of slavery is beyond question. No white writer has dramatized more powerfully, diagnosed more intricately, the collapse of white racist patriarchy. Yet Faulkner narrates this failure largely through the minds and hearts of white men who suffer from it. If race is the cardinal theme of *Absalom* (the motor of its tragedy), class determines the novel's representational focus.[11] Sutpen is first and last a figure shaped by class realities, and his epiphanic vision of Southern racial relations is class-enabled. "It was not the nigger," he keeps saying to himself. His humiliation is caused by a white master/white trash dynamic. All at once he sees clearly the structure of the life that he has been innocently living as mere experience: that blacks are better fed, better clothed than his own motley white family, and that his sisters have long known this: "a certain flat level silent way his older sisters and the other white women of their kind had of looking at niggers, not with fear or dread but with a kind of speculative antagonism" (190). Replaying a scene in which his sister refused to get out of the way of the lordly white carriage that was passing, he returns "home" and enters that unbearable state in which sight sears as recognition: "and his sister pumping rhythmic up and down above a washtub in the yard, her back toward him, shapeless in a calico dress and a pair of the old man's shoes unlaced and flapping about her bare ankle and broad in the beam as a cow, the very labor she was doing brutish and stupidly out of all proportion to its reward" (195).[12]

The material details are visualized with unforgiving precision. Sutpen registers once and forever the class-shaped penury of his life—the places his people live in, the clothes they wear, the labor they do, the wages they are paid, the absence of ceremonial dignity. Later Wash Jones will see, in Sutpen's abuse of his granddaughter Milly, a kindred class-shaped brutality. Here again Faulkner's representation will be full, generous, understanding. What the text cannot attend to at this level of domestic, material detail (detail that tells so much) is the black slave's experience of the same patriarchal codes. Faulkner knows that blacks pay the price of lower-class-white anger and that the object of the anger is really white—the white planter you cannot hit, the black servant you abuse in his place. "We whupped one of Pettibone's niggers," Sutpen remembers his father exulting late one night, and when the boy asks which one and what had he done, the father answers: "Hell fire, that goddamn son of a bitch Pettibone's nigger" (191). So far as they are concerned, he has no other name, and the boy suddenly realizes: "no actual nigger, living creature, living flesh to feel pain and writhe and cry out" (192). As often, no one knows Faulkner's omissions better than Faulkner himself, for the lineaments of this "living creature" are never represented in *Absalom*. What does he give us in their place?

The "wild negroes" of the novel's early chapters get replaced by domestic slaves, produced usually through a set of similar brush strokes: a butler's uniform ("monkey niggers"), an impenetrable face ("balloon-like," with a face merely painted on it, holding something that will rush out and envelop you if you strike that face), and a sinister capacity for "mellow laughter meaningless and terrifying and loud" (192). All these are accoutrement, not the "living creature" itself but the effects encountered everywhere by poor Southern whites. These blacks are dressed according to white code, seen acting in white-imposed roles (butlers, drivers, plantation laborers). They register as factotums representing the will of the silent and invisible white master. From that angle they seem protected, guaranteed, ratified. Their laughter echoes as the indecipherable sign of their superior insertion in the social fabric, and it drives Sutpen and his kind mad. Of the blacks' own pain, the shabbiness of their cabins, the makeshiftness of their clothes once the white uniforms have come off, the complex emotional relations they bear each other and the flux of notions they entertain toward themselves—of all of the lineaments of their own shared culture *Absalom* can tell us nothing. For it can enter the subjective dimension of black lives only through a single talismanic condition: that the black in question be, however unrecognizable as such, Sutpen-spawned.

Clytie and Charles Bon are the two black offspring who would seem to bear out this claim, yet what is strange is not that Bon rarely seems to be Sutpen's black son (*Absalom*'s elaborate plot keeps us from knowing this for hundreds of pages), but that Clytie is so sparingly represented as his black daughter. The human aspect of the interracial intercourse that produced her is effaced from the text. We never hear of her mother, never eavesdrop on either her feelings for her father or his for her. The nearest she comes to familial acknowledgment occurs through Rosa ("*And you too, sister, sister?*" [116]), not through one of her own white siblings. Not that she is ever anything but planted within that setting (only she will have the authority to torch it to the ground), but rather that, "being" black, she is scrupulously denied acknowledgment: ceremonious recognition of her subjective familial existence. Integral to keeping the household intact during the miserable War years, instrumental in seeking out and bringing up (bringing down) young Charles Etienne St. Valery Bon, faithfully on hand to care first for the hopeless idiot Jim Bond and last for the wasted Henry Sutpen when he comes home to die, Clytie is crucial to the articulation of a plot that never once articulates her. It is Clytie who finally "tells" Quentin (a telling that bypasses the ceremony of shared talk, moving one-directionally from her observed black body to his observing white mind) that the entire Sutpen disaster is racially based: "And she didn't tell you in so many words because she was still keeping that secret for the sake of the man who had been her father too as well as for the sake of the family which no longer existed . . . she didn't tell you in the actual words because even in the terror she kept the secret; nevertheless she told you, or at least all of a sudden you knew—" (288–89). We get no closer than this to Quentin's penetration of the mystery. He takes the racial key handed him by Clytie (that if her father had spawned one black child, he might well have spawned another), and with it he decodes (at Harvard, with Shreve's help) the secret of Charles Bon's parentage.

Unlike Clytie's, Bon's subjectivity is prodigally accessed by *Absalom*'s narrators. Invented and reinvented, he emerges as extravagantly overdetermined: American yet New Orleans French, male yet seductively female, white yet ineffaceably (if invisibly) black.[13] How far Faulkner has had to remove him from normative Southern black culture in order to invest him with so many tantalizing, if foredoomed, possibilities. On the one hand, this removal is fatally limiting, for it means that Bon cannot in any communal way "be" black. It means even that Faulkner was incapable of finding Bon among (what he knew about) available black resources. Yet Bon's removal from the racial norms of the South is also extraordinarily enabling in this novel of "might-have-beens" unacted by the real. Bon emerges as what could not be, yet what was and is (so long as repressed) all the more desired. His easy New Orleans sensuality (hopelessly envied by the puritanical Henry Sutpen) carries, beneath the surface, an inadmissible white admiration for a black capacity to accept and delight in the body's resources; his epicene demeanor signals a merging of male and female propensities that no white Southerner (male or female) can even dream of compassing; his sophisticated skepticism rejects fanaticism without falling into impotence in a way that Mr. Compson cannot follow. Judith loves him, so does Henry, so does Rosa. If he "were" black, he would be a slave and none of this would be possible. Since he "is" black, we see simultaneously the absurdity and the brutality of racial prejudice: absurd because Bon so transcends that prejudice, brutal because the normative imposition of that prejudice prevented Southern blacks from ever becoming Charles Bon. Faulkner has created, in the guise of this socially impossible figure (once identified, he must self-destruct), so much that the social cannot possibly put together.

I have suggested how Quentin learns that Charles Bon "is" black. But how does Quentin imagine Bon himself "discovering" it? Here Faulkner's most strenuous stylistic experimentation comes into play, for *Absalom* is of all his texts the most structurally inventive. The point of so much of this invention is to postpone authoritative comprehension (to keep it flexible, revisable) in view of newly found data, newly proposed lenses upon the data. We are indeed all but finished with our reading when we learn that Bon is not just brother but black brother: Faulkner has heroically suspended, kept occluded, that discovery. Not that he has concealed it, and no reader comes upon this information with the sense of having been fooled (or fooled with) up to that point. All the previous paradigms remain intact—*Absalom* is cumulative rather than self-correcting—in that each operates a viable cultural key upon intractable materials. Each makes its kind of sense. But the racial lens is both the most decisive (the one that can most swiftly command life-altering behavior) and the last Faulkner can afford to supply: to Bon himself, to the other characters (save for Sutpen and his mother) who surround him, and to the reader seeking to come to terms with him.

It must come last because he, we, and the others will therefore experience him otherwise until the end. We internalize (as Henry does) the developing emotional value of his becoming a brother before he can be unmasked as black (his fraternal identity compels Faulkner's imagination even more than his loverly identity), and we live inside his subjectivity as a black man who doesn't know he is black. He figures it out, finally, because the abusive treatment he receives at the hands of his father (a refusal of the ceremony of acknowledgment) tells him, gradually, by a process of elimination, that he must be suffering from the one condition no white patriarch *can* acknowledge: black blood. He is, belatedly, a "nigger" for the same reason Joe

Christmas is all during his infancy: because he is subjected to a cultural paradigm that treats him as one. Entertaining other options until the end, he and we both have had the time to register the outrageous constructedness of such racial identity. To read *Absalom* is thus to undergo a racial education that moves into tragic recognitions.[14] We are far from any illusion of unvanquishment. Yet, given Faulkner's stubborn allegiance to a Southern history he can neither repudiate nor accept, this tragic insight opens up no options in the real, however compellingly it reveals its deficits. In *Go Down, Moses*, this critique of racism joins even more achingly a diffuse conviction that—almost eighty years after 1865—no escape is yet possible. Once a slave, always a slave: from Old Carothers to Roth Edmonds, Pharaoh is still in charge.

Faulkner: *Go Down, Moses*

Here the canvas widens, and the racial diagnosis deepens. The aristocratic games that held sway in *The Unvanquished* turn into outrageous episodes—at once humorous and sinister—in *Go Down, Moses*. Chasing after stolen silver and horses becomes chasing your brother and betting your sister. The genteel pretensions of Rosa Millard's antebellum rhetoric ("There is little of refreshment I can offer you, sir. But if a glass of cool milk after your ride . . . Louvinia, conduct the gentleman to the diningroom and serve him with what we have" [*U*, 341]) become the wackiness of Sophonsiba Beauchamp's Warwick grandeur: "[saying] something about Uncle Buck was a bee sipping from flower to flower and not staying long anywhere and all that stored sweetness to be wasted on Uncle Buddy's desert air, calling Uncle Buddy Mister Amodeus like she called Uncle Buck Mister Theophilus" (*GDM*, 11).

The title of this later novel signals that we have moved from the (fantasied) domain of an intact and unvanquished South to the realm of dislocation and recognizable loss: South defeated by North, black by white. Death as the ultimate defeat of the will haunts *Go Down, Moses*, and surely Faulkner so prizes the hunt here because (in its finest form) it ceremonializes death, acknowledging the (always potentially fatal) bond between hunter and hunted, both of them exposed and fully realizing themselves through acceptance of the exposure. Old Ben, Lion, Sam Fathers: each of these figures lives his authority as an acceptance of death, a fearless refusal to hoard his being against some future payoff. The dignity with which they accept their own immolation compels Faulkner's attention, and in this regard Sam Fathers emerges as the tutorial spirit of the text.

If the racial diagnosis deepens, it remains open to recurrent failures of insight, never more so than in the unfolding of Sam Fathers's racial trajectory. This figure has already received copious critical commentary, but no discussion of Faulkner's representation of slavery can bypass him. For Sam represents in small (as Lucas Beauchamp does at large) an incoherent fusion of achieved independence and inalterable despoliation. Sam is both royalty and slave. The entire wilderness is his, yet there is nothing this motley figure can call his own. Half Indian, three-eighths white, one-eighth black, he carries in his body the incoherent racial history of his land, and he is conceived (as a slave would be conceived) to be decisively marked by that last one-eighth:

> "And all of a sudden one day he found that he had been betrayed, the blood of the warriors and chiefs had been betrayed. Not by his father," he [Cass] added quickly. "He probably never held it against old Doom for selling him and his mother into slavery, because he probably believed the damage was already done before then and it was the same warriors' and chiefs' blood in him and Doom both that was betrayed through the black blood which his [quadroon] mother gave him. Not betrayed by the black blood and not willfully betrayed by his mother, but betrayed by her all the same, who had bequeathed him not only the blood of slaves but even a little of the very blood which had enslaved it."   (GDM, 124)

Remarkably, the father's pharaonic selling of the child into bondage is read by Cass as unresented by the orphaned son. In place of this literal abandonment we get a conceptual betrayal at the abstract level of the blood itself. "Not betrayed by the black blood," yet what else is this but betrayal by the black blood, the mother instrumentalized into a pure carrier of that blood, her nurturing of this child of no moment beside the guilt she carries in her veins, while the father's actions—disturbingly similar to any number of white slaveholders' selling of their own illegitimate black offspring into slavery—escape critical reflection? Blackness seems coded as so inferior to Indianness that it accounts for all of Sam's pathos and none of his virtue. As with Charles Bon, Faulkner crosses the baseness of blackness with the nobility of other cultural resources (here an aristocratic Indian heritage, there a resilient French-sensual training of the body). In both cases the admixture permits the diagnosis to move beyond pity, raises the stakes (so to speak) of the defeat that must nevertheless occur. "Mere" blackness remains pure deficit. This racial stereotyping does not dominate Go Down, Moses—the text would have little to tell us if it did—yet variations on it do recur, specifically in the black characterization in the McCaslin ledgers, more generally in the text's incapacity to see in blackness a set of enabling cultural resources.

Ike's racial education is founded upon his reading of the McCaslin ledgers—this activity accounts for the novel's core sequence of insights—but he discovers there more about white brutality than about black capacity. The ledgers (kept by Buck and Buddy from the early 1830s until the outbreak of the War) are punctuated by the conventional refrain of manumitted slaves who can do nothing with this "gift" of freedom and who beg to remain on McCaslin land ("Son of a bitch wont leave . . . Dont want to leave . . . Dont want to leave . . . Wants to stay and work it out." [196–97]). We have seen this stance operate as the ideological core of *The Unvanquished*—its demonstration of white generosity toward blacks—and it is disturbing to find it here.

Yet these unprobed details pale beside those of another racial drama, which, in being probed, will henceforth remain unforgettable, changing the course of Ike's life. Eunice, drowned in the creek on Christmas Day of 1832, elicits from Buddy six months later the following ledger entry: "*June 21th 1833 Drowned herself*," to which Buck rejoins, "*23 Jun 1833 Who in hell ever heard of a niger drownding him self*," to which Buddy later returns with finality: "*Aug 13th 1833 Drownd herself*" (198). Pressing harder on these cryptic details that flaunt the typographic and imaginative limitations of Buck and Buddy, Ike (at age sixteen) succeeds in envisaging the entire tragic scene: his grandfather's widowhood and loneliness, his traveling to New Orleans to buy Eunice, the birth of Tomasina hard after (supposedly sired by Eunice's black mate Thucydus), the drowning of Eunice some twenty years later, six months before her daughter Tomasina gives birth to Turl (and dies in the process), and finally the old man's cryptic bequest of a thousand dollars to Turl, to take place on the latter's twenty-first birthday ("twenty-one years too late," Ike thinks, "to begin to learn what money was" [199]). Ike puts it together: the old man as Eunice's lover (her first lover), thus as Tomasina's father, and then as Tomasina's lover too; Eunice's intolerable discovery of her daughter's impregnation by her own father, leading to her own suicide; the old man's belated bequest of money rather than love: "So I reckon [Ike thinks] that was cheaper than saying My son to a nigger" (199).

Ike's father and uncle may be incapable of imagining "a niger drownding him self," but once Ike envisages it he can never forget it. How far we have come from *Absalom*'s casual "Juno or Missylena or Chlory." The abuse of Eunice and Tomasina radiates the racial crime at the core of *Go Down, Moses*—the white impregnation of black, followed by the white refusal to acknowledge black. The offspring of that second impregnation, Tomey's Turl, who is being hunted by his brothers Buck and Buddy, is where this novel begins. The offspring of Tomey's Turl, Tennie's Jim (who is the grandfather of the "doe" in "Delta Autumn"), takes us to the novel's end. (It ends again, in a final coda story, with yet another child blood-bonded to Old Carothers through that originating act of miscegenation, this time Samuel Worsham Beauchamp, virtually dead on arrival, executed in the 1940s but set on his orphaned path more than a century earlier.) The repercussions of the first crime are inexhaustible.

I have sought to trace thus far the way in which the racial imagination of this huge text alternates between blindness and insight, cliché and perception. The same mix characterizes Faulkner's grasp upon the career of Tomey's Turl's female offspring, Fonsiba. Ike witnesses her being claimed in the commissary by a grammatically insistent black Yankee for his bride ("I inform you [this said to Cass], notify you in advance as chief of her family. No man of honor could do less. Besides, you have, in your way, according to your lights and upbringing . . ." [204]). The scene of Fonsiba's departure is full of the young Ike's frustration, and the older Cass's anger, that one of their blacks is abandoning them for such un-Southern hands. (That the black man whose "uppity" discourse so infuriates Ike and Cass might be a freed Southerner rather than an intrusive Yankee is a narrative possibility simply inaccessible to Faulkner's regional piety, though not historically improbable.) At any rate, Ike determines—those incriminating ledgers still reverberating in his mind—to track down Tomey's Turl's departed children, so as to give them their share (never claimed by Turl himself and now a thousand dollars for each child) of the original Carothers guilt money.

It is as the patriarchal white benefactor, then, that Ike comes upon Fonsiba and her husband. He finds them in a barren and hopeless Southern setting that radiates the text's larger critique of Reconstruction practices: a black Yankee with a government pension who intends to farm but knows nothing about farming, who wears a pair of glasses that contain no lenses and who speaks an ornate English with no common sense to give his words substance (the lensless glasses Faulkner's mean-spirited mockery of this black man's pretended culture); a white father figure who cherishes his real (not abstract) bond with the fleeing black woman who had been part of his family. Ike dominates the scene, lecturing the black Yankee sternly (it is the single scene in the book where Ike not only seems to have more common sense than his interlocutor but also appears manly, potent, his black adversary significantly incapable of honoring his earlier boast to Cass). The latter's ineptitude registers on Ike as something "permeant, clinging to the man's very clothing and exuding from his skin itself, that rank stink of baseless and imbecile delusion" (206). Just when we are ready to ask whether that "rank stink" isn't really the stubborn white cliché about black body odor—so loaded seems the scene against a second chance for this ex-slave and her mate—Faulkner suddenly turns it all upside down. Ike asks, "Fonsiba, Fonsiba. Are you all right?" She responds, in words that conclude the scene by making all further argument impertinent, "I'm free" (207).

Faulkner's blindness alternates with his insight because, it may be, his nostalgia for immolated white innocence sometimes runs deeper than his compassion for black suffering. Those doomed and impenetrable males—Old Ben, Lion, Sam, Buck, and Buddy—remain innocent forever (no experience has the power to alter their interior accents), and Hubert Beauchamp joins them on his deathbed. His gradual decades-long pilfering of silver coins from the cup he would bequeath to his nephew Ike fairly registers the diminishing utility of that larger cultural inheritance, its promise and its pathos. As Hubert's death approaches, Faulkner's text draws near his supine body and proceeds with a sort of slow-motion fascination to describe him. Silhouetted against "Tennie's inscrutable expression" (226), Hubert's face radiates a tortured and inexpressible significance:

> the pillow, the worn and ravaged face from which looked out still the boy innocent and immortal and amazed and urgent, looking at him and trying to tell him . . . the eyes saying Yes Yes Yes now . . . the eyes still trying to tell him . . . the hands clinging to the parcel [covering the emptied cup] even while relinquishing it, the eyes more urgent than ever trying to tell him but they never did.   (227)

Immortal and innocent boys: how something in Faulkner wants to view those departed ancestors thus, as beings undone but unchanged by powers they could not defeat, and become beautiful in their very immolation. In like manner the wilderness so dilated upon in this text seduces not least because of its imaginary innocence, its status as prehuman (presexual and preracial) uncontaminated space. Writ large, it appeals as the still unpopulated, virgin continent itself—prior to the raced and gendered despoliations that come with property—and the text looks back upon this diminishing resource as a sanctuary you have to be as old as Uncle Ike to remember. (And in remembering, misremember, for such troping itself engages in an erasure, a forgetting of the ancient host already upon the land when the visitors first arrived: the Indians who themselves were erased so that the land could be imagined as virginally awaiting its white destiny.) For Ike, ensconced in his still innocent memories (his sense of himself as nonpossessing), "there was just exactly enough of it [the wilderness]" (261) to last out his life. Or so he thinks until the "doe" arrives to bring back race and history and guilt into his immaculate dreams. It is fitting, then, that the text's final racial recognition is triggered by her telling him that her family took in washing to support themselves:

> "Took in what?" he said. "Took in washing?" He sprang, still seated even, flinging himself backward onto one arm, awry-haired, glaring. Now he understood what it was she had brought into the tent with her. . . . He cried, not loud, in a voice of amazement, pity, and outrage: "You're a nigger!"
>
> (266)

How far back it goes, black women who take care of white people's dirt. For seven generations blacks have been cleaning up white McCaslin dirt. This, of all of Faulkner's novels, is the one that most patiently narrates the racial debt incurred in the time of slavery and still being evaded in the time of the writing (the 1940s). Even as Ike flings her away (and again we have the hint of the odor of race—"something intangible, an effluvium" [263]—that she stereotypically carries), he finds himself, nevertheless, a few minutes later reaching out to touch her hand so that he might feel there the throb of her past—a past he now knows is his as well: "the gnarled, bloodless, bone-light, bone-dry old man's fingers touching for a second the smooth young flesh where the strong old blood ran after its long lost journey back to home. 'Tennie's Jim,' he said. 'Tennie's Jim' " (267). Her grandfather James Beauchamp ("you called him Tennie's Jim though he had a name" [266]), the only child of Turl and Tennie they could not find, may be lost to narrative, yet his blood is in this young woman's arm, and he compels Ike as the missing piece, finally, of a family destiny.[15] Narratively absent, like most of the other slaves and ex-slaves who suffer so variously in this novel, he means most as the symbolic embodiment of more than a century of white abuse and nonaccommodation. In Go Down, Moses, the extent of that abuse and nonaccommodation reaches epic proportions. For the subjective black counterpart to suffering on this scale, the dimensions of a diaspora that began before the Civil War and shows no signs of ending, we must cross the color line and attend to Morrison's biblical saga of displacement and longing.

Morrison: *Song of Solomon*

The topic and time of slavery might not seem to go beyond 1865, but *Song of Solomon* understands this trauma as fractured into innumerable shards rather than unitary and as still living a century later in the beleaguered psyches of its contemporary characters. Macon Dead and his obsession with property, Corinthians and her long-instilled conviction that she is to marry only a high-class black man, Guitar and his haunting words to Milkman about the condition our condition is in, Milkman in rural Virginia focusing as he has never focused in his life upon the ritual dismemberment of a bobcat: these current instances of stress all circulate around an originary distress. They serve unknowingly as prisms upon the sustained humiliation that blacks endured for more than three centuries, a humiliation that fuels and often deforms the cluster of contemporary projects for recovering dignity that Morrison explores in *Song of Solomon*. The opening page's mention of Not Doctor Street, for example, testifies casually to white society's systemic attempt to deny black names to its urban space, to delete as unworthy the racial dimension of its own history. But the black experience to be erased by this official gesture (the city fathers' decree that this street "had always been and would always be known as Mains Avenue and not Doctor Street" [SS, 4]) refuses erasure. The blacks adroitly signify on "not Doctor Street," turning it into "Not Doctor Street," a negation become a proposition. The not-named take the not-name as their name. In a more complex way, this is the drama encoded in the naming of Macon Dead.

It begins as a humiliation grounded in slavery itself: the first Macon Dead (his remarkable lineage kept from us at this point, as it has remained lost to his own family) stopped by a drunken Yankee official as he crosses into Northern territory. In Macon Dead Jr.'s bitter rehearsal of this story, the actors are white, the victims black. His illiterate father is abused through his very illiteracy (his place of birth becoming his first name, his father's death imposing his surname). Even the pride of Macon's "I'm free" disappears into the official's undoing response, "born in Dunfrie." The son can see nothing empowering in his father's resonant words, and his own lifelong model of white/black relations is shaped by such scenes that took place before he was even born: whites as owners of discourse, dispossessors of black dignity.[16] Macon's own project— like Sutpen's, to combat the strong ones by owning all that they own—springs from this humiliation, bringing its equally bitter mix of success and failure. The past registers not as resource but as annihilation, and it will take the reader another two hundred pages to discover on what epic (again, virtually

Sutpenian) terms this freed black slave did indeed claim his freedom. In the meantime, though, the grandson Milkman has inherited from his father a slave-focused history of humiliation. He rehearses it thus for Guitar:

> "Say, you know how my old man's daddy got his name?"
> "Uh uh. How?"
> "Cracker gave it to him."
> "Sho 'nough?"
> "Yep. And he took it. Like a fucking sheep. Somebody should have shot him."
> "What for? He was already Dead." (89)

Orlando Patterson speaks of slavery as "social death"—the systemic erasure of one's membership in the social—and Morrison explores this legacy through terms all the more powerful for being literal. Unnamed, given their owners' surnames or cynically renamed by other whites, their inheritance a mockery through its bequeathing only insult, the Deads are born extinguished. "Anything dead coming back to life hurts" (35), Amy Denver says in *Beloved*; what can the Deads do to sustain life against a death sentence pronounced before they were born?

Guitar is named with similar inappropriateness, for an instrument he wanted to (but could not) play, but, unlike Milkman, he makes his way past names and into substance. Rejecting Milkman's admiration for Malcolm's insistence on an X that is his own, Guitar takes on his other-bestowed appellation as ineffaceable: "I do accept it. It's part of who I am. Guitar is *my* name. Bains is the slave master's name. And I'm all of that. Slave names don't bother me; but slave status does" (SS, 160). This acceptance brings Guitar no peace, though, and he ends less by resolving the Deads' identity dilemma than by disappearing into a larger ideological structure—one of the fatal Days, anonymous—that grants him power by stripping him of what an effective name is meant to provide: personal identity as an unforeclosed reaccenting of familial resource. Morrison embroiders this theme through Pilate's naming as well, these local instances preparing us for the virtually symphonic resonances of "Solomon" as the recovered talisman, simultaneously, of a family, a community, a geography, and a more-than-hundred-year history.

Solomon denotes both a famous biblical figure and a famous song. This is not the place to pursue the connections between song and novel, but no consideration of slavery can omit the resonance of the song in the novel's exploration of alienation, longing, and love. As powerfully as Faulkner, Morrison exploits the allusive frame of a marginalized people, ill at ease on the land they know but do not own, kept apart lover from lover, parent from child. The *Song of Songs* registers alienation as the beloved's passionate longing for the absent lover, her reverie of escape from present pain—from potential betrayal—once the lover returns. Her love is articulated as the experience of unbearable frustration. *Song of Solomon* pursues the connection between slavery and lovelessness in stunning ways, for it understands that the kinds of incapacitation and abuse stemming from that original wrong wounded blacks in their capacity for self-endorsement, without a measure of which there can be no giving or receiving of love. Need one say that Faulkner does not find his way into this interior wound, his focus on white shame blinding him to its intricate black counterpart?

"I love ya, I love ya all" (26), the distraught Porter screams from the attic window in the book's opening chapter, following this outburst with a whimpering, tearful plea: "Gimme hate, Lord. I'll take hate any day. But don't give me love. I can't take no more love, Lord." *Song of Solomon* encloses this scene in a comic frame (as Faulkner's "Was" seems at first to be comic), but we learn eventually to resee this same Porter as one of the Days almost suicidally buckling under the pressure of racial wrongs that he has taken into himself and that he is pledged to avenge. The hate that fuels such revenge is hard to tolerate, but love is harder, for love reopens the psyche to the torment of feeling itself, while hate at least closes off the portals of human responsiveness, mechanizing the self into an instrument of vengeance. Milkman and Guitar are the two central male figures through whom Morrison dramatizes this agon, Guitar's Seven Days' project frightening Milkman with its inhuman aridity:

> "What kind of life is that?"
> "Very satisfying."
> "There's no love in it."
> "No love? No love? Didn't you hear me? What I'm doing ain't about hating white people. It's about loving us. About loving you. My whole life is love." (159)

Later he will say it again: "It *is* about love. What else but love?" (223), for in Guitar Morrison has caught, so to speak, the politics of love—love's vexed relation to the larger society's racist practices. How, when brought up as an orphan (his father brutally killed in a mill accident, the two parts of his mangled face not even properly aligned in the coffin, the recompense being four ten-dollar bills that his mother must smile in cringing gratitude to receive), his adolescence a sustained experience of penury at the hands of whites and of the desire among blacks to get some of their own back, how can Guitar manage the complex human art of love? His response, echoing Malcolm X, is that there is no way beyond such injustice but through it, and that the only authentic love he can feel must first be directed toward his slaughtered kind: to that redress he devotes himself with an abstract and purifying intensity that he calls love.

Damaging though this project for self-recovery be, it remains available to black males in *Song of Solomon*.[17] The women's options seem even more pinched, and in Ruth Dead Morrison achieves perhaps her most moving portrait of abortive love. Disregarded by her celebrated doctor-father (as he, despite his success, was disregarded by the city fathers), shunted aside by her husband's relentless property project, abandoned by her son's desire to flee the nest, Ruth has no capacity to endorse herself outside the endorsement of the men who have shaped her life—an endorsement that is not forthcoming, given their need to find their own sanction elsewhere. Supplicant, begging for love from all three of her men, Ruth looks her son in the face and speaks her truth: "And I . . . prayed for you. Every single night and every single day. On my knees. Now you tell me. What harm did I do you on my knees?" (126). Corinthians, who has been trained since childhood to "display" her father's success, and Hagar, who will perish without the endorsement of a male: these two women join Ruth as figures damaged indirectly and long ago by slavery itself, delivered into the world with no birthright to call their own, able to imagine selfhood only in the mirror of others' acknowledgment. In themselves they are nothing, stillborn, "dead" before they exit from their mother's womb—their solitude resembling what Baby Suggs in *Beloved* thinks of as "the desolated center where the self that was no self made its home" (B, 140). This is the song of *Song of Solomon*, the longing to establish selfhood securely enough to take on the risks and rewards of love, within a slave-marked history that turns community into diaspora and that issues less in reciprocated desire than in the separate careers of males in flight and females suffering abandonment.

Against this backdrop of affective damage and inherited scars *Song of Solomon* stages its lyrical recovery of the past, its rewriting of the racial legacy. Not Faulkner's focus on the written word as trace of a buried history—his letters, ledgers, and engraved tombstones—but an oral history enacted through the spoken memories of Danville, the children's play and song of Shalimar. It emerges as a communal history everywhere surrounding Milkman. His task is not to strain upward to decipher its elusive messages but to relax downward and hear the boys and girls chanting in the playground:

> *Solomon and Ryna Belali Shalut*
> *Yaruba Medina Muhammet too.*
> *Nestor Kalina Saraka cake.*
> *Twenty-one children, the last one Jake!*   (303)

Hebrew and Christian, African and Islamic, Greek and sweets, sacred high-culture allusion and secular demotic corruption: it merges together as a multicultural game to be performed, with the flights and falls of voice and body providing that much more pleasure to be savored. It lives only communally. The sounded song rehearses a hundred years of remembered black culture, locating the lost tribe of wandering Deads as sprung from the mythic ancestor Solomon, its youngest offspring finally returned to his turf. Urban alienation is replaced by rural community; even the landscape knows Solomon and Ryna, while the children sing of them.

This Solomon figures the transcendence of slavery's ills. Mythically capable of flight, he returns unbruised to Africa. With unfettered agency, he decides to leave the American shores, reversing the slave-laden tide of history. Morrison's deployment of Solomon enacts one of her most breathtaking risks, as history is reshaped—lyrically—to accommodate folklore. Blacks bent to their knees and suppliant are now seen to descend from a released black body so charged with life that, Daedalus-like, it defies gravity and rides in the air of its own sovereign will. This ancestor is as forceful as Carothers McCaslin in *Go Down, Moses*, and he is equally unlimned psychologically. But where Carothers's human weakness is writ large in his abuse of a black woman and of her offspring, Solomon remains radiantly unknowable, like one of those carven gods whose empty sockets—whose lack of personalizing eyes—only add to their strength.

His strength is without compassion, however, and we are not allowed to forget the pain inflicted on his family by his departure. Ryna sobs eternally. Beneath Milkman's exultation—"You think Macon Dead was something? Huh. Let me tell you about *his* daddy. You ain't heard nothin' yet" (329)—we may measure the unnegotiated cost of male transcendence: "You just can't fly on off and leave a body" (147). Sing, sing, this book keeps quoting, remembering, enacting. The song is simultaneously performance, identification, declaration of loss. Sing as the weeping Ryna filling the land with the lament of her flown-away man, Sing as the overdetermined command passed from the orphaned Jake/Macon to his orphaned offspring Pilate (signifying both the departed woman—Jake's wife, his children's mother—and the need to turn disabling loss into enabling song), Sing finally as the performance of Morrison's prodigiously sounded novel itself: achieved voice yet at the same time the lyrical reminder of what is missing, the diaspora that has not ended, the lovers still apart from each other and from the land that would ground them. It would be hard to imagine a more powerful treatment of the fallout of slavery. In *Beloved*, nevertheless, Morrison goes further yet, giving us not the consequences but the unspeakable thing itself.

Morrison: *Beloved*

Inasmuch as this is Morrison's masterpiece and everything in it contributes to the representation of slavery, I recur to it often, inevitably focusing on slavery. I here propose as specific an analysis as possible (rather than the indirect consequences of slavery explored in *Song of Solomon*), beginning with the figure of Sethe herself. Morrison's fundamental strategy for showing black capacity to survive slavery inheres in this portrait, for Sethe has weathered it all and her speech registers this authority on almost every page. She is the "one who never looked away" (B, 12) from disfigurement: a man being stomped to death outside Sawyer's restaurant, a sow eating her own litter, Here Boy being slammed by the baby's spirit so hard his legs break and his eyes dislocate. She can take on this violence in front of her because she has had to absorb its counterpart within her.

Unlike Macon's family, who is born dead, Sethe undergoes and survives death in her own lifetime—in the crisis with her child—and this ordeal unspeakably ratifies her. To Paul D she rings out:

> I got a tree on my back and a haint in my house, and nothing in between but the daughter I am holding in my arms. No more running—from nothing. I will never run from another thing on this earth. I took one journey and I paid for the ticket, but let me tell you something, Paul D Garner: it cost too much! Do you hear me? It cost too much. Now sit down and eat with us or leave us be.   (15)

The elemental authority here has been potential in Morrison's black women all along (Eva Peace and Pilate and Ondine are forerunners of Sethe), but it is as though Morrison touched down, in Sethe, on the thing itself that the later ones have inherited: black women are indestructible (not all of them, but not just a remnant either) because they have survived and found internal terms for the worst that slavery could do to them or make them do to themselves and others. "Black women have held, have been given, you know, the cross," Morrison said recently in an interview. "They don't walk near it. They're often on it" (*TM*, 384). Emerging from this crucible, they have been weighed and found adequate. And they know it: Sethe, Baby Suggs, and Ella suffer from and are empowered by a terrible knowledge.

With a few radiant exceptions, no women in Faulkner's world muster such authority, for the experience they articulate is in a crucial way chimerical. Defenders of honor (which "must be defended whether it was or not since, defended, it was, whether or not" [*RN*, 545]), they tend to grow shrill in behalf of standards that are verbal alone—words that "go straight up in a thin line, quick and harmless, [in contrast to] how terribly doing goes along the earth" (*AILD*, 117). Only Addie and Charlotte (and to a lesser extent Ruby) speak the terribleness of doing. Faulkner's other women are more likely either to collapse into silence or inarticulate desire (Caddy, Dewey Dell, Eula) or to stand tall and speak the rules (Mrs. Compson, Miss Jenny, Rosa Millard).[18] In Faulkner, to discover the outrageous truth on the other side of verbal paradigms is, typically, to be speechless or incoherent: Benjy best incarnates that truth, Quentin stutters it, Joe Christmas and Thomas Sutpen suffer it. Only the law is utterable as a discourse. Faulkner's great work stages a sympathetic yet necessarily ruthless sabotage of that law—stages it in the form of the ferocious stylistic experimentation that characterizes his texts from *As I Lay Dying* through *If I Forget Thee, Jerusalem*. When he finally turns from the sabotage of discourse to the eloquence of its articulation, when the Ikes and Gavins become his central speakers, what they speak, however individually accented and partially resisted, is the law. By contrast, Morrison's indomitable black women not only break the law but they speak that rupture unforgettably. This can only be because the law they are breaking is itself patriarchal, white, and grounded originally in slavery. Morrison's hold upon her audience today draws upon this eloquent rebuke of such law.

Sethe has absorbed into herself the brutality one race inflicted upon another, and she has made of it her bitter and compelling wit: "The [escape] plan was a good one, but when it came time, I was big with Denver. So we changed it a little. A little. Just enough to butter Halle's face, so Paul D tells me, and make Sixo laugh at last" (197). Likewise, she confronts her own probable annihilation with comparable wit. Exhausted and on the verge of collapse during her escape from Sweet Home, she hears a noise (it is actually

Amy Denver approaching) and gathers herself to face this enemy, thinking: "That on a ridge of pine near the Ohio River, trying to get to her three children, one of whom was starving for the food she carried; that after her husband had disappeared; that after her milk had been stolen, her back pulped, her children orphaned, she was not to have an easeful death. No" (31). Unbearable knowledge has been disciplined by wit into survival orientation. Sethe does not dilate upon her wrongs; rather, she compresses them into brief phrases, enabling insights, travel guides.

What Sethe knows is common knowledge among this black community. (Once again the contrast with Faulkner is telling: his rebel figures' unspeakable rejection of their community's shared knowledge ensures their alienation.) Stamp Paid or Baby Suggs or Paul D or Ella: any of these may know and speak the race-based truth they all share. Here is Paul D thinking about where and what Beloved may have come from, remembering his own experience in Rochester a few years earlier:

> The War had been over four or five years then, but nobody white or black seemed to know it. Odd clusters and strays of Negroes wandered the back roads and cowpaths from Schenectady to Jackson. . . . Some of them were running from family that could not support them, some to family; some were running from dead crops, dead kin, life threats, and took-over land. Boys younger than Buglar and Howard; configurations and blends of families of women and children, while elsewhere, solitary, hunted and hunting for, were men, men, men. Forbidden public transportation, chased by debt and filthy "talking sheets," they followed secondary routes, scanned the horizon for signs and counted heavily on each other. Silent, except for social courtesies, when they met one another they neither described nor asked about the sorrow that drove them from one place to another. The whites didn't bear speaking on. Everybody knew.   (52–53)

No small measure of Beloved's hold upon us derives from passages like this one. Morrison's capacity for pithy summarizing fills this novel to bursting with historical data that has been digested into the common subjective experience of the race itself. ("Everybody knew.") When Stamp Paid reflects back on the arrival of the four whites come to retrieve Sethe and her offspring, he thinks: "Not Ella, not John, not anybody ran down or to Bluestone Road, to say some new whitefolks with the Look just rode in. The righteous Look every Negro learned to recognize along with his ma'am's tit. Like a flag hoisted, this righteousness telegraphed and announced the faggot, the whip, the fist, the lie, long before it went public" (157). So intensely marshaled are the racial data in this text that we measure, here, not only the coding that knits together a black community (their shared recognition of "the Look"), but also the community's betrayal of its own standards. I shall explore in the last chapter Morrison's brilliant notation of black language in *Beloved*, but already we see how those who make up "the same" (white folks) yield a semiotic knowledge (the Look they unknowingly carry on face and in gesture) available only to the trained gaze of those who make up "the other" (black folks). If you were black you had to know whites as they did not have to know themselves. Morrison need do nothing exotic to invent a black speech beyond white ken. Half of it is already available in the thrown-away and unrecognized maneuvers of the whites themselves, knit by black need into a coherent and trustworthy skein of signs.

If Sethe represents the black encounter with slavery in its heroic guise, Baby Suggs represents a wiser and sadder version of that encounter. Unlike Sethe, she has lost all of her children but Halle, and she learns in the course of the novel that she is losing him too. "Anybody Baby Suggs knew, let alone loved, who hadn't run off or been hanged, got rented out, loaned out, bought up, brought back, stored up, mortgaged, won, stolen or seized. So Baby's eight children had six fathers" (23). Morrison bestows upon Baby Suggs's thought process a linguistic compression that matches Sethe's and testifies to an equivalent power of subjective will: unbearable, inhuman experiences compassed and accommodated (though never accepted). She does her best not to remember the sentient details connected with those disappeared offspring, and Morrison analyzes through her what kind of selfhood remains when your dearest others have been taken from you: "Sad as it was that she did not know where her children were buried or what they looked like if alive, fact was she knew more about them than she knew about herself, having never had the map to discover what she was like" (140). How would she know? Subject formation is inescapably a negotiation with other (internalized) subjects, and her children were stolen from her before she could draw the map of who they were, learn who she was through her reflexive relation to that map.

All these deprivations resonate when the Garners "give" her her freedom. "What you call yourself?" Garner asks her—a novel question he never needed to pose when still her slaveholder—and she answers, "I don't call myself nothing" (142). Once, though, she answered to "Suggs," and she stubbornly knows her true name to be on the map composed by her relation to him—Baby—rather than the name the Garners call her, Jenny. What it means to be so impotently inserted into the symbolic (to be married to Suggs yet have no clue where his owners have determined his place in the social) emerges in her search, now that she is free, for her disappeared husband: "After two years of messages written by the preacher's hand, two years of washing, sewing, canning, cobbling, gardening, and sitting in churches, all she found out was that the Whitlow place was gone and that you couldn't write to 'a man named Dunn' if all you knew was that he went West" (147). *Song of Solomon*'s tracking of the Dead heritage seems by contrast facile—its soaring mythmaking transcends these knotty geographic obstacles—whereas Baby Suggs founders over the tiniest injuries imposed by slavery: a changeable name she cannot trace through the postal system, a trajectory she cannot map since her errant husband was its victim, not its shaper. She knows as well that the freedom proudly bestowed by her erstwhile owners has been cunningly mortgaged: "thinking, But you got my boy and I'm all broke down. You be renting him out to pay for me way after I'm gone to Glory" (146).

Baby Suggs told her congregation that the only grace they could have was the grace they could imagine. In like manner, the only freedom some of these beleaguered blacks may count on is the freedom they can wrest from within the necessity of slavery itself. Sixo beautifully demonstrates the powers and limits of this enterprise. Owned from birth to death, he remains free within this servitude—free to find, court, and make pregnant Thirty-Mile Woman; to steal back (in small installments) from what has been hugely stolen from him ("Improving your property," he explains to schoolteacher when he is caught with the purloined shoat); to plan the slaves' escape from Sweet Home; and to direct the scene of his own immolation. He takes the rifle pointed at him and puts it in his mouth (necessitating his death rather than his return to slavery), then sings his own death song, and finally dies (he is being burned to death) with a joke on his lips: "Seven-O! Seven-O" (226). A joke that only Paul D recognizes (this sign system is beyond white comprehension): "because his Thirty-Mile Woman got away with his blossoming seed" (228–29), guaranteeing a continued black lineage as triumphant here as its contemplated continuation at the end of *Absalom, Absalom!* is terrifying.

If Sixo's insistence on freedom despite enslavement is dramatic, Stamp Paid's way of staying intact despite slavery's ravaging is more intricate, ultimately more suggestive. His crisis, as he tells Paul D, involves a name change, and in that symbolic operation we witness, in small, the meaning of civilization as a set of resources for making bearable a condition otherwise unbearable. His wife, who was taken from him so that the young master might play with her, is returned a year later:

" 'I'm back,' she said. 'I'm back, Josh.' I looked at the back of her neck. She had a real small neck. I decided to break it. You know, like a twig—just snap it. I been low but that was as low as I ever got."
"Did you? Snap it?" [Paul D asks.]
"Uh uh. I changed my name." (233)

All moves in the real being unacceptable, and therefore finding himself entirely enslaved, Stamp Paid makes his move in the only arena remaining, the symbolic. He takes the wound into himself (a classic self-castration, a revelation of the imposture at the heart of masculine mastery), which is the only way it can be borne: he changes his name from Joshua to Stamp Paid. This lateral gesture of accommodation, when any forward exercise of the will has been foreclosed, enacts an exquisite sense of masculine adaptability, one simply beyond the imagination of any male in Faulkner and of most males in Morrison. Its racial and gender implications are considerable, inasmuch as it finds its way past the honor/dishonor binary at the heart of slavery itself, making impotence a situation still permitting options (the direr the constraint, the more remarkable the adaptation) compatible with male dignity.

Stamp Paid's self-ordained new name literally announces that he has paid all debts, owes nothing to anyone, but it does its real work figuratively—enabling him to conceive himself anew, absorb this blow, and become free again. Reenergized, the slate not so much cleaned as refocused, he then bequeaths his self-proclaimed state of debtlessness to other blacks, serving as the Hermes of his community. (It is he who rescues Sethe, passes messages back and forth, tries to persuade Baby Suggs not to give up, tells Paul D of the murdered child.) If manhood is defined as the adequation of behavior to will—a definition I explore at length in the next chapter—then black slaves (and ex-slaves) learn painfully that their experience of impotence is an unmanning whose redress will require a radically different set of terms. Stamp Paid learns to be a man, as Paul D will, on terms no white male is ever forced to discover.

I have been exploring the remarkable resources that Morrison finds within a slave community that Faulkner's Ike McCaslin could defend only in terms of "endurance . . . and pity and tolerance and forbearance and fidelity and love of children" (*GDM*, 218). Morrison not only goes further than any writer I know in accessing the range of black enterprise within white shackles. She also presses beyond the limits of realism to invent a uniquely capacious form for expressing the wound that was slavery. The name of that form is Beloved, its genre romance. "Romance," Morrison argues in *Playing in the Dark*, "offered writers not less but more; not a narrow a-historical canvas but a wide historical one; not escape but entanglement" (37). Why does this genre offer her opportunities unavailable in realism?

First, there is the documentary premise at the heart of realism, the conviction (rarely stated, usually operative) that the single career, presented with responsible material and psychological verisimilitude, conveys the generic situation. This is realism's dependence on the status quo, on the shared recognition of its données as indeed given: a canvas whose props and behavioral mode are already naturalized by its audience. Before everything else, realism is immediately recognizable. Like Faulkner, who for different reasons found this form inadequate, Morrison must convey an experience that can only be betrayed within the norms of always-recognizable realism. Not that Faulkner or Morrison writes wholly outside the conventions of realism (they would be illegible if they did) but that certain aims require another mode. (Denver's career, for example, is largely represented within realistic conventions.)

Second, the experience of slavery (like that of the Holocaust) will not accede to conventional formulae. The assurance of realism's formulae—their promise of representational mastery, of knowing in advance "what it looks like"—constitutes an arrogance that any artist alert to the problem will beware. If idiocy could be represented through correct grammar and familiar thought patterns, Faulkner would not have needed to invent the ferocious rhetoric of *The Sound and the Fury*. Likewise, an experience of untold millions murdered or mangled, most of them leaving no records (their very speech acts incomprehensible to the American ear that would later seek to "hear" them): this experience is ultimately "unspeakable," and the only way to speak it at all is to acknowledge the unbridgeable gap between the language available and the referent one can only gesture toward.[19] For this, one needs innovative techniques.

Beloved emerges, then, as a radically overdetermined figure—psychologically compelling but at the same time aligned nonpsychologically within several other meaning structures. Who is she? Is she a crazed and abused black girl who believes Sethe to be her mother? The text gives us details that support this reading, and there is every reason—statistically, so to speak—to believe that such damaged children would bond with damaged mothers.[20] Is she Sethe's murdered daughter come back from the dead, seeking both maternal embrace and filial revenge? This reading is undeniably invited, and for most readers this may be the only reading that matters. Note, though, that with this reading (and a fortiori the one that follows) we have exited from realism and entered romance: that space where Newton is superseded not by Disney but by Shakespeare. In Shakespearean romance you are given a second chance, you can return to your mistake (your mistake can return to you) and revise it, do better the next time. It is an autumnal form for revisiting error and offering apology, as Shakespeare's kings and Morrison's Sethe know.

Finally, is she the symbolic embodiment of all those shipwrecked and injured slaves whose voice was never recorded, whose silenced cry began with the nightmare of the Middle Voyage and whose trace we must translate to descry at all? The most haunting passages in the novel suggest she is indeed this kind of revenant, not personal but emblematic of her race's ordeal:

> I cannot lose her again   my dead man was in the way like the noisy clouds when he dies on my face I can see hers   she is going to smile at me   she is going to   her sharp earrings are gone   the men without skin are making loud noises   they push my own man through   they do not push the woman with my face through   she goes in   they do not push her   she goes in   the little hill is gone   she was going to smile at me   she was going to   a hot thing.   (212)

Without pretending to decode this language completely (for it resists the conventions that permit authoritative decoding: orderly punctuation, identified speaker and interlocutor and referent, recognizable setting and behavior, et cetera), one can note the following: that it is a passage of loss and upheaval in several keys—a woman separated from the child-speaker (the original mother kept from the enslaved child?), a dead man (on the slave ship?) pressing on the speaker's face, the incomprehensible sounds and actions of white men (the "men without skin"), the throwing of dead bodies overboard, and (as a kind of refrain) the entry of the woman (the mother?) into the water, rupturing the infantile bond with her child: a bond whose intensity seems to be signified by that recurrent phrase, "a hot thing."[21]

How inadequate psychological verisimilitude—with its statistical accuracy, its one-to-one ratio, its pretense that the general crisis can be measured through the local case—would be for the expression of experience on this scale. Insofar as Beloved shadowily figures forth the tragedy of a race, she cannot be psychological. If she were simply a person, she would only be that person. Morrison's triumph is to make her credible in all of these arenas, despite their mutual incompatibility. Through this extraordinary portrait she gives us, then, "not a narrow a-historical canvas but a wide historical one; not escape but entanglement." Dead and alive, single and plural, real and mythic,

Beloved incarnates at every level the tragedy that was American slavery. In her the unspeakable speaks, unspeakably.

Finally, Morrison represents slavery not only through the invention of a Beloved ("which was not beloved") but also through the capacity of her black characters to register, conceptually and emotionally, slavery's penetration of their very marrow. The gap between the innocent Bodwin's knowledge and the tragic Sethe's knowledge cannot be bridged. Sethe knows, as Bodwin never will, that this centuries-long disaster can be survived but not erased. She tells Denver that the substance of "rememories" never goes away:

> "Where I was before I came here, that place is real. It's never going away. . . . The picture is still there and what's more, if you go there—you who never was there—if you go there and stand in the place where it was, it will happen again; it will be there for you, waiting for you. . . . That's how come I had to get all my children out. No matter what." (36)

This is a vision of space not as virginal, innocently awaiting its (white male) destiny, but as a medium soaked in time and human suffering. Faulkner's precious, inhuman wilderness is Morrison's history-haunted Clearing. Time does go forward in *Beloved* (Denver is launched into forward-moving time), but not in a way that would resolve the horror of past enslavement. Unlike Faulknerian tragedy, though, this enslavement—however disabling—brings forth acts of humanity, rituals of acknowledgment, more compelling yet. Sethe and Paul D do indeed have "more yesterday than anybody." On what but this would they build "some kind of tomorrow" (273)?

Speculative Conclusions

I have been intent upon suggesting the role played by race and gender within these two writers' representation of slavery. Equally, their work is affected by the pressures of their own historical moment, and this chapter can conclude by briefly relating its internal findings to a number of outer coordinates. The differences between Faulkner's early-twentieth-century South and Morrison's midcentury Ohio are considerable. Faulkner's later years witnessed a ferment in American race relations that he stubbornly sought but failed to comprehend; his best work, furthermore, was already behind him. Morrison's formative period embraces the decades of segregation (the 1930s and 1940s) and integration (the 1950s), while her fictional output begins (with *The Bluest Eye*, 1971) on the other side of a decade of "black power." If slavery is a phenomenon that reached its crescendo before 1865, these two writers' ways of accessing it are nevertheless marked by twentieth-century frames of reference.

The monolithic racial institution within which Faulkner came of age was Southern segregation. Born in Mississippi in 1897—the same time that, following *Plessy v. Ferguson*, Jim Crow laws began to sprout up all over the South—he experienced a schizoid world of whites fanatically separated from blacks, on the one hand, and, on the other, a domestic economy of a black mammy who doubles as a mother, who treats the needs and vulnerability of his body with a care that his own mother cannot provide. He loves "his" blacks, yet grows up in a culture that keeps him from knowing in any depth what black life might mean outside his own narrow yet intimate relation to it. This orientation enables, I believe, the extraordinary tension in his great work between normative racist practices and subjectively felt, guilt-fueled analysis of them. Such analysis registers, necessarily, within the tormented subjectivity of his narrators rather than at the level of a tragic plot unfolding that he found himself powerless to alter, to envisage as alterable.

The stories that make up *The Unvanquished* seek and find the easiest solution to the contradiction between antebellum culture's confident norms and its abusive practice. Despite brilliant flashes of pain, this novel works to anneal racial suffering, representing slavery as an institution coming to its fitting end, yet lived out beneficently within Sartoris precincts. Race-fueled chaos may rage outside, but Sartoris slaves do not want to be "abolished." The drama Faulkner focuses on instead tends to center on white male values—an honor/shame drama of aristocratic chivalry and poor-white betrayal—and this drama concedes the loss of the War in such a way as rarely to take the measure of why it had to be lost. The ideological work of *The Unvanquished* consists in proposing that the externally vanquished South remains internally, morally, unvanquished.

Absalom, Absalom! and *Go Down, Moses* refuse the blandishments of this fantasy, portraying black slaves as belonging to the white family in a way that has become unbearably guilt-ridden. It is as though the more Faulkner bore down on Sartoris, the more he saw Sutpen and McCaslin—men whose dynastic drive is inseparable from their owning, abusing, impregnating, and refusing to acknowledge the black lives that surround them and let them become who they are. In this new perception, repudiation of the black slave is simultaneously (by way of a double vision that constitutes Faulkner's greatness) amputation of the white dynasty. White mother and black mother, white offspring and black offspring: these are inextricably same and other, beloved and repudiated, producing in the tormented beholder (Henry, Bon, Quentin, Ike) a racial vertigo unamenable to therapy.

Yet, even in these texts, Faulkner never fully escapes (how could he?) the cultural pressures that simultaneously sting him into articulation. The abiding facade of segregation (one drop would make you black) underwrites his creativity, serving as the visible key to concealed horrors. His tragic theme is miscegenation not least because that is the taboo truth of declared segregation. More, his representation of white feeling toward black runs the widest gamut between illicit desire and sanctioned repudiation. All this, finally, takes place within the family itself: Sartoris order turned inside out as Sutpen and McCaslin disorder, serving no longer as sanctuary against outer stress but as inner revelation, diagnostic X-ray of the larger culture's norm-justified racial madness. All of Faulkner's art is lavished upon this topic, for he first came into power as a writer of the emotionally ravaged Southern home (Compson, Bundren), and he eventually brings to that damaged and damaging space the ultimate element explaining dysfunction and awaiting inclusion: miscegenation.

Segregation as social system gives Faulkner his racial frame, shapes what he does not know even when its own blindnesses become his major insight. Like Racine, who required the prison of the Alexandrine for his richest expression, so Faulkner interrogates Southern forms as only someone also within them and sharing their emotional hold could. He sees that the white house, built upon a black foundation, is divided against itself and cannot stand. But he cannot produce a narrative of any house that might replace this doomed white one, and he has trouble envisaging a black house grounded outside the parameters of white sponsorship. Dilsey and Nancy, Lucas and Molly—these black portraits are etched in the slave-retainer mold, and their living quarters are conceived within its frame: outposts constructed upon white property. Even the precious "fire and hearth" of Lucas and Molly is white-oriented, vulnerable to a call in the night from the white planter, the pharaoh whose authority remains operative, however gullible.

Segregation decrees a social scene whose falseness inspires Faulkner's diagnostic powers, yet whose primary terms inflect his own. He may reveal the fantasies (alternately poignant and cruel) supporting the properly segregated Southern family, but he never doubts the primacy of the putative white family itself. If this primacy eventually allows him to write the tragedy of racial nonacknowledgment at the core of Southern family, it also nourishes the blindnesses that follow from reading race through the lens of family. Like all lenses, that lens is angled, carrying an *ideologeme* that places black necessarily within the triple schema of damage, disinheritance, and nonacknowledgment.[22] From *Flags in the Dust* through *Intruder in the Dust*, these blacks are "our" blacks, offspring of our family. To care for them is our pride, to disown them our shame and eventually (since we are inextricably bonded) our downfall. No one has told this story more powerfully than Faulkner, but it remains a story whose primary players are white and male.

It is not difficult to point to the omissions of such a narrative, and in the next chapter I shall pursue the meanings of racial legacy—the fallout of slavery—in both writers' work. Suffice it for now to say that a narrative lens focused on family keeps Faulkner from reading his black portraits outside the themes of damage, disinheritance, and nonacknowledgment. More sinister, that lens eventually loses its (always limited) flexibility, and the narrative of "our" blacks reveals its defensive component: our blacks, not yours. As Faulkner grappled with the increasing racial ferment of the 1940s and early 1950s, his family frame widened and rigidified. The family tended to become the postbellum South itself, black and white, a coherent region (despite its tensions) that no one from elsewhere could understand. (Shreve's bewildered refrain in *Absalom*—"Because it's something my people haven't got" [*AA*, 297]—may be anachronistic for 1910 but is perfectly fitting for 1935, the more region-beleaguered year in which Faulkner finished the writing.) *I'll Take My Stand* had come out in 1930, Cash's *Mind of the South* would appear in 1941. We are witness to the mythologizing of a region into a Culture, a mythologizing that—under great pressures both internal and external—would seek to anneal racial difference into family understanding. Faulkner's work in the 1930s and 1940s incoherently both supports and attacks this myth. On the one hand, you'd have to be born there to see it steady and see it whole. On the other hand, its vaunted integrity is a tissue of fantasies covering over deep (and deeply divisive) experiences of racial pain.

This double stance punctuates the representation of race in Faulkner's supreme attempt to understand the meaning of slavery, *Go Down, Moses*. Ike contemplates Lucas Beauchamp's face (in "The Fire and the Hearth"), and he realizes: "It was not at all the face of their grandfather, Carothers McCaslin. It was the face of the generation which had just preceded them: the composite tintype face of ten thousand undefeated Confederate soldiers" (*GDM*, 83). I used to read this description as pure fantasy—a Southern black of 1895 (the year of this represented scene) having the face of a Confederate soldier—but it now seems to yield its fantasy logic. That logic is of 1940, the year of the writing, and it proposes Lucas Beauchamp as not only fiercely Southern but white Southern, Confederate Southern, "undefeated" Southern.

Insofar as Lucas's face can be reinscribed within this unreconstructed Southern family frame, it signals a warning to Faulkner's contemporary public, the agitated North of the 1940s: go slow now, do not interfere with a regional racial struggle inexorably working itself out in Southern terms, family terms.[23] Yet Faulkner cannot sustain this mythic (and reactionary) belief in regional unity, as "Delta Autumn" closes on the specter of the ruined delta: "This land which man has deswamped and denuded and derivered in two generations . . . where white men rent farms and live like niggers and niggers crop on shares and live like animals . . . [where] Chinese and African and Aryan and Jew, all breed and spawn together until no man has time to say which one is which nor cares" (269). Yeats claimed that out of our quarrel with ourselves we make poetry, and *Go Down, Moses* makes memorable art out of Faulkner's conflicted family stance, his South at once an elegiac source of race-annealed value and an ongoing scene of racial humiliations. *Intruder in the Dust* will press harder on both ends of this contradiction, arguing explicitly for a "homogeneous" culture while producing everywhere—at the levels of sentence structure, class hostility, age and gender barriers, the near-total absence of blacks from the story—a canvas of uncohering parts.

Faulkner's representation of slavery is saturated in a self-divided twentieth-century Southern experience of segregation that, so to speak, moves determinedly toward but never gets past *Brown v. Board of Education*—a representation keyed to the family vocabulary of abused and unacknowledged offspring. Morrison, for her part, reads the original disaster as a black woman writing at a later time, in other places, and with different cultural narratives at her disposal. Unsurprisingly, these different orientations enable different versions of the story of contemporary America that is covertly operative in each writer's treatment of nineteenth-century materials. Not the victim Emmett Till (whose murder Faulkner decried) but the activist Malcolm X (whose message reaches Guitar in *Song of Solomon*) whispers in Morrison's ear as she seeks to recover and turn into narrative form the experience of slavery in America.

Born in 1931 in Lorain, Ohio, Toni Morrison has lived through a number of times and places and professional identities before becoming a practicing novelist.[24] She is in one sense a generation further than Faulkner from the experience of slavery, yet her knowledge of that institution—both sets of grandparents from the nineteenth-century South, inevitably marked by slavery before 1865 and racism after—comes to her free of racial translation (white reading black) and possesses an emotional breadth and depth outside his range. More, her later work at Random House leads to her helping to edit *The Black Book*, a compendium of wide-ranging information about American slavery and a sourcebook for *Beloved*. She has not only grown up, like Faulkner, with tales of slavery; she has also studied it.[25]

If Faulkner's understanding of slavery is inseparable from his region's experience, Morrison's practice correlates less easily with (or against) regional attitudes. Lorain, Ohio; Washington, D.C.; New York—she has lived at length in each of these (and other) places, coming to her material as well through a sequence of unprecedented racial upheavals. Unlike Faulkner's essentially segregated Southern experience from childhood through his twenties and thirties, in which the horror of white abuse toward black was typically mediated by regional norms rationalizing white supremacy, Morrison's prenovelistic years span segregation, the first ferments of integration, the fiery years of freedom marches, and the advent of "black power." By the time of Martin Luther King's rise in the 1950s, Faulkner had ceased to write fiction focused upon race. In contrast, King, Stokely Carmichael, and Malcolm X had all come into prominence and passed into martyrdom or silence before Morrison begins *The Bluest Eye*. There were, of course, other currents affecting both of them—my aim here is to gesture toward a field, not to characterize it thoroughly—but we can already see that, apart from their different race and gender positioning, their historical moments are deeply dissimilar. In suggesting their differences, I have not even spoken of Morrison's sustained professional achievement as a woman of letters: editor at Random House, professor at several universities, and now holder of a distinguished chair at Princeton. We are far from Faulkner's lifelong dislike of academics, his insistence, both surly and shy (and despite the fact that he read deeply and was anything but an untutored genius), that he was a farmer who happened to write books.

Keeping in mind both the urban racial upheaval of the 1960s and the many-stranded interest in an authentic black experience descended from Africa, we can recognize some of the stakes involved in *Song of Solomon*'s narrative emplotment of the phenomenon of slavery. (Alex Haley's *Roots* had appeared in 1976, too late to influence the writing of *Song of Solomon* yet too close in time not to imply a larger cultural current to which both texts were responding.) The city on which the novel opens is hollow, unsustaining. Its white authorities seek (by way of renaming streets and racially quarantining social spaces) to repress its own biracial history. The city does not nourish the fragile racial identity of those who, like Macon Dead Jr., would model themselves upon its capitalist terms ("A nigger in business is a terrible thing to see," Guitar's grandmother says [SS, 22]). What Milkman learns from this father is so alien to the text's aims as to be literally unrepresentable (we may see Milkman at his father's office but never at his father's work). Instead, the immediate lifelines are all female: Milkman's prolonged nursing from his mother, his absorption of Pilate's wisdom. To orient himself properly within his race's culture will involve a reshaping of his relation to time and place, and this will take him past both Macon Dead Jr. and Macon Dead Sr.—toward the original father, Solomon.

Getting to Solomon (as I shall explore more fully in part 3) involves a Faulknerian relinquishment of gold, to be replaced by an investment in the land itself deeper than any exchange commodity the land might yield. The Shalimar sequence of Song of Solomon enacts a mythic repossessing of the land—a coming to human terms with its natural terms, its foliage and trees and beasts, in the midst of a strangely all-black biblical community of Saul and Solomon, Calvin and Luther. Such repossession reverses, point for point, the dispossession of property that cost Macon Dead Sr. his life and that metonymically replays the larger dispossession of slavery itself. Macon Dead Jr. still lives the fallout of that antebellum dispossession. His urban properties bring him only anomie and hunger, no connection with the land they lodge upon or with fellow blacks whom he views through a capitalist lens as tenants, not distant kinfolks. The root ill of impotence came from slavery's psychic and material disenfranchisement and can only be reversed by a return to that originating wound.

Solomon himself embodies Morrison's lyrical rewriting of black disinheritance. African slaves were forcibly removed from their homeland and taken in ships to America; Solomon makes this journey in reverse, flying homeward from captivity. Home is, moreover, what the blacks in Shalimar and Danville, however impoverished, draw upon as a rooted dwelling. Their rural bonding with the land itself contrasts eloquently with the urban politics and anomie that fill the foreground scenes of the novel. (Pilate's elaborate inoculation of her urban home against city networks—a small circle of black neighbors but no phones, no house number, no clocks, no white norms—shows how difficult it is to live in this city and retain any of the rootedness of her black culture.) The Solomonic myth connects the seeker with his past, makes the sequence from Africa to the American 1960s continuous and narratable, makes chronological time make familial sense. But this myth accommodates the damage of slavery by transcending it. Only in *Beloved* does Morrison make good on the passionate promise that concludes *Song of Solomon*: that you engage disaster not through flight but through an all-risking encounter—"For now he [Milkman] knew what Shalimar knew: If you surrendered to the air you could *ride* it" (337).

Beloved deepens and completes the journey begun in *Song of Solomon*. After constructing a narrative of black return to Africa, Morrison now constructs a prior narrative of African voyage to America—the Middle Passage. In myriad ways she shows that an original African heritage never entirely died; indeed, that death never entirely occurs ("anything but forgetfulness" [*B*, 4], as Baby Suggs characterizes it). In *Beloved*, black Americans reach back to folkways, enduring (when they do endure) the ordeal of slavery because they could (and had to) draw upon resources for survival not available to white Americans. The antelope in Sethe's belly points simultaneously backward and forward, to the African dance her ma'am participated in and to the rambunctious fetus restless in her stomach and eager to get on with things. It thus epitomizes the sense of Sethe's moment-by-moment movement as invisibly oriented, rooted in an African diaspora (her ma'am's dance itself a ritual of memory and adaptation) and heading toward a difficult yet unstoppable future.[26]

The songs Paul D sings with the other slaves and which the whites cannot fathom, the strange language Sethe's mother spoke and whose meaning Sethe somehow retained, the humming of thirty women come together to liberate one of their own, in search of "the right combination, the key, the code, the sound that broke the back of [white] words" (*B*, 261)—all these daily yet irrepressible moments of adaptive agency show slavery to have produced in the black subject something quite other than the "natal alienation" intended by all slaveholders. Rather, much as W. E. B. Du Bois argued at the turn of the century and as dozens of black spokespersons proclaimed throughout the 1960s, Africa provided a veiled and yet enabling set of cultural resources for black Americans decades and generations removed from its shores. It could be, could not but be, remembered. Its legacy of resources led to engagement with, not transcendence of, slavery's worst inflictions. These same resources would later nourish that extraordinary riding of the air that is jazz/*Jazz*.

PART 2
Legacies

I opened this book on personal memories of the segregated world of Memphis in the 1940s that I was born into—what I knew before I knew what I knew. This segregated world gave me Vannie; and I have tried, some twenty-five years after her death, to understand both the strengths and the limitations of the bond that developed between us. Drawing on Vannie as my fundamental childhood engagement with race, I went on to propose, as a suggestive counterpart, Faulkner's coming to his grasp upon race and maternity in the South through the formative encounter with Mammy Callie. The real Mammy Callie leads to fictional Dilsey and Molly. More, she first embodies for her creator the inextricable mix of same/other that will characterize his most powerful representations of race. The opening chapter concluded with Morrison's significantly different interest, first in maids (she sees past their role as mammies), then mothers. Part 1 then turned to historical beginnings by focusing upon slavery as the inaugurative disaster of American history. Neither Faulkner nor Morrison lived the experience of slavery, yet its repercussions shape their lives and their work. I sought to show how, as twentieth-century writers, white and black, male and female, Southern and non-Southern, they turn this nineteenth-century material into revealingly different narratives.

I turn now to legacies, as understood in a number of ways. First, there is the historical legacy of slavery itself—the brief decade of Reconstruction followed by an eighty-year postbellum experience of segregation. Faulkner and Morrison are born into this latter period; its assumptions and practices mark their work decisively. Second, there is legacy in the traditional sense of the territory of the father as this passes to his progeny: the entry into custom and law, the inheritance of property. Differences coded to race could hardly be starker in this domain, for the role of the postbellum black father is burdened by a unique set of pressures. Both Faulkner and Morrison recognize and seek imaginatively to resolve the lack of power that slavery has imposed (before and after the Civil War) upon black men.

The first chapter of the section, " 'Mister,' " explores their different strategies for thinking through the dilemma of black male powerlessness. These differences spring, I believe, from racially different stances toward the Oedipal itself. For the Oedipal operates as the normative psychic model underlying white Western patriarchy's design for regulating the descent of gender identity and the tripartite cultural inheritance that gender subtends: the proper, propriety, and property. This model was not designed, so to speak, with blacks in mind; and black males aspire to it at their peril. This last problematic—the Oedipal paradigm for male maturation and its vexed relation to the descent of gender identity and cultural inheritance in both writers—serves as the center of the next chapter, "David and Solomon." Here I explore Faulkner's and Morrison's construal of fathering by asking: What is a father? What material and emotional legacies pass from fathers to their offspring? How does a white father differ from a black father? How does a black female writer engage these questions differently from a white male writer?

My alignment of masculinity with legacies is of course not absolute, for I explored throughout part 1 the resonant role of the mother's legacy in both writers' work. In any event, a separate treatment of male and female spheres only shows—no matter what their differences—the interpenetrability of male and female domains. I turn now to the historical legacy of slavery, the world of segregation I was born into and more or less unthinkingly accepted in the 1940s and early 1950s.

Historians often remind us that conditions we take to be changeless are inscribed in an ongoing process. Southern segregation seemed during the first forty years of this century to have been in place forever. Yet, as Joel Williamson remarks in *The Crucible of Race*, "The word 'segregation' apparently was not much used before 1899, and when it was used it had no special racial connotation" (254). This is so because the phenomenon we know as segregation—an exhaustively worked-out, Jim-Crow-law-supported skein of barriers separating black and white—did not exist during either the centuries of slavery or the Reconstruction decade that followed the Civil War.[1] The condition that fomented segregation—black enfranchisement—was recent, and the Jim Crow laws were even more so. Rather, throughout the eighteenth and most of the nineteenth centuries in the United States, whites and blacks (the great majority of whom lived in the South) lived more in each other's presence. The differences between them tended to be vertical rather than spatial.

Such inequality, though continuous throughout the slaveholding South, did not always rest upon an absolute distinction between white and black blood. In South Carolina in the seventeenth century, for example, there was genuine resistance to categorizing on the basis of blood alone. "We cannot say what admixture of blood will make a colored person," Judge William Harper declared in 1635. "The condition of the individual is not to be determined solely by distinct and visible mixture of negro blood, but by reputation, by his reception into society, and his having commonly exercised the privileges of a white man."[2] What would by the segregated time of Faulkner's Joe Christmas become a source of ungovernable anxiety—the 1930s possibility of a man's racial identity not being visually accessible—was closer to a normative situation two hundred years earlier (and equally in the Deep South).[3]

I emphasize the fact that blacks and whites lived in each other's presence for almost three centuries in the South not to mitigate the abuses of slavery, but to distinguish them from those of segregation. Slavery remained damaging on an unspeakable scale, and Williamson's *Crucible of Race* has established that, with its cessation after 1865, the incidence of miscegenation dropped dramatically. Freed black women were no longer available for coercive intercourse or rape in anything like the appalling earlier numbers (307). Yet slavery—which in hindsight certainly appears to be the fatal flaw of the American design—was itself not lived for over two centuries as an institution uniformly endorsed in the South. The Virginia parliament voted as late as 1831 to affirm slavery by a margin of only 65 to 58. Four changed votes would probably have led to the abolition of slavery in the leading Southern state, which contained at that time one-fourth of the black slaves in America. Williamson speculates that such an alternate scenario (what Faulkner would call a "might-have-been") might have radically altered the career of slavery, inaugurated a process of racial integration, and averted the need, some thirty years later, of the Civil War (15–16).

The pertinent point is that the "solid South," with its all but hysterical consensus upon segregation, dated only from the 1890s. The Jim Crow laws were at first resisted in many white quarters. C. Vann Woodward's *Strange Career of Jim Crow* rehearses the range of liberal Southern voices that the eventually uniform imposition of segregation would blanket into silence. There is retrospective pathos in a North Carolina black editor's being persuaded by these

1880s white voices and commenting, "The best people of the South do not demand the separate car [carriage] business" (32). At the other end of the class scale, a Texas politician could recognize, as late as the 1880s, an economic kinship underlying pigment difference: "They are in the ditch just like we are" (43). The populist Tom Watson put it even more succinctly to a mixed audience: "You are made to hate each other because upon that hatred is rested the keystone of the arch of financial despotism which enslaves you both" (44–45). With the advent of uniform segregation, however, these tentative recognitions of class commonality ceased to command attention, and there arose something at the end of the nineteenth century that slavery itself had depended on, yet never needed directly to nourish: racism. This phenomenon, having incubated for centuries, swiftly spread beyond the South. It has remained a pervasive, if (since the turbulent 1950s and 1960s) less spectacular, dilemma of the American scene, and its capacity to substitute racial terms for economic ones continues to bedevil us today.

The abolition of slavery thus opened up the widest social chasm. How would a majority white society come to terms—emotionally, politically, economically, conceptually—with a newly enfranchised black minority? For some twelve years (1865–1877) Northern enforcement had made the South grapple with this issue, but national resolve faltered in the face of social adjustment required on so vast a scale. Increasingly, issues of racial justice were relegated to state jurisdiction. It was as though the federal government in a dozen different decisions was saying to the defeated South: we are tired of this issue, it is your problem and you take care of it. How spectacularly the South failed to take care of it, Faulkner's work testifies eloquently. How unsuccessfully it has been taken on elsewhere in the country, Morrison's work (among other data too numerous to mention) shows us. As though unresisted, the Jim Crow mentality extended its domain throughout the 1890s and the first decades of the twentieth century. The *Richmond Times* greeted the new century by thundering: "God Almighty drew the color line and it cannot be obliterated."[4] From one-quarter to one-eighth to one drop: this is the amount of black blood it takes, during a hardening of American racial thought from the seventeenth into the first half of the twentieth century, to make you black. One drop carries the plague much as a virus would. Into such a racially virulent world Faulkner and Morrison were born, inheriting it as their tormenting and unwanted birthright.

3

"Mister"

The Drama of Black Manhood in Faulkner and Morrison

The present argument first began quite locally, focused upon a single resonant word, *Mister*.[1] Negotiating a critical moment of racial humiliation in both *Go Down, Moses* and *Beloved*, this word implicates—I eventually realized—a larger schema of inequality that circulates about the issue of inheritance. For the term *Mister* is a birthright of white boys who will grow up to be white men. During most of American history this term has not been available to blacks. The respect lodged at the core of this appellation is founded, I propose, upon the possible ownership of property. Ownership and property, moreover, are not only etymologically twinned—that which one owns, that which is proper to one—but together they can be said to be indispensable terms of a Western discourse of identity: one's self as that which is one's own. The pride of identity itself is inseparable from the possibility of self-ownership: an equation, I shall argue, that both posits identity as wholly self-contained and sheds a lurid light upon the ordeal of identity undergone by an enslaved people who could not own themselves.

Postslavery segregation both alters and continues this identity/property dynamic, for it is a schema that envisages the "enfranchised" black as deprived of all properties but one (and that one unchangeable): his essential black identity as carried by his undilutable black blood. As Eric Sundquist argues in *To Wake the Nations*, late-nineteenth-century attitudes toward miscegenation (the mixing of "properties") are decisively shaped by a fetishizing of blood as an immutable racial property: "In transforming race into an intrinsic and changeless entity signified by blood," Sundquist writes, "miscegenation jurisprudence defined it as inheritable property" (248). Inheritable and contaminating: black blood-property to be kept scrupulously separated (one drop from the wrong vat could be devastating) from white blood-property that descends in patriarchal fashion from lily-white wives. The descent of goods, of patriarchal legitimacy, and of racial identity, then, is conceived in each case as the descent of an intrinsic and bounded property.

Finally, I want to introduce at the outset a missing term that we require if we would meditate upon a more flexible poetics of identity: *identification*.[2] I wish to conceptualize identity as a self-relation that oscillates between two poles—the boundedness of possession (of self and of the other) versus the fluidity of identification (of self with the other). At one extreme, identity—one's own, that of others—is imagined as a possessible property. At the other extreme it is an aleatory, interpenetrable, and frighteningly vulnerable resource. The one is solid, with the strengths and weaknesses that attach to solidity. The other is liquid, with the strengths and weaknesses that attach to liquidity. Treating them both as psychological propensities, Freud distinguishes in *Group Psychology* between possession and identification as the desire to *have* the other versus the desire to *be* the other. Though he also stresses that "identification . . . is ambivalent from the very first; it can turn into an expression of tenderness as easily as into a wish for someone's removal" (105), he makes it clear that possession accesses the other as object while identification seeks (impossibly) to access the other as subject. These two polar stances—never wholly separable, both of them at work in how we construct our world and construe our relation to self and other—take me to the body "proper" of my argument about *Mister* and the drama of black manhood.

> Years after the [Civil] war white southerners sighed with relief when Booker T. Washington received a doctorate. They had too much respect for him to call him "Booker" and could not call any black man "Mr."; but "Dr. Washington" presented no problem.
>
> (Eugene Genovese, *Roll, Jordan, Roll*, 445)

Mister: the term puts before us, as in this early twentieth-century white dilemma over how to address Booker T. Washington, a host of racial/gender norms. Descended from *master*, *mister* performs as an address of respect.[3] Whatever ironic inflections it may take on notwithstanding, the term acknowledges a sustained distance between self and other, a minimal space surrounding the male who is designated *mister* that keeps him, so to speak, intact within a field of address. Children are not yet misters, not yet inserted into the social network securely enough to receive this deference. Thus *mister* both betokens male adulthood as achieved insertion within the symbolic order—one can only be *mister* within a larger community of misters—and simultaneously declares a certain measure of autonomy. To be addressed as Mr. is to be addressed properly, with propriety, with the implication of property. All three of these notions—property, propriety, the proper—are legacies reserved (well into our century) for whites only. Together they constitute the mastery that stands behind *mister,* and they point to those aspects of (white) manhood denied explicitly to the black male slave and implicitly to the black freedman.

Mister further implies, at the deeper level of psychic identity, a completed negotiation of the Oedipal crisis itself. All misters are deemed to have passed through the crucible of potentially crippling infantile confusions and to be credentialed as successfully individuated human beings within the social order. They have internalized the father's authority (in the form of the superego), become capable of policing themselves, achieved adult identity. Propertied or not, misters are assumed to be self-owning and entitled to larger ownership; fathers or not, they may occupy paternal terrain. They may inherit and they may bequeath.[4] The refusal of Southern white culture at the turn of the century to call Booker T. Washington "Mr." is a refusal to grant him manhood within that culture's registers of property, propriety, and the proper: the potential property of goods and land that define the birthright of white post-Enlightenment males, the propriety of membership within a community of white misters, and the proper (the *propre,* "one's own") of achieved masculine identity itself. These are the larger stakes at issue in the drama of black manhood.

Property, propriety, the proper: perhaps the greatest of these is property. Before moving forward to the specific resonance of these notions in Faulkner's and Morrison's texts, I want briefly to rehearse the larger American claim for property as a defining attribute of free men. That claim derives from the European Enlightenment; its best-known source is probably John Locke's "Second Essay Concerning Civil Government" (1690).[5] Seeking (in the wake of a century of religious war) to shore up the individual Englishman's rights against unpredictable vagaries of the Crown, proposing an argument of natural law that supersedes all monarchical constraint upon the subject, Locke writes: "The *natural liberty* of man is to be free from any superior power on earth, and not to be under the will or legislative authority of man, but to have only the law of Nature for his rule" (283). Deeper than any covenant imposed by church or king, Locke argues, is our natural, inalienable liberty. This liberty acquires focus and grounding through the concept of property: "Though the earth, and all inferior creatures be common to all men, yet every man has a *property* in his own *person*. This nobody has any right to but himself. The *labour* of his body, and the *work* of his hands, we may say, are properly his. Whatsoever, then, he removes out of the state that Nature hath provided, and left it in, he hath mixed his *labour* with, and joined to it something that is his own, and thereby makes it his *property*" (287–88). Given these convictions, which are almost Marxian in their understanding of subjective identity enacted through objective labor, Locke has no difficulty in assigning to government its foremost (and far from Marxian) purpose: "The great and *chief end*, therefore, of men uniting into commonwealths, and putting themselves under government, *is the preservation of their property*" (350–51).

It would be hard to overestimate the appeal of this argument to America's Founding Fathers. Louis Hartz, seeking to characterize this country's liberal tradition, calls Locke "America's philosopher" as he could never have been Europe's: "When Locke came to America . . . a change appeared. Because the basic feudal oppressions of Europe had not taken root, the fundamental social norm of Locke ceased in large part to look like a norm and began, of all things, to look like a sober description of fact. . . . History was on a lark, out to tease men, not by shattering their dreams, but by fulfilling them with a sort of satiric accuracy."[6] Our labor, the activation of our personal resources, the goods we individually gather through such expenditure of energy: these are to be thought of (with a literalism inconceivable in the Old World) as our inalienable property, central to our unfettered, self-shaped identity. British refusal to recognize—through appropriate representation—this American right to property led to what was seen as a justified war of independence. The individual possession of property is not only what Americans went to war to protect, it is also what the forefathers believed would most securely keep the peace. "Government, thought the Fathers, is based on property," Richard Hofstadter writes in *The American Political Tradition*. "Men who have no property lack the necessary stake in an orderly society to make stable or reliable citizens" (13). Property both knits together the domain of the self and inserts the individual properly within the larger social fabric. In a 1787 commentary on the Constitution, Noah Webster describes the maintenance and regulation of property rights as the very basis of American freedom:

> Wherever we cast our eyes, we see this truth, that *property* is the basis of *power*; and this, being established as a cardinal point, directs us to the means of preserving our freedom. Make laws, irrevocable laws in every state,

destroying and barring entailments; leave real estates to revolve from hand to hand, as time and accident may direct; and no family influence can be acquired and established for a series of generations—no man can obtain dominion over a large territory—the laborious and saving, who are generally the best citizens, will possess each his share of property and power, and thus the balance of wealth and power will continue where it is, in *the body of the people. A general and tolerably equal distribution of landed property is the whole basis of national freedom.*[7]

If property is proposed as the grounding concept of both peace and freedom, we might begin to note the anxieties and omissions that hedge this claim in Locke and more openly in Webster, and that have bedeviled it ever since. Suppose that each did not possess his share, that property were not spread through "the body of the people . . . [with] tolerably equal distribution," that one man did take more than he could actually make use of? Suppose he did obtain "dominion over a large territory"? Locke feebly argues that "he was only to look that he used them [the goods that make up his property] before they spoiled, else he took more than his share, and robbed others. And, indeed, it was a foolish thing, as well as dishonest, to hoard up more than he could make use of" (300).[8] But this rejoinder had no more force in 1690 than the following one penned 245 years later and put into the mind of young Thomas Sutpen: "And as for objects, nobody had any more of them than you did because everybody had just what he was strong enough or energetic enough to take and keep, and only that crazy man would go to the trouble to take or even want more than he could eat or swap for powder and whiskey" (*AA*, 179).

Somebody always does have more than you do, and Sutpen stumbles down from the mountain upon a Tidewater drama that sharply subverts Locke: the spectacle of a white man so engorged with property that his power is revealed not in his labor—Locke's crucial justificatory term—but in his indolence: a man whom others fan and feed, who lords it over "a country all divided and fixed and neat with a people living on it all divided and fixed and neat because of what color their skins happened to be and what they happened to own" (*AA*, 179). Here the defects of Locke's property schema leap into visibility. Far from a natural right of every human being, it is always selectively distributed: first to industrious white males who underwrote England's bloodless revolution of 1688 and our bloody one of 1776, thereafter to white males (even those originating from the Old Bailey) cunning or hungry enough to acquire it. Not only do propertied white men grow greedy for more property, but there have long been other, gaping omissions on the American scene: poor whites who lack property; women who both lack property and are property; slaves who were nothing but property; their offspring still in search of property. History only seemed to be on a lark, for what beckoned as a manageable fact—the effective accumulation of property—would for many Americans never be more than a dream. Founded on a Lockean premise destined to implode—to make of class, gender, and race the very factors that will cause the project of identity-as-property to collapse—this American dream functions from the beginning as a white male drama with its tragic exclusions already inseparable from its intoxicating promises. Faulkner and Morrison were conceived centuries before they were born. Before turning specifically to Lucas Beauchamp and Paul D, I would like briefly to probe the larger repercussion, in both writers' work, of a model of identity premised upon the notion of property.

Faulkner becomes Faulkner, paradoxically, by finding his way into the drama of radically failed self-ownership—a consequence inseparable from the failure of parental legacies. The voices of Benjy and Quentin Compson testify eloquently to the collapse of the American dream of identity-as-property. Rather than the Lockean premise of successful labor, of a thrusting male will that subdues and shapes an estate in its own image—that knows and ratifies itself through what it possesses—Faulkner gives us the drama of interior dispossession. Caught up within a stream-of-consciousness technique that produces them not as subjects with a coherent project but as cacophonous sites of cultural interference, Benjy and Quentin never do or own anything. Instead, they are done to, they suffer the consequences of previous cultural designs gone awry and no longer regulatory. The burden of generations of Compson dysfunction comes to rest upon their ineffectual minds and bodies. "I was trying to say" is the hallmark of Faulknerian voice, and it can find utterance only when a culture's legacies—its descended norms of saying (of articulating social possibility as achievable personal project)—have failed. Early Faulknerian voice is an unforgettable way of saying No after a host of conventional ways of saying Yes have proved bankrupt.[9]

Benjy, Quentin, Darl, Joe Christmas: these are the subjectivities the early Faulkner most brilliantly produced. Each signals the unavailingness of cultural designs as maps for achievable selfhood. If in Western culture the Oedipal crisis is the ordeal the male child must go through in order to emerge as a candidate for paternity and its perquisites—property, propriety, the proper—then each of these characters remains arrested on the threshold of that journey, dancing around a wound that precedes the Oedipal. Damaged by defective or disappeared mothers, insufficiently birthed into the culture's symbolic orders (or birthed into the culture's insufficient symbolic orders), they cannot manage the simplest tasks of self-ownership. The legacies they do manage to inherit incapacitate.

Insecurely gendered, incapable of separating internal from external, resolutely untrainable, these boy children career across the Faulknerian canvas, revealing fissure and contradiction wherever they touch down. Desiring their mother or their sister or their brother, they are hopelessly enmeshed in incest schemas, and such schemas only deepen as scandal if the sibling turns out to be black as well. Indeed, Faulkner found his way into the ordeal of race through the ordeal of family: the ordeal of illicit sameness residing in the precincts of the other (incest)—or intolerable otherness residing in the precincts of the same (miscegenation)—the home itself a hothouse where the most intimate bondings and aversions cohabit. In a certain sense he never ceased to view racial torment as an epiphenomenon of family torment. In both domains the structures that sustain individual identity by maintaining coherent distinctions between races, genders, and generations have collapsed. Incest and miscegenation are the prime motives fueling his narrative, guaranteeing its subversion of Lockean proprieties by contaminating all definitions of the proper. If there is one thing his most memorable characters share, it is the knowledge that they do not possess themselves.

Is it too much to say that a fear of contamination—an all but hysterical sensitivity to odors and touches that have already invaded and deformed before they are even recorded by consciousness—coils at the core of Faulknerian sensibility? Or should we say that this fear of contamination registers simultaneously an impossible (because ideologically taboo) longing—a desire to cross illicit boundaries (incestuous, miscegenous) in which successful transgression could only mean the death of the "proper" subject? At any rate, from Donald Mahan in *Soldiers' Pay* to the reporter in *Pylon* to Chick Mallison in *Intruder in the Dust*, a characteristic male note is to be moved beyond control, overwhelmed internally and externally, besides oneself: hardly traits on which a fiction committed to the masculine pursuit of intrinsic identity through attainment of fixed property could be built.

Even if we grant that Faulkner's work is irretrievably invested in a model of identity as failed self-owning, however, we might concede his work's yearning for achieved selfhood, attained project, the successful maturation of child into property-bearing adult. *Go Down, Moses* manages in its portrait of Ike

McCaslin to attend with equal generosity to why he must repudiate the contract and what social price he pays in repudiating it. Who better than Faulkner could understand a refusal to take on the guilt attaching to propertied Southern adulthood, even as he shows both that property repudiated remains property someone else will accept and abuse—the names change but the racially unjust social order remains in force—and that the pursuit of property could be an epic male undertaking, however disastrous its consequences?

As for Morrison, her texts likewise recognize that identity on the model of self-contained property tends to foreclose one's emotional resources (think of Macon Dead Jr. in *Song of Solomon*). Yet, on the other hand, identity as unchecked identification with others threatens to run rampant over the fragile boundaries of one's selfhood. No one who has imagined the damage done to individual identity by the institution of slavery—the attack upon sustaining psychic boundaries, the undoing of one's own self-possession, the imposition of impotence—will discount the preciousness of self-owning and thus the power of the freed Baby Suggs's discovery: "But suddenly she saw her hands and thought with a clarity as simple as it was dazzling, 'These hands belong to me. These *my* hands' " (*B*, 141). Hers to own, to make plans for, take charge of: the text's most lyrical passage rehearses Baby Suggs's sermon of self-ownership, of reclaiming your body from the institution that had controlled it. *Claim* is a term that punctuates Morrison's text: "Freeing yourself was one thing; claiming ownership of that freed self was another" (*B*, 95).[10] The radically unclaimed self—unable to count on its free labor as its own property—is rudderless, a creature of others' will, what Locke quite deliberately calls a slave.[11]

Beloved both endorses and provocatively calls into question this model of achieved self-ownership—calls it into question not least because no people who had experienced three centuries of enslavement could afford to envisage their subjectivity in such immaculate terms of self-management. If you had to own yourself to be yourself, and if this model could actually be realized only for a certain class of white males, then what goes on inside the mind and heart of all those others—unpropertied white males, women, slaves—for whom such a definition of who they are is only a mockery of what they are? This is exactly the question I want now to pursue, more deliberately, through Faulkner's and Morrison's black males. Unable to be a Mister, how does an unpropertied black male negotiate his manhood? I turn to Lucas Beauchamp in a scene from "The Fire and the Hearth" in *Go Down, Moses*.

"Are you the husband?" the Chancellor said.

"That's right," Lucas said.

"Say sir to the court!" the clerk said. Lucas glanced at the clerk.

"What?" he said. "I dont want no court. I done changed my—"

"Why you uppity—" the clerk began. . . .

"Not now," Lucas said. "We don't want no voce. Roth Edmonds knows what I mean."

"What? Who does?"

"Why, the uppity—" the clerk said. "Your Honor—" Again the Chancellor raised his hand slightly toward the clerk. He still looked at Lucas.

"Mister Roth Edmonds," Lucas said.   (*GDM*, 124)

"Are you the husband?" The question resonates in the mind, inasmuch as the deepest crisis Lucas Beauchamp undergoes in this novel revolves around his status as Molly's husband. If he were Molly's husband as a white man is husband of a white woman, Zack Edmonds could never have presumed upon Molly as his own property (a presumption the text produces as normative more than as transgressive). And Lucas would never have needed to wonder, "How to God . . . can a black man ask a white man to please not lay down with his black wife?" (58) *Please*: the word betokens not personal timidity but a structured nonmastery, a pleading with the master to abrogate a right that is his in some way deeper than the law itself. Of course until 1865 it was the law itself: during slavery there were no legal black marriages. Despite the overwhelming reliance of black families upon this ceremony, it was for obvious reasons illegal.[12] In the eyes of the law the offspring of slaves belonged to the white master. "Are you the husband?" Earlier in the South he would not have been, and Faulkner saturates this 1940s court scene with Lucas's continued eccentricity to legal norms. We have here a Chancellor, a clerk, a Mister— and Lucas. Each of these white titles conveys entitlement within the segregated social system, and the scandal Faulkner delights in is Lucas's nevertheless insisting on agency. Pressured as to juridical identity, menaced as to courtroom manners, Lucas insinuates his own purpose into the scene: "Roth Edmonds knows what I mean," and Roth does. The price Lucas pays registers not in his checkbook—Edmonds pays court costs—but in that required term of respect he must utter yet can never himself receive from the lips of white men: "Mister."

Faulkner dramatizes Lucas's pursuit of an independent identity as an ongoing struggle with the white symbolic implicit in *mister*. His origin, already announced in the ledgers of "The Bear" as white-bestowed, is what he seeks to rewrite:

> not *Lucius Quintus* @c @c @c, but *Lucas Quintus*, not refusing to be called
> Lucius, because he simply eliminated that word from the name; not deny-
> ing, declining the name itself, because he used three quarters of it; but sim-
> ply taking the name and changing, altering it, making it no longer the white
> man's but his own, by himself composed, himself selfprogenitive and nom-
> inate, by himself ancestored.   (*GDM*, 269)

We should note the desperate illogic of this premise. How can a man change
his name from white-imposed Lucius to black-invented Lucas and be imagined as therefore free, "selfprogenitive and nominate"? Lucas's white grandfather, the original old man, Lucius Quintus Carothers McCaslin, dominates Lucas's psychic life. All alterations relate to this white origin.[13] But
Lucas strives to relate to it on equal terms—Lucas to Lucius—whereas Ike
McCaslin's very name places him in a structure of biblical sonship (Isaac to
Abraham): his moves limited to submission to or withdrawal from the
parental narrative.

Lucas, by contrast, would step into the entitlements of that narrative; this
requires, however, taking on its originary white male terms. To put it starkly,
Faulkner redresses Lucas's race and gender marginality—his lack of entitlement, of land, of secured wife—not by immersing him within the living
resources of a native black culture but by phantasmally aligning him with the
authority of his white male soul mates. Locked in an embrace that harbors this
text's deepest yearning, Lucas is dramatized in unforgettable encounter with
Zack across the marriage bed and with Old Carothers over the upholding of
masculine honor, just as in *Intruder in the Dust* he will be dramatized in
charged relation to Chick, his childlike suitor, and to Gavin, his garrulous and
frustrated brother. White to black, male to male, each of these pairings figures
the bond that Faulkner has invested in, and each represses from view its
excluded other: black to black, male to female. "Are you the husband?" is the
surface question—are you capable of enforcing your claim to your wife?—but
the underlying question is different: "Are you the man?"—can you hold your
own with Old Carothers?

Thus when Lucas makes his way through Zack's challenge to his manhood
by a ritual encounter of honor-bound moves, advantages offered first by one
and then by the other and accepted by neither, the enemy cherished even as
he is pursued (all of this enacted over the wife-empty bridal bed)—when
Lucas terminates this love scene to his own satisfaction, he thinks: "*Old
Carothers . . . I needed him and he come and spoke for me*" (*GDM*, 57). This
focusing moment locates Lucas's self-possession within the fantasy of a white

male structure of subjectivity. He becomes himself by being spoken/spoken for by Old Carothers. He comes into his legacy, and it is pure white. Defiantly risking his own life and Zack's, Lucas answers—as no one else in *Go Down, Moses* does answer—the old man's original challenge.

That challenge was shaped, precisely, to the American property model: simply to take all you wanted and could get, to bend your will to no man's rejoinder, to map the world and name its creatures as though you were indeed impenetrable and omnipotent—yourself your own ancestor and all others your progeny or property. *Go Down, Moses* testifies eloquently to the inhumanity of this project—its way of treating others as instrumental extensions of one's own will—but perhaps we have overlooked the text's covert longing for it nevertheless. Old Carothers, Du Homme, Sam Fathers, Old Ben, Lion: these impervious male icons grant no quarter, absorb no insult. Figures of imaginary wholeness, they are archaic or marginal within the realm of the ongoing social—a solution at one level that is a collapse at another. Is there any doubt that Lucas reincarnates the hard sufficiency of these figures when he silences Roth by saying: "I'm the man here" (*GDM*, 116)? In my reading, *Intruder in the Dust* continues this phantasmal (white) project, resolving Lucas into a monument of fixed manhood, a phallus without the complications of interiority, immovable, impervious, self-owned: imprisoned in the social yet unbroken in the imaginary. It is as though, by 1948, the only Man Faulkner could envisage among the puling boys and men he gazed upon—the only figure beyond social co-optation and therefore capable of genuine self-possession—would have to be black, immolated, and unconquerable. I turn now to Paul D in *Beloved*.

> "Mister, he looked so . . . free. Better than me. Stronger, tougher. Son a bitch couldn't even get out the shell by hisself but he was still king and I was . . ." Paul D stopped and squeezed his left hand with his right. He held it that way long enough for it and the world to quiet down and let him go on.
>
> "Mister was allowed to be and stay what he was. But I wasn't allowed to be and stay what I was. Even if you cooked him you'd be cooking a rooster named Mister. But wasn't no way I'd ever be Paul D again, living or dead. Schoolteacher changed me. I was something else and that something was less than a chicken sitting in the sun on a tub." (*B*, 72)

Like Faulkner's totem animals that radiate an imaginary integrity, Mister impresses Paul D as immovably centered, and therefore free. Even eaten, Mister stays what he is, remains intact, a feat beyond Paul D's capacity.[14] Paul D has lost his proper, his own. Owned and invaded by schoolteacher, he has been remade into a being he can no longer recognize as himself. Why has his identity project failed and how does Morrison propose its recovery?

We begin again with names. Garner named them all, bestowing both their names and their manhood. Others' slaves were treated as boys; Garner's were trained as men:

> "Beg to differ, Garner. Ain't no nigger men."
>
> "Not if you scared, they ain't." Garner's smile was wide. "But if you a man yourself, you'll want your niggers to be men too."
>
> "I wouldn't have no nigger men round my wife."
>
> It was the reaction Garner loved and waited for. "Neither would I," he said. "Neither would I," and there was always a pause before the neighbor . . . got the meaning. Then a fierce argument, sometimes a fight, and Garner came home bruised and pleased, having demonstrated one more time what a real Kentuckian was: one tough enough and smart enough to make and call his own niggers men.   (B, 11)

Garner performs exactly the definition of manhood he pretends to offer his slaves: the maintenance of physical integrity, the capacity to make good on your word, to prove it through bodily prowess. White manhood is, precisely, the maintaining of self-possession, the adequation of one's behavior to one's will, the ability to patrol one's property—one's self at all times, one's wife in this instance—and guarantee that she remains one's own. The fights break out over just this, the other men's realization that Garner has insulted their capacity to patrol their wives in the presence of nigger men, not boys ("I wouldn't have no nigger men round my wife," they say, and when Garner responds, "Neither would I" [i.e., if I were you], the fight breaks out). A "real Kentuckian" looks remarkably like Old Carothers. He makes people do his bidding, assigns their names and object status in relation to his subject control, remains inalterably himself.

Paul D's crisis stems from his having been trained to believe himself to be such a man.[15] Choices had been made available to him, he was never forced. Rather, he had subjectified the proffered model, assented to the hailing, imagined himself in charge of himself. Only later, after Morrison has exposed him to the full brunt of slavery, does Paul D sees that on this model he can never be a man. The black experience of slavery simply disallows the equation of male identity with male will. As Genovese puts it, "The slaveholders deprived black men of the role of provider; refused to dignify their marriages or legitimize their issue; compelled them to submit to physical abuse in the presence of their women and children; made them choose between remaining silent while their wives and daughters were raped or seduced and risking death" (490). The list continues. Paul D's experience of such impotence is harrowing.

The text produces him as a man invaded, treated like an abusable woman. Things are put into male slaves: a bit in their mouths, a penis in their mouths, irons upon their legs. If manhood means self-ownership, Paul D is owned by others, raped repeatedly. He ceases to be a single entity; his body shakes uncontrollably (as Temple Drake's does after her rape in *Sanctuary*). He becomes a site of overrun boundaries: "Paul D thought he was screaming; his mouth was open and there was this loud throat-splitting sound—but it may have been somebody else. Then he thought he was crying. Something was running down his cheeks. He lifted his hands to wipe away the tears and saw dark brown slime" (*B*, 110). Liquids pour out of him, over him, into him; his own, those of others, those of nature. Out of control, venting without knowing it just as Sethe's urine "breaks" without her consent, Paul D undergoes a self-undoing that grotesquely reverses the Oedipal crisis. Rather than struggle with taboo desires and succeed in imposing a boundary upon them—a boundary enabling eventual entry into language, individuation, manhood, paternity, and property—Paul D reverts, under such pressure, to a chaotic, prehuman economy of liquids. At the extreme, when a male slave is confronted with the utter incapacity of his will to affect his reality, forced to watch impotently while his wife is beaten and milked, he becomes—like Halle—simultaneously not-male and insane (his identity no longer his own), a creature smeared in butter, undone by a liquid economy erasing all boundaries, disfiguring a face and a mind once male.

This critique of the Oedipal model seems as profoundly Morrison's intention as the re-imagining of the Oedipal model seems Faulkner's.[16] As the grounding norm of white society, the Oedipal stabilizes patriarchy itself. It does so by providing Western culture's central paradigm for justifying the male child's endurance of (rather than rebellion against) libidinal repression imposed by authority: justified because in time that child will achieve the individuation of centered selfhood, will take on the structural position of the vacated father, and will inherit his power and his possessions. To become properly oneself, to move from infantile polymorphous perversity to adult conventionality, is to discipline desire, to accept as legacy the strictures of the father, and to enter the genealogical field of property descent. Morrison shows that this gender economy—geared to the patriarchal notions of propriety, property, and the proper—must be reconceived if it is to nourish disenfranchised black subjectivity. *Beloved* contributes in a number of ways—and not just through the figure of Paul D—to such a reconception.[17]

There is, first, the tension between loving small and loving large. Morrison's commitment to the historical Margaret Garner materials radiates from a slave woman's refusal to love small. A sentimental writer would have exonerated such large love, a lesser writer would have criticized it: Morrison explores both its cost and its necessity.[18] She shows that for black slaves to love large is to enact an identification that risks insanity when the loved ones are abused: "He saw a witless coloredwoman jailed and hanged for stealing ducks she believed were her own babies" (*B*, 66). At the same time Morrison shows us that Paul D's heart cannot be confined within that rusted tin can. So long as he believes this, Paul D is on the run, unwilling to invest his feelings where he cannot, manlike, maintain his will. Indeed, his initial indictment of Sethe—"You got two feet, Sethe, not four" (*B*, 165)—follows from a sense of manhood in which the proper still reigns. Her behavior is hers to patrol, there is a right and a wrong choice, in killing her child she has made the wrong choice.

Our judicial system is founded in certain ways on such distinctions; its notions of right and wrong are intricately calibrated according to the male criterion of self-responsibility before the law. We are assumed to be individually responsible for patrolling our territory, maintaining our proper/property. *Beloved* recurrently undermines this model, perhaps most eloquently in those intense passages in part 2 where we cannot responsibly assign utterance to speaker, say what belongs to whom. This collapse of boundaries is writ with equal power in Sethe's act itself—"This here new Sethe didn't know where the world stopped and she began" (*B*, 164)—an act in which self and world are inextricably intertwined. The murder of the child explodes the boundaries without which there can be no proper itself: it is her act and yet not hers, her fault and yet not her fault. The weight of an entire institution—the institution of slavery—must be brought to bear, if we would understand how a mother might kill a child out of love and be both right and wrong in doing so. If the law is useless for sorting this out, if the law incites to violence rather than to humane self-possession, if the law proposes no credible paternal model for normative behavior, how is Oedipus to oversee our maturation by laying down our categories of gender difference and underwriting male self-possession? Paul D eventually comes to see—in washing Sethe's feet rather than counting them, in nursing rather than judging—that male and female are interdependent realms, and that a black man cannot sustain a model of white manhood.

As Hortense Spillers puts it in "Mama's Baby, Papa's Maybe," "the black American male embodies the only American community of males which has had the specific occasion to learn who the female is within itself" (80). This female-within-male calls into question gender categories in ways that go beyond the ken of all impenetrable misters.[19]

I would close speculatively. Both writers know—how could they not?—that the central damage done by slavery to black manhood was to cripple individual agency. Unable to equate self with will, black men were wounded in their own proper, their capacity to own themselves, to become full-fledged misters. "A man without force," Frederick Douglass had written as early as 1855, "is without the essential dignity of humanity. Human nature is so constituted that it cannot *honor* a helpless man, although it can *pity* him; and even that it cannot do long, if the signs of power do not arise" (286). The blow dealt by such impotence to the pride that sustains identity fuels Faulkner's intricate exploration of Lucas Beauchamp and accounts for *Intruder in the Dust*'s suturing of Lucas's authority. Morrison, by contrast, does not so much restore Paul D's manhood on the property model as reconceive its lineaments. The reconception calls into question the Oedipal economy of the achieved proper itself.

In her work—especially her theoretical work—we find, foregrounded, what we are learning to recognize in Faulkner's as well, that identity of every sort is differential rather than "properly" achieved or essential. Self-owning is rarely innocent; it is usually a juggling act. Men too often know who they are, they ratify their self-image, through repudiating the other: they are not women, they are not blacks. "I aint a nigger," little Jason says in "That Evening Sun" (CS, 297). In this casual paradigm we see the fantasy of a pure identity being constituted by a juxtaposition against contaminating others. Morrison powerfully explicates the scene, acted out in countless episodes of American history, in which the drama of immaculate white freedom requires for its unfolding a rejected and immovable black silhouette. I quote from *Playing in the Dark*:

> The need to establish difference stemmed not only from the Old World but from a difference in the New. What was distinctive in the New was, first of all, its claim to freedom and, second, the presence of the unfree within the heart of the democratic experiment—the critical absence of democracy, its echo, shadow, and silent force in the political and intellectual activity of some not-Americans. The distinguishing features of the not-Americans were their slave status, their social status—and their color.

It is conceivable that the first would have self-destructed in a variety of ways had it not been for the last. These slaves, unlike many others in the world's history, were visible to a fault. And they had inherited, among other things, a long history on the meaning of color. It was not simply that this slave population had a distinctive color; it was that this color "meant" something. That meaning had been named and deployed by scholars from at least the moment, in the eighteenth century, when other and sometimes the same scholars started to investigate both the natural history and the inalienable rights of man—that is to say, human freedom.   (48–49)

Here we return to Locke and the Enlightenment with a darker awareness that freedom and unfreedom, like male and female, white and black, are inextricably interdependent terms—that selfhood as achieved property plays itself out differentially, against a backdrop of dispossession.[20] "Before slavery," Patterson argues, "people simply could not have conceived of the thing we call freedom" (340). Surely it is because Faulkner's characters so yearn for self-sufficiency that his texts dramatize their discovery of internal rupture—their incapacity to maintain identity as a self-patrolled property—as a tragic burden. To be rudely ejected from the sanctuary of one's imaginary self-possession is to be involuntarily invaded by others, to be othered:

> But after that I seemed to see them [black people] for the first time not as people, but as a thing, a shadow in which I lived, we lived, all white people, all other people. I thought of all the children coming forever and ever into the world, white, with the black shadow already falling upon them before they drew breath. And I seemed to see the black shadow in the shape of a cross. And it seemed like the white babies were struggling, even before they drew breath, to escape from the shadow that was not only upon them but beneath them too, flung out like their arms were flung out, as if they were nailed to the cross. I saw all the little babies that would ever be in the world, the ones not yet even born—a long line of them with their arms spread, on the black crosses.   (LA, 253)

The speaker is Joanna in Light in August, but the burden she carries here is more generally Faulknerian. It is the awareness that those of us who are white are both orphaned and multiply possessed, both abandoned and penetrated by our parents and by the larger culture's unwanted arrangements. Women not only show men that they are, satisfyingly, men, but women also live within men uninvited, disturbing the propriety of male norms. And blacks, because of what those of us who are white did to them in the United States before we were even born, will forever live inside us, owed a reparation beyond our capacity to repress or repay. This too, as Joanna and her creator know, is a legacy, however unwanted. Insofar as the property model of identity may nevertheless operate in Faulkner's work—requiring the other's disenfranchisement to know itself as free—it does so outside the comforts of innocence, in the form of an overdetermined and internalized debt, an accumulating cultural mortgage—a property not at all clear but laden with insurmountable liens—one of those checks we somehow cosigned before exiting from our mother's womb, which will be called in for cashing any day now.

Morrison, by contrast, seems to register the penetrability of identity as both burden and promise. Whites may know themselves as not-black, yes, but her best work goes past this oppositional frame, opening into a complex embrace of the mutuality that funds all identity.[21] Identity as patrolled property too easily slips into figurative ossification of self or literal enslavement of others. *Beloved* shows, instead, the irresistible need to live in others, to know self through identificatory investment in others. You could be reduced to insanity by the damage done to your loved ones, but you could also survive disaster by identifying—as Sethe does in her flight to freedom—with those beings who came from your body but who are not you. They call to that in you that exceeds you, that is not your property to patrol. Sethe's breasts are not her own; they and the milk they carry link her to her offspring. The text's most terrifying image is of white boys enclosing those breasts as their own property. What is for Faulkner our human tragedy—that we are never our own, are always trying to say, always inadequate to and in excess of ourselves—is for Morrison our human possibility.

4

David and Solomon
Fathering Black and White

David and Solomon: the biblical names take us to *Absalom, Absalom!* and *Song of Solomon.* They suggest, at the outset, that Faulknerian paternity will circulate about disinherited sons as recurrently as Morrisonian paternity will involve a search for Solomonic stability and wisdom. In the pages that follow I have not sought to reconstitute the father as he arises, component by component, from a totalizing vision of each writer's texts. Rather, I have proceeded across the range of fathers that emerge in two careers full of paternal imagining. The father I pursue changes from novel to novel, shows moreover a different face when juxtaposed against the other writer's paternal figures, yet retains a certain structural insistence (there is no avoiding either his presence or his absence) tinged with pathos. He would bequeath and enable. Insofar as he is invested in a patriarchal model of paternity turned incurably dysfunctional, he cannot succeed at either task. How the white Southern male writer and the black non-Southern female writer attend to such dysfunction: that is the question underlying the analyses that follow.

The foregoing chapter has prepared the way for further scrutiny of the failure of paternal descent in both writers' work. In considering the gender crisis undergone by a single pair of black males, Lucas Beauchamp and Paul D, I sought to illuminate their ordeal by reading it within a larger framework of racially commanded cultural legacies: property, propriety, and the proper. These legacies are designed to pass from white parent to white child. The more I considered such legacies and exclusions—bequeathings and withholdings of property—the more it appeared that identity itself is inseparable from some capacity of the will to stabilize selfhood by remaining intact, the

"I" thus enacted as a sort of minimally maintained property within the public domain. "I" is always, in a crucial measure, the "I" of "I can," a self-sustaining (however brief, however fluid) witnessable within a public forum. To be essentially without such power is to risk the loss of one's identity. This is precisely the wound dealt to blacks during their enslavement. Denied self-ownership, the black slave lives out an imposed incapacity to demonstrate integrity—to enact selfhood—within a public sphere of acknowledgment. Such "dishonor" is a fundamental component of slavery itself and one of the core meanings of what Patterson calls "social death."

Why, though, should this wound be peculiarly disabling for males? What is the gender coding of this scheme of identity? We may take up these questions by pressing upon Patterson's term *dishonor*, for dishonor has its meaning within an honor-shame code that aligns human worth with the capacity to preserve one's publicly given word—one's publicly declared identity—against any challenge to it. The ethos of Southern aristocracy, as many critics have shown, certainly privileged this code in which white male will is all but deified.[1] Women's dependency and blacks' inferiority follow accordingly, serving to silhouette and stabilize the drama of white male autonomy. But the larger set of norms at work, while perhaps accentuated in the South, is broadly American—traceable in fact to the Lockean legacy of unfettered identity as the irrevocable right to property. Free men own themselves and the fruit of their labors—both self and labor understood as intrinsic property. If we would go further and unearth the gender model aligned with this property schema, we find the Oedipal paradigm.[2] The underlying pattern finally emerges, for the Oedipal serves (though Freud never said so) as the motor of patriarchy itself. It does so by providing the normative developmental model in which little boys are trained to discipline desire and endure the strictures of the law: so that they might achieve individuation (break cleanly from their mothers' hold) and come into their inheritance of the proper (centered identity), propriety (a like and lawful community of empowered white males), and property (the departed father's legacy, their post-Enlightenment birthright). I argued in " 'Mister' " that this model of identity is keyed to a white male patriarchal trajectory and that disempowered black males subscribe to it at their peril.

The Emancipation Proclamation of 1863 ended slavery without ending its legacy of inflicted impotence. For later generations of blacks such a legacy may act, in a reversal of the very intention of legacies, as a disabling parental bequest, in the form of menacing cultural memories and material humiliations. Morrison attends from the beginning of her career to the repercussions of this patriarchally inflicted wound, and she seeks increasingly to imagine her way past the gender assumptions that underlie it. At the same time, Faulkner's texts show, more vividly perhaps (because he is a postbellum Southern writer) than those of any other twentieth-century Western novelist, a white dysfunction wrought as well into the heart of the patriarchal model of property descent: a dysfunction that registers in the damage done to and (even more) by the father. This chapter on fathering, then, explores the kinds of legacy that white and black fathers leave their offspring. Examining both writers' careers synoptically, I seek to disengage the quality of paternity that such fathers embody. For both the boy child and the girl child, what gendered scheme of possibilities, constraints, or disasters does their behavior bequeath? What modes of thinking and feeling and doing, what grasp upon cultural norms, what relation to the Oedipal model do these fathers enact? In a word, what stories do Faulkner and Morrison tell when they tell the story of the father?[3] I begin with the most suggestively troubled fathers of Faulkner's and Morrison's early fiction: Mr. Compson in *The Sound and the Fury* and Cholly Breedlove in *The Bluest Eye*.

The Sound and the Fury and *The Bluest Eye*

Mr. Compson is the most engagingly impotent father in Faulkner's fiction. John Irwin, André Bleikasten, and Richard Moreland have cogently analyzed his competitive relation to his son Quentin, his unshakable alcoholism, and his reactionary cast of mind, yet his portrait in *The Sound and the Fury* is nevertheless infused with tenderness.[4] His defining attribute is incapacity; he is the one who can make nothing happen. Faulkner's representational strategy ensures this impression by severing Mr. Compson's behavior from his words. We hear him repeatedly in this novel—Benjy's notation of his telling the children to "mind Dilsey now" (16), Quentin's incessant "Father said"—but we do not see him act.

He comes into narrative focus as the father whose blueprints for behavior cannot affect the real. He cannot keep the Compson gate closed ("How did he get out?" [*SF*, 33] he asks his son Jason), leading to Benjy's castration. Here, in microcosm, we see his failure to shepherd his offspring through the Oedipal crisis, for the role of the father is to *suspend* the possibility of castration over the son's rebellious desires, leading to the latter's successful self-discipline and eventual gender maturation. He is not to permit the castration actually to happen; otherwise what are fathers for? He can't keep his daughter

Caddy in tow any more than he could Benjy, and her exit from Compson mores is steadily driving him to suicidal drink, whatever he may say about the fictitious value of a daughter's virginity. Nor, despite a continuous pouring forth of advice (much of it acute, all of it intended as enabling), can he keep his dearest son, Quentin, from suicide. Finally, he fails to imbue his name-sake, Jason, with any of his virtues. Perhaps the most revealing testimony to his failure lodges in the spectacle of his son Jason's reversal of the father's pater-nal functions. As "a different breed of cat from Father" (126), Jason systemat-ically abuses his own siblings—the offspring Mr. Compson could not protect.

There is one moment in which, through Benjy's perspective, we see the father equal to his paternal role: "Caddy and Father and Jason were in Mother's chair. Jason's eyes were puffed shut and his mouth moved, like tast-ing. Caddy's head was on Father's shoulder. Her hair was like fire, and little points of fire were in her eyes, and I went and Father lifted me into the chair too, and Caddy held me" (46). The harmony is precarious; for an instant the father serves as a sort of bodily ground uniting these three offspring, letting them nest upon him as they brush up peacefully against each other. More often, though, his sons' perspectives show us a man in bodily isolation, furtively or defiantly drinking by himself, a man whose gnomic phrases about the meaning of life lack local grounding. His children can do nothing with his advice. It comes from a source removed from their experience, and it does not help them adapt to current conditions.

This is so because the only worldview he would bequeath to them is an antiquated one in which he no longer believes. Honor is the mainspring of his behavior—he takes in Caddy's child without asking questions, quietly defying his deal-making wife—yet honor has become for him like the family watch he bequeaths to Quentin. Both are meant to signal the ceremonial ordering of time from generation to generation, but time can no longer be ordered. The watch should at least still tell time, but after Quentin smashes it it does noth-ing but tick. Its mainspring is indestructible—it keeps ticking—but it no longer orients, like Mr. Compson's irrelevant but still insistent mainspring of honor. It insists therefore in the form of its own negation: "reducto absur-dum." The dimensions of the real register on him not as possibility or even challenge but as a slap in the face—a reduction to absurdity of his once-per-tinent system of values. "Quentin and his father," Warwick Wadlington writes in *Reading Faulknerian Tragedy*, "tend to experience difference as contradic-tion, multiplicity as a stalemated war between 'impure properties.' The whole novel traces the fault line of this mental set" (69).

Mr. Compson's "reducto absurdum" offers no subjective space for grounding him in the present. His lengthy speeches are about the nonbeing of what used to be. Ungrounded, he imagines himself as not there—like a shadow or like death itself, "only a state in which the others are left" (50). Others are left alive to move about on his periphery, but he is distant from them, suspended, enervated. "It's not despair until time it's not even time until it was" (113), Quentin remembers his father saying, and this formula conveys the in-between temporality within which his father passes his life: a ticking watch/code that tells him that he no longer "is" but is not yet "was."

The mental set he can neither relinquish nor successfully bequeath is the ideology of Southern honor. Within that framework a father is a gentleman who passes on to his offspring both the proper sense of "gentle" and the resourceful, will-enabled sense of "man." Born after the War, Mr. Compson lives in a social scene that refuses both of these senses. A mercantile cash nexus (which his namesake, Jason, will actively engage) has replaced the cavalier mythology he believes disappeared in 1865, and he has withdrawn from this vulgar situation into an impotent world of books. He utterly lacks a current project. His Latin tags orient no better than his other gnomic sayings, but they at least reveal that he knows of a way of life less mean than the one before him. Meanwhile he takes to drink, sells off the land parcel by parcel, and addresses his present moment in the relentlessly ironic mode of "reducto absurdum" (as though he were saying, "I who speak to you at this moment am not really here and now but there and then, suspended in an other scene whose values have of course become absurdly irrelevant today").

Faulkner's creative energy in this text is invested less in the failed father than in the loss inflicted upon his needy children. All four of them go radically awry—the daughter unable to use her father as a buffer against her mother's attacks upon her burgeoning sexuality, the eldest son unable to draw emotional sustenance or masculine resolve from his father's nihilist stance toward Caddy's fall from honor, the middle son repelled by his father's elegant incapacity to grapple with postwar material conditions, the most helpless third son abandoned first to the castrating knife and eventually to the impersonal asylum in Jackson. So great is Quentin's need of the father's guidance that he insistently constructs his crises as appeals to the father ("Father I have committed . . ."). Indeed, he half invents this necessary judge of his defective behavior: "I am my father's Progenitive I invented him" (78). It is as though, given the intensity of his children's need, Mr. Compson's paternal blankness explodes in each of them as a social alienation beyond healing. The Southern codes he would patriarchally bequeath collapse into a quietly corrosive irony as they pass through his discourse. Yet—and this is perhaps the source of his appeal—his more aggressive wife rages with a passionate intensity next to which his lack of all conviction appears virtually benign. The mother's defection outweighs his own, and on this note we may now turn to the radically different construction of parental figures in Morrison's fictional world.

Although the destruction of Pecola Breedlove in *The Bluest Eye* reveals a cultural impasse traceable equally to the father and the mother, Cholly Breedlove fails the more dramatically. The text announces his failure immediately, informing us as early as the fourth page of the doomed daughter impregnated by her father. Even before this opening there is the Dick and Jane prologue, typographically jumbled phrases that will reappear as incoherent chapter epigraphs (in that space where the reader usually finds nuggets of wisdom). These muddled Dick and Jane passages announce that this will be a story of propertylessness, of failed proprieties. "Knowing that there was such a thing as outdoors," Claudia, the narrator, says, "bred in us a hunger for property, for ownership" (*TBE*, 18). "Outdoors" is economic territory, the unprotected space (shaped by racial injustice) to which blacks lacking income to pay their bills to white merchants are exiled. Claudia's (textually unrepresented) father passes this solvency test, but Cholly supremely fails it. Morrison paints this portrait through the misery of his ragged possessions—"the furniture that had aged without ever becoming familiar" (35). Economic defeat passes metonymically into emotional ravage. Cholly and Pauline have forged a marriage out of their mutual failures—"she needed Cholly's sins desperately" (42)—and we are urged to trace their trouble back to childhood wounds.

Cholly's wound, first mentioned just prior to the ugly fight that erupts between him and Pauline, takes on the resonance of trauma. As a young man he had been caught in his first act of intercourse by white men. Their flashlight on his behind and their sadistic sexual urging transformed desire into disgust and hatred—not for the whites who were watching but for the frightened girl beneath him. We shall return, as Morrison does, to this scene, but we can identify already a number of damaging elements that it coalesces into a single syndrome. First, Cholly's dysfunction is sexually charged—intercourse will henceforth be revenge as much as release. Second, it is white-inflected. It is as though the white flashlight reoriented his glandular and emotional systems; the act of sex is now subjectively accompanied by phantom onlookers. Third, the early sexual encounter and the present fight with Pauline circulate about the motif of a naked black body. "Black e mo. Yadaddysleepsnekkid," Maureen taunts Pecola (65), and the taunt has its disturbing edge of truth. Cholly's impotence (literal in that early scene) registers in the form of a humiliated and exposed black body. He has been seen naked—first by abusive whites, next by his cringing daughter—without the dignity provided by clothes. This early sexual dislocation seems to lead inexorably to the final sexual outrage, his rape of his daughter, Pecola.

In all of this the patriarchal/Oedipal model is failed utterly. Nakedness seems coded economically even more than sexually.[5] Cholly has nothing— no parents, no lineage, no job, no possessions, no social coherence—he can call his own and can bequeath to his child. Futureless himself, he plays no role in shaping his daughter's maturation. "How dare she love him?" he thinks, just before abusing Pecola: "Hadn't she any sense at all? What was he supposed to do about that? Return it? How? . . . What of his knowledge of the world and of life could be useful to her? What could his heavy arms and befuddled brain accomplish that would earn him his own respect, that would in turn allow him to accept her love?" (161–62). His exposed black body suggests a black man arrested in infancy, in the state of dishonor, one whose will has no efficacy in the world. A "genealogical isolate," Cholly suffered a childhood bereft of legacies that would enable his adult entry into the social. Eventually he leaves his daughter with a sexually humiliating wound similar to the one by which he reads himself. Propertyless, he respects no proprieties, he lacks the proper of achieved masculine identity. Within the white model of male self-possession so far considered, he emerges as a disastrous father, the first in Morrison's subsequent gallery of men who missed some turning in the ritual of maturation and who remain BoyBoys forever. Cholly is the most disturbing of these, yet, already, this novel is suggesting other, more provocative ways to view him. In a move all her own, yet beautifully Faulknerian, Morrison goes on to revisit the child after delineating his adult collapse. The revisiting lens transforms the portrait.

Like Joe Christmas who changes before our eyes from pain-inflicting adult to pain-absorbing infant, Cholly now comes to the reader as an orphaned child, desperately in search of a father figure. Aunt Jimmy, as the name suggests, played this role as best she could, but Cholly yearns for the missing male who would embody an adult grasp upon the social world that he could emulate and in time make his own. It is during this unsponsored state, aggravated by Aunt Jimmy's death, that the traumatic sexual event occurs: "The flashlight wormed its way into his guts and turned the sweet taste of muscadine into rotten fetid bile" (148). It would be hard to envisage a purer moment of self-alienation. The white gaze has penetrated to his guts and will henceforth (dis)orient his desires. Stung by these upheavals, he takes off for Macon, Georgia, in search of a man called Fuller—whom he believes to be his departed father. The scene of Cholly's discovery of Fuller in a card game (with other black men likewise discarded by the social system) is sublime. Cholly stares at the man whose mysterious potency begot him, amazed by Fuller's "hard, belligerent face" and vulnerable body smaller than his own:

> "What you want, boy?"
> "Uh. I mean . . . is you Samson Fuller?"
> "Who sent you?"
> "Huh?"
> "You Melba's boy?"
> "No, sir, I'm . . ." Cholly blinked. He could not remember his mother's name. Had he ever known it? What could he say? Whose boy was he? He couldn't say, "I'm your boy." That sounded disrespectful.
> The man was impatient. "Something wrong with your head? Who told you to come after me?"
> "Nobody." Cholly's hands were sweating. The man's eyes frightened him. "I just thought . . . I mean, I was just wandering around, and, uh, my name is Cholly. . . ."
> But Fuller had turned back to the game that was about to begin anew. . . . [Eventually] he stood up and in a vexed and whiny voice shouted at Cholly, "Tell that bitch she get her money. Now, get the fuck outta my face!"   (155–56)

Recoiling in a daze, Cholly wanders into an alley, trying to hold himself together. Then "his bowels suddenly opened up, and before he could realize what he knew, liquid stools were running down his legs. At the mouth of the alley where his father was, on an orange crate in the sun, on a street full of grown men and women, he had soiled himself like a baby" (157). He runs to the river, sits "knotted there in fetal position" (157), enters the water to cleanse himself and his clothes, then thinks for the first time since her death of Aunt Jimmy: "With a longing that almost split him open, he thought of her handing him a bit of smoked hock out of her dish. . . . And then the tears rushed down his cheeks, to make a bouquet under his chin" (158).

I have quoted this scene fully because it embodies a male rite of passage that perfectly fails—as prelude to going beyond—the Oedipal model. Unfathered, sexually disoriented (confused as to racial and gender identity), Cholly seeks out the father, who once again disowns him. He regresses to a liquid and infantile economy, an unlearning of the constraints that had permitted his earlier precarious coherence. He soils himself, reenters the urine and feces that normally precede birthing, then—glimpsing in his mind the woman who gave him the only fathering he would ever receive—dissolves into tears. Like Paul D, he is undone by a kind of absolute self-dispossession. Split open by longing, he loses the last shreds of individuation that allowed him to recognize himself as himself. The sequence is saturated in those infantile liquids that infants must learn to control if they would become adults. Within a patriarchal/Oedipal economy grounded in the expectation of property, an economy whose legacies guide proper gender discipline, Cholly is an unmitigated disaster, and Morrison knows it.

She also knows that "the pieces of Cholly's life could become coherent only in the head of a musician. . . . Only a musician would sense, know, without even knowing that he knew, that Cholly was free. Dangerously free" (159). His terrible way of failing a white gender model, his making of his life a series of contingent adventures rather than a cumulative sequence of projects—this is at the same time an unco-opted way of being black and male whose rhythm only a jazzman could intuit. Damaged to the core, all identity-sustaining boundaries overrun, Cholly ceases to be, on one model, and comes into being, on another. The second model is non-Oedipal and nonpatriarchal. This Cholly has received no shaping legacy, will never own anything, is incapable of parenting. He is also, and dangerously, free. Indeed, he embodies the true threat promised in Morrison's later name of Stamp Paid, for he has paid his final dues ("there was nothing more to lose" [160]), opted out of all paradigms of duty and the accumulation of goods, is in the clear. No ideology of the will, of possession, can hold him. He rewrites, as a black man, the gender pact for humanizing time, going for unrelated moments of authenticity rather than a developmental sequence that would yield maturity and mastery.

If Cholly is for Morrison a breakthrough, he is no less an unresolvable problem. The man who breaks out of the cycle of male heartbreak is also the father who abuses his own daughter. Morrison narrates this climactic event strictly from within Cholly's perspective, for even her courage might fail if she were to invite us to feel (as Faulkner's Temple Drake feels) what being raped is like. The text then dances abruptly into Soaphead Church's crazed mind (a lens upon Cholly's?), before finishing in Pecola's crazed mind. Cholly exits from the representational schema altogether, allowing this tragedy to come to conclusion but leaving open the question that will engage Morrison for the next twenty years: how can a black man achieve masculinity outside a white model of manhood?[6] The figures through whom she pursues this inquiry are not always fathers, but they share increasingly the primary paternal resource: the capacity to enable others' growth. Stamp Paid and Paul D are stepping-stones toward her latest musically paced attempt at an answer—Joe Trace of *Jazz*.

Repercussions

In 1970 (the year of *The Bluest Eye*), Stamp Paid, Paul D, and Joe Trace are a long way off, hardly beckoning as eventual solutions. Instead, in a brilliant turn that focuses and releases a new source of power, Morrison transfers the dangerous masculine freedom of Cholly Breedlove to the female sphere. Cholly's first inheritor is Eva Peace, and this gender shift enables a social one. As Kathryn Stockton has suggestively argued, the "Bottom" in *Sula* is central to an organizational departure from white norms that is simultaneously economic and libidinal. ("The little nuclear family," Morrison argued in a *Time* interview, "is a paradigm that just doesn't work";[7] the savaged Dick and Jane snippets of *The Bluest Eye* were already pointing this way.) Eva's domestic sphere cuts loose from the organized libidinal repression of patriarchal models. Taking that model's masculine prerogative into herself, paying its male price (the castration/loss of her leg), she achieves separation on her own terms and becomes the architect of her black realm, sovereignly giving and taking life. Whites—and white ways—are kept out.

Black males enter her world freely, but always under the sign of economic incapacity (kept down by the patriarchal model), BoyBoys in the social sphere however Ajactive their sexual prowess. Chicken Little, the Deweys, Tar Baby, Plum, Shadrack—these are males shattered by or kept on the nearside of the social contract for white males. Orphaned, disowned, picked up (if at all) only by Eva, they have inherited nothing and they bequeath nothing. They cannot, in Stockton's words, "convert the penis to the phallus" (104). Like Tar Baby, each enacts a version of "drinking himself to death" (S, 40). They are as futureless as Hannah's husband, Rekas, a "laughing man . . . who died when their daughter Sula was about three years old" (41): a male whose textual introduction serves equally as his epitaph, whose novelistic life lasts all of one vivid sentence. Failed fathers here are colorful, epitaphic ("a laughing man"), not the material of sustained analysis. It is as though nothing further is expected of them, as though, knowing they will turn emasculate—will deflate from Ajax to Albert Jacks—when forced to negotiate the patriarchal sphere,

Morrison prefers to leave them their penis intact, not ask of them the social stability and norm-providing authority that only the paternal phallus brings.[8]

Sula leads—even more than her mother and grandmother—a life outside of patriarchal constraints. Cut off like Cholly from all legacies, she becomes, like him, dangerously experimental:

> As willing to feel pain as to give pain, to feel pleasure as to give pleasure, hers was an experimental life—ever since her mother's remarks sent her flying up those stairs, ever since her one major feeling of responsibility had been exorcised on the bank of a river with a closed place in the middle. The first experience taught her there was no other that you could count on; the second that there was no self to count on either. She had no center, no speck around which to grow.   (S, 118–19)

In Cholly this experimental stance was foredoomed. A man without connection, yet with a family, is in trouble; his ultimate trouble will be to experiment with his own daughter. But Sula is intoxicatingly free of her family. The novel's most tonic passages are all enactments of familial disowning—of Chicken Little's unregretted disappearance into the water, of Plum's maternally engineered and incandescent departure, of Hannah's flaming dance that her daughter, Sula, watches with interest. Early in adolescence Sula had invaded masculine as well as occupied feminine territory, wielding the knife upon her finger as her grandmother had done on her leg, testifying to an unchecked will (capable of limitless damage to self and other) that makes antagonists shrink from her. She is radiantly herself alone. To her grandmother's petulant plea—"When you gone to get married? You need some babies. It'll settle you"—she answers, "I don't want to make somebody else. I want to make myself" (92).

I want to make myself. The figure of Sula lets Morrison raise the fatal questions concealed beneath the articulate surface of *The Bluest Eye.* How does an unaided human life essentialize itself, purify itself of all excrescences, finding its way to the naked and inhuman loam (past flesh, past even bone)? What possibilities lie outside of all legacy (much of which has been white-deformed), such that the old stories are overthrown and a new one can come into being? What resources are available on the other side of orphanhood—the mother refused and the father all but unknown? How does a death sentence become—once it is embraced rather than resisted—life-enabling? Of all of Morrison's novels this is the most death-centered, the most lyrically committed to encountering with style, without fear, the annihilation of self that is death. If *The Bluest Eye* is a complaint launched from the shadow of a death always to be inflicted, *Sula* is an affirmation rising from within the substance of a death already imposed and accepted. In this book death is taken in, turned inside out, and reborn as a life-form. No more victimization at the hands of white convention; black life will issue (will issue only) from native black resource. There are no more laws, no more authorized values, no guiding legacies. Morrison will not rest here—a self that is no self, recognizing no family and no lawful values, offers little resting place—but she could never have found her way into the generosity of Pilate without passing through the crucible of Sula. As for the indistinguishable BoyBoys who accept their non-manhood, they will reappear as the paired hunters—Milkman and Guitar—in search of the father.

If one of Morrison's abiding projects, from *Sula* forward, is to free black experience of maturation from the shackles of a white value system, we may return to Faulkner by saying that the collapse of this system generates the inexhaustible fallout of his fiction. He makes his tragedies out of an encountered outrage—a humiliation of inherited values and of the masculine will that sustains them—that Morrison seeks increasingly to read in other terms. Such outrage has long been recognized as Faulkner's keynote. There has been less scrutiny, however, of the emotional and intellectual syndrome subtending outrage: the syndrome of innocence. From Donald Mahan through Chick Mallison, Faulkner's commitment to male innocence is absolute, however complex his judgment of it. This innocence involves, always, a dream of the intact will, a fantasy scenario in which subject and world coincide as though meant for each other—the world obediently submitting to the subject's mastery.

As a black woman who has virtually absorbed the defeat of the sovereign will with her mother's milk, Morrison differs fundamentally. She is as repelled by innocence as Christians are by corruption. In her work it casts an equivalent and indicting odor: "An innocent man is a sin before God. Inhuman and therefore unworthy. No man should live without absorbing the sins of his kind, the foul air of his innocence" (*TB*, 243).[9] The contrast becomes clear. On the one hand, the Faulknerian project of the father, involving the indispensable twin features of innocence and outrage, unfolds as a drama of the disinherited son's humiliated will: a white male story of American failing. On the other hand, the Morrisonian project of the father, beginning with Cholly Breedlove, involves not the failed transmission of a once-intact legacy but the suspended threat of an impotence descending from slavery itself.

John Irwin and André Bleikasten have given us our most cogent readings of the damaging Faulknerian father, and Carolyn Porter has recently proposed a compelling revision of their claims. Irwin reads the Faulknerian father as a grown-up son, authoritative only in the eyes of his own rebellious offspring. Irwin's Mr. Compson embodies a generations-repeated imposture. Appearing powerful to his son, he in effect confesses to him that he too was undone earlier by the apparent power of his own father, that no father is powerful inasmuch as every father is a son caught between his own father on whom he would seek revenge and his own son seeking similar revenge. Irwin draws on Nietzsche to propose a model of time as Chronos, the inhuman power that eventually undoes all sons grown first to fatherhood and then back into the impotence of old age. Bleikasten's Faulknerian father is equally beleaguered, mainly because he comes at a time—after the Civil War—in which he has no authority left to bequeath. Insofar as the father can pass on to the son only those legacies that the larger culture has kept intact, the postwar South guarantees Mr. Compson's impotence. Bleikasten reads Faulkner's antebellum fathers—the Hightowers, Sartorises, Sutpens, and McCaslins—as serenely unapproachable by their confused twentieth-century progeny: of no use whatsoever for current cultural adaptation. Porter's revision involves, by way of a politically slanted Lacanian lens, a reseeing of the paternal dynamic. Moving from *The Sound and the Fury*'s question with respect to Mrs. Compson—*who* is this mother?—to *As I Lay Dying*'s larger question with respect to Addie Bundren—*what* is a mother?—Porter sees Faulkner in *Absalom, Absalom!* turning from the mother to the generic question of the father: what is at stake in his making and unmaking? By the time of Sutpen, the Faulknerian father emerges as the figure of cultural authority itself. His power is based upon a successfully survived Oedipal ordeal—the eventual occupation of the position vacated by the original and hostile father that characterizes every Oedipal passage—which is itself the psychological motor of patriarchal politics, the logic of the descent of property and other perquisites from father to son. When *this* father comes apart, Porter argues, his self-destruction and destruction of others reveals nothing less than Faulkner's extraordinary diagnosis of patriarchy's racial and gendered injustice.

Without further complicating this portrait of the father (for I do not know how to improve on these analyses), I would point to the three sequences of Faulkner's fiction (all of them circulating in different ways around the son's outraged innocence) to which fatherhood gives rise. First there is the sequence of the impotent father, he who fails to protect the son. Mr. Compson inaugurates this lineage, though we may say that the all-but-absent Judge Drake in *Sanctuary* and the present-but-useless Old Bayard in *Flags in the Dust* are preparatory figures. Their paternal ineptitude (Porter elaborates on Lacan's definition of the father as the father who does not know he is dead[10]) underwrites the assault—at once substantive and stylistic—that these novels deliver. (Indeed, what would better motivate such ferocious assault than the twin insults of a culture gone bankrupt both in the substance it would bequeath and in its very style of bequeathing?) Malraux knew long ago that Faulkner's subject was "the irreparable," to which I would add that "the irreparable" becomes dramatic only when the drama of outraged innocence in its presence is supplied. Rape and rupture—a humiliation of will, a failure of legacy—are the obsessive events, and Faulkner's art is lavished upon showing that there is no getting used to these abuses. Benjy Compson embodies most purely a nonadaptation equally visible in Quentin and Jason, in Darl and Jewel, in Joe Christmas and Temple Drake.

When Faulkner returns to Temple, some twenty years later in *Requiem for a Nun*, the failed legacy and humiliating wound remain beyond adaptation. Indeed, the wound has festered, poisoning the lives it touches—Temple's, Gavin's, Nancy's, the baby's. As Temple says to the doomed Nancy late in the novel, "Why do you and my little baby both have to suffer just because I decided to go to a baseball game eight years ago?" (658). Despite its endless circulation around this question and its cognates, the text can come up with no answer beyond Nancy's mysterious "Believe." There may be some ultimate sanction justifying this suffering, but it is beyond knowing, even perhaps, the text may suggest, beyond white believing. What strikes me is Faulkner's unresisted urge to keep the wound mortal, to collapse the intervening days and years into so much inauthentic time passed under the shadow of a concealed self-betrayal. We are in the presence of an authorial insistence upon disaster, one focused not on the event's further possible meanings (for the event reduces here to pure evil), but rather on its irreparable consequences. The pretenses of a recentered self (Temple's, Gowan's) are tirelessly torn apart. The text all but revels in its protagonists' pain and in the futility of any parental figure's attempt to alter that pain.

The pattern I have been tracing—the humiliation of the will, the discovery of impotence consequent upon a failed legacy—begins arguably with the paralyzed Donald Mahan and nourishes many of Faulkner's characteristic portraits. Bayard (of *Flags*), Benjy, Quentin, Horace, Joe Christmas, Henry Sutpen, Charles Bon, Ike McCaslin: these are, above all, disappointed sons, young men orphaned and humiliated by the parent or the parental culture. They lack resource, they are overwhelmed by the trouble they find themselves in, they tend toward the denouement of the corporal in A *Fable*: crucifixion. Out of this overwhelming Faulkner makes very great art, perhaps his greatest. There may be no better way of indicating the magnitude of cultural bankruptcy that he witnessed (the South's incapacity to diagnose its dilemmas and reroute its legacies) than by creating a gallery of unavailing male protagonists. Yet, without derogating the significance of such failure, we might note its insistent racial and gendered assumptions. For we are dealing with what is mainly a white male topic, an infatuation with immortal wounds suffered by those who had such other expectations. And we are asked, in the reading, to register the priceless value of male hearts and minds going down to defeat. Charles Etienne St. Valery Bon—he of the long name and short life—epitomizes the beauty and hopelessness of this Faulknerian agon, and something of this figure lies concealed within the entire gallery of failed young men I have been examining. They find themselves radically unparented, with no resources for encountering the collapse of their dreams, the defeat of their innocence. "His trouble was innocence," it is famously said of Faulkner's Sutpen. The diagnosis bespeaks a trouble common to the larger white male illusion of an intact will. When, by contrast, Morrison speaks of "the foul air of innocence," she gestures toward a territory on the other side of that illusion, a space in which the broken will—an absorption of "the sins of one's kind"—is inaugurative rather than conclusive. For reasons that have nothing to do with biology and everything to do with cultural placement, this latter territory is black.

Faulkner produces other paternal configurations as well, one of which (to which I shall return) might be called "the ameliorative." Figures in this group include the later Ike McCaslin, the amiable Ratliff, and the indefatigable Gavin Stevens. But the most famous Faulknerian fathers, the "giants before the flood," remain Sartoris, Sutpen, and McCaslin. As I argued in " 'Mister,' " these figures suffer not from an incapacitation of the will but from its hypertrophy. Taking what they want, brooking no query, self-possessed to a fault, they not only exercise their own freedom at others' expense, but they can come into their own, it seems, only through others' expense. Sartoris's heroic statue makes no reference to the murdered Burdens, but we may mentally supply those two corpses, just as we eventually see that the grandiose marble tombstone of Sutpen omits reference to the murdered Charles and the abused Eulalia and Rosa (figures who make him what he is), and just as Old

Carothers's ferocious self-sufficiency (so sought after by Lucas Beauchamp) requires, as its complementary features, an immolated Eunice and an impregnated but disowned Tomasina and her offspring. It takes a passel of abused people to account for three solitary heroes, and Faulkner's texts work carefully to produce the pathos of the missing corpses. Such epic fathers leave a violence-filled legacy that their twentieth-century offspring (forced to confront the racial and gendered consequences of an unchecked male will) can neither accept nor escape. As Faulkner puts it with unforgettable force:

> Yes. Maybe we are both Father. Maybe nothing ever happens once and is finished. Maybe happens is never once but like ripples maybe on water after the pebble sinks, the ripples moving on, spreading, the pool attached by a narrow umbilical water-cord to the next pool which the first pool feeds, has fed, did feed, let this second pool contain a different temperature of water, a different molecularity of having seen, felt, remembered, reflect in a different tone the infinite unchanging sky, it doesn't matter: that pebble's watery echo whose fall it did not even see moves across its surface too at the original ripple-space, to the old ineradicable rhythm thinking Yes, we are both Father. Or maybe Father and I are both Shreve, maybe it took Father and me both to make Shreve or Shreve and me both to make Father or maybe Thomas Sutpen to make all of us.   (AA, 216)

Perhaps the entire Faulknerian dilemma is here. We have the insistence upon disaster, upon an unhealing wound and an unavailing legacy, in its purest form. The vignette is eloquently, maybe even unknowingly, gender-figured, revealing a structure in which agency is male, reception female. The key event is the pebble's fatal entry into the water; the repercussions of that phallic penetration are immortal. Water-ripple is mere effect to pebble-cause, and the various pools' differences over time, however considerable, can be no more than superficial. The drama is rigorously commanded by a single (sovereign) male action forgotten yet generative of a foredoomed genealogy: "maybe Thomas Sutpen to make all of us." Omitted at every level but the figurative is female agency, for the passage's essential hubris is to imagine a procreative descent—a virtual orgy of begettings—enacted exclusively through male couplings. This incapacity to give name to the women who make generation possible (an incapacity at the heart of *Absalom's* plot) is quietly upbraided by the figurative logic of the passage, in which, insist as they will, male pebbles remain indebted to a liquid structure that permits echo to occur. For this is simultaneously an umbilical scene, deep in the territory of the female. But if only the white male players are named, if action is coded white and male and reaction coded black and female, then what would the result be but the repeated outrages that constitute *Absalom, Absalom!*? Morrison, for her part, narrates this drama of the sought-after father's bequests and omissions but once—with differences as marked as the similarities. For this narration we turn from David to Solomon.

"The fathers may soar / And the children may know their names"—so reads the epigraph of *Song of Solomon*. The epigraph cues us to the transcendent father sought after in this text, Solomon, a figure so epic that even his immediate offspring, Macon Dead Sr., appears (in memory) as larger than life:

> He had come out of nowhere, as ignorant as a hammer and broke as a convict, with nothing but free papers, a Bible, and a pretty black-haired wife, and in one year he'd leased ten acres, the next ten more. Sixteen years later he had one of the best farms in Montour County. A farm that colored their lives like a paintbrush and spoke to them like a sermon. "You see?" the farm said to them. . . . "Here, this here, is what a man can do if he puts his mind to it and his back into it. . . . Grab it. Grab this land! Take it, hold it, my brothers, make it, my brothers, shake it, squeeze it, turn it, twist it, beat it, kick it, kiss it, whip it, stomp it, dig it, plow it, seed it, reap it, rent it, buy it, sell it, own it, build it, multiply it, and pass it on—can you hear me? Pass it on!"   (SS, 235)

The passage is resonant, and if it sounds familiar that is because the first sentence uncannily echoes the advent of Sutpen, equally from nowhere, equally boundless in his ambition. Macon Dead appears here in poignant contrast both to the fleeing youth first sketched to us in the naming scene, and to the desiccated sequel embodied a generation later in his son Macon Jr. In between, after the War and before the rise of segregation, something marvelous has happened. The tendering to blacks of the American dream (during the period of Reconstruction) has been accepted and exploited. We witness a self-making focused on the will and on the Lockean dream of identity-as-property. A black dynasty is being envisaged, its rhapsodic phrases not to be sounded by Morrison again until Baby Suggs's sermon in *Beloved*. Macon's farm focuses and enables a virtual explosion of the will, that penultimate sentence lavishing twenty-three different verbs in the imperative mode—each a call to action, a celebration of black identity as a capacity enacted through the possession, improvement, and bequeathing of property.

The exercise of will, the insistence of claim in Macon's property project are transformative (there is no self-ratifying without a measure of these virtues), yet such self-making is menaced on all sides. As Morrison well knows, this was a short-lived (barely one-generational) dream for blacks; Macon Sr.'s property claim is also his undoing.[11] His last soaring is five feet into the air, rent apart by a white man's shotgun while trying to protect his property. His soaring and his falling are inseparable. He leaves, like his transcendent father, orphans behind.

Macon Dead Jr., in fact, never recovers from the murderous theft of his father's land. Taking from his father only his passion for material possession, dedicating his life to the pursuit of property, he urges his own son: "Let me tell you right now the one important thing you'll ever need to know: Own things. And let the things you own own other things. Then you'll own yourself and other people too" (55). Envisaging human value as a possessible thing, abstracting the energies of will and claim from the relational web that keeps them healthy, Macon Jr. subtly deforms all the lives that come into his domain. His urge to own is simultaneously competitive and paranoid—what he cannot bound frightens him—and he remains locked in a contest with his father-in-law, Dr. Foster, that lasts well beyond the old man's death.

Dr. Foster and Macon Jr., however inimical, resemble each other finally, sharing the next black generation's twentieth-century yearning for success at any cost and on white terms. Both men achieve such success, and in so doing complete an alienation from cultural roots that orphans those nearest them. Morrison brilliantly explores a black class system coded to the lightness of skin color, a system on whose tenets Corinthians and Magdalena are splayed/displayed as crucified exemplars. Macon Jr. may be incapable of forgiving his light-skinned father-in-law's white airs—he dilates obsessively on the repellant whiteness of the doctor's corpse—yet, like Sutpen, he emulates what he detests, driving the Packard to prove his class superiority, withholding his daughters from darker-skinned or uncultivated suitors. In some repressed part of himself, moreover, Macon Jr. knows that his financial success masks a human failure. Covertly watching from outside, as though hypnotized, he sees his disowned sister, Pilate, move through dinner with her family with a rhythmic grace—alternately singing, eating, braiding, sewing, none of this programmed, all of it pleasure-producing—long since banned from his will-governed and white-routinized life.

If Dr. Foster and Macon Jr. both fail as parental guides (their model for success being premised upon an erasure of their racial heritage), there remains one further paternal claim in the midst of this novel's midcentury racial turbulence: the Seven Days. A paramilitary group intent on revenge against the whites, the Days propose simultaneously a reading of black history, a recovery of black dignity, a model of black masculinity, and a task for black males that (as the name suggests) gives order to time.[12] In the name of community they band together, a sassing and amiable group of black men congregating around the pool bar and the barbershop when not on a mission. Milkman's only friend, Guitar, is their youngest convert, and this would be a different novel if Morrison could see in such parentage a successful nourishing. To measure the depth of the need to which the Days respond, even if finally without success, we must turn to the third generation of black males in search of grounding, Milkman and Guitar.

"Everything in the world loves" a black man, Sula told a disgruntled Jude (S, 103). Men white and black, women white and black—all dilate, with whatever different motives, upon the black man's charged body. ("Somewhere beneath all that daintiness, chambered in all that neatness, lay the thing that clotted their dreams" [S, 51].) I use the verb "charged" to convey a body never neutral in the imaginary of both races and genders, and to convey as well, and in consequence, the body on which so many claims are charged, so much violence is discharged. It is a body riddled with imaginary over-investments, and Morrison's phrasing intensifies when, three years later, she has Guitar echo Sula: "Everybody wants the life of a black man" (SS, 222). The grim insight in this phrasing accommodates both Faulkner's understanding of white insanity (male and female) over black male bodies and the wry self-awareness of the black male subject himself. A player in everyone else's fantasies, what is left over for himself? What unsought legacy could possibly serve as a mirror for his own self-unfolding? This problem becomes a crisis when his model of manhood would equate identity with unfettered potency, and when everywhere he finds himself economically cut off, racially and sexually stereotyped, a participant only in the projects of others. Is it any wonder that the radical solution proposed by the Days—eye for eye, act for act—has its appeal?

Morrison shares with Faulkner the courage to follow her insights absolutely, to refuse compromising resolutions, and she ends this novel (as Faulkner ends Absalom, Absalom!) in a moment of perfect tension—Milkman leaping into an apotheosis whose outcome we simply cannot predicate. Whether, and on what terms, he lives or dies is unsayable.[13] But we can note that her exploration of fathering in the Faulknerian key of supreme authority imposes considerable costs. Not only are Corinthians and Magdalena virtually undeveloped in this text of the son, but Milkman's triumphant recovery of Solomon is ringed round with female suffering and exclusion. How, for example, are we to respond to Hagar's sudden death, to Pilate's smiling subordination to

Milkman at the end (accompanying him to her death), and to Ruth Dead's continued exile from the text? How, further, should we read the text's sexual offer of Sweet as Milkman's earned (and remunerated) male reward? And, finally, what are we to make of the closing fraternal embrace—"My main man" (337), Guitar murmurs as he moves toward Milkman—an embrace paid for by a certain number of dead and disowned black women? "We don't off Negroes," Guitar had assured Milkman (161). Yet something in the internal binary logic of this text understands the saved life of a black man in terms of the yielded life of a black woman.[14] Henceforth Morrison will approach the male search in different terms. From Son through Paul D and Stamp Paid to Joe Trace—this drama proposes, increasingly, the black male's recovery of his manhood less through pursuit of the father outside than through reconciliation with the woman within.

Later Developments, Tentative Conclusions

I would conclude this study of fathering tentatively because Morrison's career—while amply before us—is still in the making. Yet she seems to have reached her own version of an autumnal stance that permeates Faulkner's later work as well. What appears in *Jazz* as a nostalgia funded by the middle years reveals the paternal principle in a different—softer, less urgent—light. Commenting briefly on three texts, *Intruder in the Dust*, *Beloved*, and *Jazz*, I want to explore the bearing of these later developments.

Lucas Beauchamp in *Go Down, Moses* runs the gamut from youth to age. He stands as figurative counterpart to Ike McCaslin, as literal father to black offspring, and as symbolic father (or is it competitor?) to Roth Edmonds. When Faulkner takes Lucas up again in *Intruder in the Dust*, he is older yet, and this time carefully lifted clear from his black culture. "Solitary, kinless, and intractable" (*ID*, 301), the text delights in calling him. Later we read: " 'I aint got friends,' Lucas said with stern and inflexible pride" (331–32). Removed from a black web of identity-shaping associations, Lucas can thus be inserted in a white web of values.[15] In *Intruder*, that web is insistently parental and filial: parental insofar as he emerges as Chick Mallison's fantasy-father (Chick falling into Lucas's creek, being covered with Lucas's cloak), yet filial insofar as Gavin Stevens (the other symbolic father in this text) will insist on seeing and renaming him as the entire South's offspring: Sambo.

As fantasy-father, his portrait is suffused in the same admiring terms earlier bestowed upon Faulknerian male icons. Regardless of the scene we find him in, Lucas is inscrutable, impenetrable—at his own fire and hearth or imprisoned in the Jefferson jail. Rising out of the water as though into a second birth, Chick first discovers Lucas's eyes upon him, "watching him without pity commiseration or anything else" (287). Lucas's face has no pigment, his bearing is "not arrogant, not even scornful" (288); and these "not" formulas do their work of producing him textually without penetrating within. "Within" is a sanctuary of maintained self-sameness that no stress can violate, and the text cooperates in preserving this male bastion of virginity. He remains immaculately self-possessed, assuring Gavin that "never nobody knocked me down" (531), aligning himself insistently with his trusty "Colt 41" (an heirloom from Old Carothers). Three times he presses to have this pistol back, as though that phallic accompaniment would take care of all problems, whereas it is in fact his vanity over the pistol that allows Crawford Gowrie to entrap him in the first place. Finally, this is a virtually silent father whose authority is constructed outside the field of speech.

The inevitable segue here is to Gavin Stevens, the other father figure in *Intruder in the Dust*. Gavin tells Chick; Lucas shows him. Lucas's enactment of dignity counters Gavin's talk of dignity, and this split is suggestive. It is as though the social realm itself—the space of law, education, culture, politics— were becoming for Faulkner increasingly garrulous and unreal at the same time; its name is Gavin. Perhaps the sadness that saturates the later novels (*Sanctuary* is bitter, it is not sad) locates itself most precisely in this figure whose unflagging energy never quite conceals a deeper hopelessness. But if Gavin is sad, he is not (like Mr. Compson) nihilistic, and his advice seems followable. John Irwin has recently commented on Gavin as an older and mellower Mr. Compson, and Jay Martin has urged us to recognize, especially in later Faulkner, a reliance upon the male mentor.[16] Avuncular rather than more closely blood-related, liberated from the complicities of marital involvement, freed as well of the need to do, Gavin tirelessly advises. The bachelor caretaker of the realm of culture, he will yet never complete his translation of the Old Testament back into its original Greek. He too is virgin.

The father in the social realm of endless talk is white; the father in the fantasy realm of focused silence is black. Both are free of the female (the one widowed, the other incapable of marriage), both are innocent. The political implications of this split in the figuring of authority are considerable. The "homogeneous" white South that Gavin would preserve from Northern interference is itself anachronistic, a retreat (as the rabidly Latinate-insistent vocabulary and ceaseless syntax of Gavin's speech are a retreat) from New

South vulgarities that nevertheless will have to figure in the region's future. Intact himself, Gavin projects a similar intactness upon his culture. In both cases the intactness screens a deeper impotence—indeed, the absence of any intrinsic Southern culture left to be bequeathed. Lucas, for his part, is accessed by Faulkner in such a way as to be alienated from his own black culture; he despises "field niggers" as wholeheartedly as whites do. More, he is ushered into white protection on a single, all-encompassing condition: that he cease to be a "nigger." The mob, of course, would leave him be if he would only act like a "nigger," but Gavin and the privileged few who know better see his eventual emancipation in reverse terms, as a transcendence of his racial legacy. The Negro must "learn to cease forever more thinking like a Negro and acting like a Negro," Faulkner wrote later in the 1950s; this stance recurs in *Intruder in the Dust*. Black smell, black food, black irresponsibility: all these "habits" can be unlearned, surpassed, and Lucas's masculine courage testifies to such a surpassing (which is in reality an erasing).[17]

If Gavin's white model of authority is latently impotent, so then is Lucas's black model. His power is more openly revealed as illusory by his other textual name, Sambo. Faulkner incoherently envisages his region's racial future as a sort of improved return to the past. He sees the white South (no Northerners needed, thank you) eventually freeing its silent and dignified blacks. Lucas, the plot of this novel elaborately guarantees, is incapable of freeing himself. Indeed, what kind of authority could he possess if his virtues are imagined as outside the realm of speech?

Within the Oedipal framework that I have developed, we see two fathers who, in equal and opposite measures, succeed on the surface but fail at a deeper level. Lucas is the archaic imaginary father, the figure of unblinking courage ready to face death with his manhood intact. Gavin is the impotent symbolic father, the weaver of words and speaker of the social drama, yet inept, a well-intentioned mentor at best. Chick apparently learns from both of them, though Faulkner cannot show us anything bearing on race that Chick (or any other character) might learn, for he never writes a fiction seriously attentive to racial turmoil on the other side (post-1948) of Lucas Beauchamp's crisis. The Oedipal legacy ends by being bypassed rather than secured. Faulkner is simply unable, in the South of the late 1940s, to imagine a successful transmission of cultural values for which the Oedipal paradigm would be the blueprint. Bypassed, not dismantled, not even attacked: Lucas and Gavin both retain a masculine integrity perhaps all the more poignant for its inability to affect the real. Protected from a more damaging immersion in the racial currents of their time, they survive intact, and in so doing leave behind the Faulknerian tragedy of humiliated will, the outrage to male identity that has virtually served as this writer's novelistic signature. Faulkner finishes, thus, upon the sweetness of *The Reivers*, where the legacy of male innocence returns unchecked (that is, checked only in ways that can be overcome). For a take upon manhood outside this protected register, we turn to Morrison's *Beloved* and *Jazz*, texts saturated in a racial experience that ensures that "no man should live without absorbing the sins of his kind, the foul air of his innocence."

Paul D is a man in profound touch with women and a man who has lost his innocence. These go together inasmuch as innocence is a notion lodged within a white male paradigm of values. (It was men, Mr. Compson tells his son, who invented virginity, not women.) Morrison introduces Paul D as "the kind of man who could walk into the house and make the women cry" (*B*, 17). Women find themselves confessing to him, Sethe soon realizes that his hands are wise enough to take on "the responsibility for her breasts" (18). His gift is an empathic quickness that registers the shifting feelings of the other: "as though all you had to do was get his attention and right away he produced the feeling you were feeling" (7–8). More, this capacity to enter others' emotional range is not limited to females; he is a lover but he is not just a lover. His name (however slavery-imposed) intimates as well that, unlike a Faulknerian isolate, he lives in a fraternal world, sharing his identity with other males. He touches men's bodies casually, engages in a kind of intimate horseplay with the other Pauls that seems outside the range of Faulknerian white male behavior. This somatic/fraternal ease allows him to step into the space vacated by Halle (almost another brother) without competitiveness or stress, and it allows him as well to survive the ordeal of slavery. Shackled men must come to terms with their own bodies and those of others as free men never need to. He may vomit at the threat of a white penis in his mouth, and he may go half mad at the imposition of the bit upon his tongue; but he has bonded with his black confederates and he has come to terms with that chain.[18] Moving together, their bodies synchronized, the slaves work with the chain, not against it, to secure their freedom. Their singing together, their sign language for checking on each other's bodily endurance—these betoken a body regime, an achieved and shared somatic intimacy, beyond the experience (outside the training) of Faulkner's white males.

His is also, as I explored in the last chapter, an experience of self-annihilating abuse. Owned and manhandled by slaveowners, forced to realize his radical impotence, he sees he cannot be a man on the terms proposed by Garner. If he would become a man on other terms, he must yield up his white model and its judgmental code—cease viewing Sethe as a creature with four legs, not two—and begin to reconceive manhood on the other side of an intact body and an intact law. This involves the relinquishment of identity as a maintained possession, an intrinsic property, and its replacement by a model of identity shaped to the pressures of psychic and bodily interpenetration. In this second model the would-be creator—the male whose identity is synonymous with the reach of his will—cedes some space to the actual creature: the male who must learn to live his identity as a variable resource dependent upon an identificatory and reciprocal commerce with others. On this schema, identity operates relationally or not at all. Stamp Paid, as I argued, has learned to resee himself in such communal terms. Joshua was extinguished by a wound to the male ego too deep to be borne, but this wound need not extinguish life as well. Reemerging as Stamp Paid, he managed to accede, as only the pain of nonintactness could teach him, to another way of being male: one beyond the luxuries of innocence and outrage. The institution of slavery, I wish to argue, taught black people to acknowledge a kind of radical interdependency of identity without which they would have perished: an interdependency at the core of survival itself (for none of us makes it all alone) but one from which Western white males are still fleeing in numbers too vast for counting.

In my reading of Morrison's career, *Beloved* is the novel in which she finds her way into this new vision of black manhood, with its potential for a different kind of paternity. She finally turns off that white flashlight coiling in Cholly Breedlove's guts (telling him he must be male on the white master's terms or not male at all). She starts to envisage a recovery of paternal dignity that moves, not through the heroic mastery of Macon Dead Sr. and his mythic father, Solomon, but rather through Paul D and Stamp Paid, toward the damaged but indestructible Joe Trace. All these males are orphaned, but they are, at the same time, increasingly immersed in the resources of a shared community. Morrison's novelistic trajectory makes its way past the innocence and outrage of *Song of Solomon*, issuing into the shamelessly fallen world of *Jazz*.

As insistently as the surname of Paul D, Joe Trace's surname reveals his status of nonmastery. His orphaned identity is founded upon a void itself—a mother who disappeared "without a trace" (*J*, 124). Joe lives in the contingent: "Before I met her [Dorcas], I'd changed into new seven times" (123), each identity change dependent upon a change in time and place. Contingent, yes, but not to be confused with Camus's Meursault or any other figure suffused in white Western alienation. Joe is cut off but not alone, unsponsored but not unrelated. The mother Joe would "trace" is herself Wild, and her unapproachable blackness whispers of Africa further back. A hunter's hunter, Joe has picked up the Shalimar virtues as well—his orphaning does not read as an abandoning—and this figure, when we follow him in the City, is no victim of urban anomie. Rather, he is all but limitlessly open to a shaping context, and his emotional quickness echoes Paul D's:

> A sample-case man. A nice, neighborly, everybody-knows-him man. The kind you let in your house because he was not dangerous, because you had seen him with children, bought his products and never heard a scrap of gossip about him doing wrong. Felt not only safe but kindly in his company because he was the sort women ran to when they thought they were being followed, or watched or needed someone to have the extra key just in case you locked yourself out. He was the man who took you to your door if you missed the trolley. . . . Who warned young girls away from hooch joints and the men who lingered there. Women teased him because they trusted him.
>
> (73)

Like Paul D (but a generation later), living domestically in the City, Joe Trace is yet capable of betraying utterly the aura of reliability radiated by this passage. In a different kind of novel—a mystery story, or even Conrad—that betrayal would reveal the true figure behind the conventional facade. But *Jazz*'s commitment to the mobile surface of things, to the pressures and possibilities of contingency, is absolute. There is no master model for sorting Joe's surfaces from his depths. He is trustworthy, yet he could do anything—a twentieth-century black man both hemmed in and seething with life. A current runs through him, and that current is the African-American genius that Alain Locke saw in the 1920s as shaping the "New Negro" of the Harlem Renaissance.[19] The deepest achievement of *Jazz* registers not in the plot or the characters but in the music of the black language itself. "What was meant," the narrator says of a black parade charged with pride and anger, comes not from the hoisted banners: it comes "from the drums" (53). Joe Trace's emotional life and characteristic moves are nourished by these same drums. As he himself acknowledges, "You could say I've been a new Negro all my life" (129).

If we seek to understand why Joe killed Dorcas, we find ourselves far from any interior psychoanalytic paradigm of isolated and repressed motivations. No (white) model of individual depth operates here; no Faulknerian exploration of the psyche's secrets. Rather, the explanations (insofar as they exist) are cultural and temporal: outside pressures affecting them all. The cultural context is the intoxicating black culture of the City itself, resulting from a migration from the South that reached its headiest moments in the 1920s and that seems to turn America's largest urban space of that time into a village. Joe (like Violet and Dorcas and Alice and the others) lives immersed within a ceaselessly humming communal world made up of migratory strolls for business and pleasure, vibrating chords of street and bar music, the casual interlocking of male and female lives, the rhythmic circulation of alternately fanned and repressed desires, and the thickened medium of black urban folkways of the 1920s. Morrison works to get us to take in this story of romance, heartbreak, and murder as a black folktale of the city, if not a piece of jazz itself.

The pressures upon Joe Trace are temporal as well as cultural, though; his story is saturated in the passage of time through his sensibility. Seeking his unknown mother's hand, wanting just the touch of acknowledgment but not receiving it, he enters (chronologically decades later, but textually on the next page) into the relationship with Dorcas as a renewal, in a different key, of the search for the mother. Though he is on the far side of fifty and she on the near side of twenty, Joe and Dorcas are both orphaned, and they pass their evenings released through mutual memories as well as passionate lovemaking. It is their own gathered incompleteness that they pour into each other, and Joe needs this since his wife, Violet—fiercely battling her own menopausal changes and now hopelessly childless—has withdrawn from him. Dorcas is represented fleetingly (tentatively) as the withheld mother, the fantasy daughter, the momentary lover; they each play multiple roles. It all makes for an indecipherable explosion of violence, next to which the assessing of Sethe's murder of her child seems tolerably clear:

> "Why did he do such a thing?" [Alice to Violet.]
> "Why did she?"
> "Why did you?"
> "I don't know."   (81)

Such not-knowing denotes not ignorance but the opening into mystery. It is radically not clear why people do what they do, though we see the age-old pressures (both cultural and universal) at work upon their incurable incompleteness. Orphans all, exiled from Oedipally descended norms of right and wrong, of achieved identity, these characters move musically, so to speak, in an almost tangible atmosphere of physical and emotional interpenetration.

This is Morrison's supreme novel of touch, and touch—the root of contingency—seems not only to replace knowledge, it brings a sort of experience unamenable to knowledge.[20] Unlike Faulknerian dramas built upon the collapse of innocence, the outrageous refusal of the real to meet one's dreams of mastery, *Jazz* circulates about a cast of characters who have long ago lost their innocence and who have ceased to judge the real by the criterion of innocence. Their negotiations with the real are instead steeped in an accommodation of the irreparable in which wound and dance—injury and performance—are inseparable constituents.

If we call this condition tragic, we miss its most stunning dimension: that it turns the collapse of mastery into the enabling framework of the music. The narrative begins rather than ends there. Not the dream innocence of a single male's intact will, then, but the shared life intensification that follows the breaking of the law. Here is Joe to Dorcas:

> I told you again that you were the reason Adam ate the apple and its core. That when he left Eden, he left a rich man. Not only did he have Eve, but he had the taste of the first apple in his mouth for the rest of his life. The very first to know what it was like. To bite it down, bite it down. Hear the crunch and let the red peeling break his heart.   (133)

Solomon does not speak in *Song of Solomon*; only in *Jazz* do we get the words he might have uttered. Heartbreak as wealth, love as necessarily including betrayal, any life worth living as one transgressing the law that prohibits the apple, any identity worth enacting as one born of an accommodated self-shattering. By the time of *Jazz*, the commerce of parent and child involves not the legacy of lawful property and propriety, not the dream of an individual's intact descent, but instead a larger community's taking hold and savoring of its lived adulteration, transforming those who are often seen as last into the first, "the very first." Beyond innocence and outrage, this Solomon would speak—if he spoke—the survival of a people who have taken into themselves everything that white America could impose upon them: and made of it an unsentimental, unspeakable music.

Faulkner's David withholds his legacy, or he suffocates his offspring in bequeathing it, or his legacy (like Hubert Beauchamp's cup of silver) has lost its value by the time it is drawn upon. Whatever the case, when Faulkner thinks of David, his mind turns to Absalom. He sees several sons, some legitimate and some not, all clamoring for the father's blessing. The tragedy of these needy sons balked of their inheritance gives Faulkner the substance of his fiction, and that substance registers as the outraging of innocence. The inheritance is Oedipal/patriarchal, and its model for the descent of property and the proper excludes women (politely) and blacks (brutally) from positions of acknowledgment. The deepest thing Faulkner knows is that the women and blacks will suffer from these exclusions in such a way as to dispossess the men as well. His greatest fictions present and re-present a racial and gendered nightmare—a design gone irreparably wrong and yet uselessly repercussing rather than replaced by something better. This is his tragic story of America. He is incapable of revising it, for nothing in his culture's norms or in his relation to those norms positioned him to see his way past this disaster. His last fathers are less disabling, and his last sons are better instructed, but these are scenes of descent in which the blacks have been removed and the women kept on the margins. The fiction of his final decade (apart from the brilliant intrusion of an unassuageable Mink Snopes) becomes pastoral; it plays for lesser stakes.

Morrison's Solomon rarely speaks. The black father first enters her work in the desperate form of Cholly Breedlove, and Morrison somehow manages to see this damaged and damaging figure with remarkable generosity. It would take a musician to find the coherence in Cholly's contingencies, she writes, and rather than take up that task in *Sula*, Morrison transfers the vital principle from male to female. But *Song of Solomon* pursues again the father and the music he implies (it is a song in search of Solomon)—this time a figure of achieved power mythically removed from Cholly's errancies. Finally, *Beloved* and *Jazz* begin the work of reconceiving the black male outside the Oedipal/patriarchal frame in which he is doomed to fail. A male broken into and dispossessed of the dream of innocence in which his identity might be coextensive with his intact will, a male who has learned to be in touch with others' bodies and their minds (male and female), a male whose creatural experience has taught him to recognize the woman within, a male for whom identity begins on the other side of adulteration and the broken law—such a figure starts to beckon in her work. He is not yet a father, but he has something to bequeath. He does not yet speak, but his life seems to cohere as an African-inspired music.

PART 3
Encounters

"The language, only the language," Morrison answered when she was asked, "What makes [fiction] good?"[1] How one says it, "the words to say it" (*PD*, xiii), these tiny, endless acts of craft underwrite the largest cultural reach of any writer's work. In order for the work to be everything else it is, it must first be an artful arrangement of words, an achieved form. If the words are not compellingly ordered, the fiction, however ambitious, is not good. Faulkner matters most to Morrison because he was an extraordinary arranger of words; all his other claims on her attention flow from this claim. Part 3 stages, therefore, three different textual encounters between Faulkner and Morrison. The simplest realm is constituted by (what I take to be) Morrison's specific reshaping of Faulknerian materials (less at the level of discrete phrases than at the level of the conceiving and molding of episodes). More complex and diffuse is a second realm constituted by a general resemblance of the two writers' concerns and forms for addressing those concerns. Finally, and perhaps most telling, there is a third realm of significant differences that virtually constitute Faulkner's and Morrison's writerly identity as they embark on the task of representing racial turmoil. In each of the chapters that follow, I draw on a different pair of novels to explore these three realms.[2]

At the level of specific reworkings, I explore a crucial episode of *Song of Solomon*—Milkman's rite of passage at Shalimar—as a reprise of Ike McCaslin's rite of passage in *Go Down, Moses*. Thereafter, I pair *Absalom, Absalom!* and *Jazz*, first as texts that share a similar episode (Golden Gray's search for his black father replaying and revising Charles Bon's search for his white father) and then more broadly as texts with similar strategies and concerns with respect to the representation of race. Finally, the third chapter compares *Light in August* and *Beloved* as each writer's most incisive rendering of racial disturbance.

This last comparison is the most elusive, for in it I seek to map, so to speak, the "circulation of social energy" itself—the ways in which each text catches up (and is caught up in) crucial ideological currents of American culture. I aim, in this last pairing, to produce a reading in which aesthetic value emerges less as a sign of disinterested mastery than as the effect achieved when a socially embedded text transforms into verbal texture some of that society's deepest tensions and convictions and passes these into readerly experience. In this reading, value is a coefficient not of purely formal achievement but of the degree of ideological disturbance that a text can summon forth, significantly interrelate, and formally convey. "The language, only the language," yes, but as the medium of a haunting, a registering upon the reader's subjectivity of the culture's conflicting circuits of social energy: a culture's nightmares brought by ordered words to the light of day.

5

"The Condition Our Condition Is In"
Bedrock in *Go Down, Moses* and *Song of Solomon*

Song of Solomon does not conceal its reprisal of Faulknerian materials.[1] A mysterious and ancient black caretaker named Circe harks back unmistakably to the inscrutable Clytie in *Absalom, Absalom!* More, a scene in which one of the characters is named Calvin and another (the protagonist) puts on black brogans recalls *Light in August*'s pair of Calvin Burdens (not to mention the Calvinistic McEachern), as well as Joe Christmas's donning of black brogans preparatory to his fateful return to Mottstown and Jefferson. But *Go Down, Moses* remains Faulkner's novel most intricately at play in Morrison's shaping of *Song of Solomon*. Both of these texts reach their furthest insights, touch down on bedrock, through the episode of a self-transforming hunt. When Morrison rewrites Ike McCaslin's wilderness drama as Milkman's Shalimar ordeal, what accents have changed, what transformations been wrought, such that the first writer's frame serves as the second writer's vehicle? The result is neither borrowing nor theft, but something closer to alchemy, for Morrison rewrites Faulkner's moves only to make them appear her own.

Faulkner's text invests the wilderness—the enabling ground for Ike McCaslin's maturation—with sacred significance. Ike enters it (with Sam Fathers his guide) as though into a new world: "the two of them wrapped in the damp, warm, negro-rank quilt while the wilderness closed behind his entrance as it had opened momentarily to accept him" (*GDM*, 143). This space on the other side of the social is trackless, all-embracing, "drowsing, earless, almost lightless" (143): a second womb replacing that contaminated first one, and within which "at the age of ten he was witnessing his own birth" (143).[2]

If this unmarked new world functions to erase the burdensome alignments of a prior world, we might ask, in the Thoreauvian sense of "economy," what this urge to essentialize has discarded as dross. Mainly it provides an escape from women: the Southern hunting ritual was (and to some extent remains) integral to the gender politics of a culture committed to male honor. "Three things . . . drew sons and fathers together," writes Wyatt-Brown in his study *Southern Honor*. "They were a passion for the hunt, a loyalty to family honor, and a mistrust of women" (195). More broadly, escape to the wilderness allowed white males to escape the class- and race-inflected scene of ownership, production, and competition in the New South: routines understood in *Go Down, Moses* as sterile and contaminated. For two weeks a year the men escape the frustrating compromises, routines, and headaches endemic to the social, and they enter the territory of wilderness. At its finest, the dream underwriting this sacred space of wilderness is the desire to reaccess abandoned roots, that germ of animal nature lodged beneath cultural overlay, so that—face to face, cultural coding supposedly discarded—they encounter as fraternal beings the beasts that they hunt. The element of tonic self-risk is central to the experience.

Yet the coding of gender and race, the ordering of rules, are not actually left behind. Ash, the single black man included in the hunt (Sam appearing as Indian, not black, during this ritual), plays emphatically the dual role of woman and not-hunter. He does all the cooking, and we see repeatedly his incapacity to master the hunter's gun. More, the ritual itself is (like all ritual) rule-governed and mnemonic, designed to "remember" as natural recovery what is in fact cultural training. When the hunting party discovers the slaughtered colt and believes it is the work of Old Ben rather than Lion (the dog who will eventually hunt the bear to his death), Major de Spain reacts: "I'm disappointed in him. He has broken the rules" (*GDM*, 157). These are of course the rules of honor—of parry and thrust, of shared risk and scrupulous refusal to take advantage: a mutual respect between gentlemen. These rules descend from an aristocratic male model of reciprocal menace and courtesy, beyond the conceptual and behavioral possibilities of Faulknerian women and blacks. Not just anyone can participate in this November hunt. (Indeed, the fantasy of a ritual that would take one cleanly outside the social networks of gender, race, and class is itself raced and gendered: white and male.)

Morrison's first significant change is to launch Milkman's rite of passage not in Faulkner's exotic wilderness but in the oddly described—half biblical, half class-saturated—town of Shalimar, Virginia. Kids play in the lanes, the town coheres around a general store, women are present as well as men. Both obscurely sacred and overtly secular, the town of Shalimar will let Milkman discover something new, but—following his unintended insult of its men—it will also make him recognize something old: his unconscious assumption of class superiority:

> His manner, his clothes were reminders that they had no crops of their own and no land to speak of either. . . . He was telling them that they weren't men . . . that eyes that had seen big cities and the inside of airplanes were the measure. . . . He hadn't found them fit enough or good enough to want to know their names, and believed himself too good to tell them his. They looked at his skin and saw it was as black as theirs, but they knew he had the heart of the white men who came to pick them up in the trucks when they needed anonymous, faceless laborers. (SS, 266)

If Faulkner's wilderness is shaped to transcend class and gender demarcations, Morrison's Shalimar is shaped to make them erupt. Macon Dead Jr.'s entire middle-class project comes to its logical dead end here, as his urban, moneyed, deracinated son confronts the people he has sought to leave behind. This is the black underclass he is meant to be superior to, to collect rents from. Theirs is a form of unpropertied black masculinity he has never needed to respect.

The knife fight that erupts establishes Milkman as capable of growing beyond his coddled (milked) adolescence and holding his own with his own. His father's economic influence provides him no protection here. The fight alludes as well to the (usually urban) class violence only apparently transcended in this sleepy village: black men wounded in their proper (their capacity for self-ownership through possession of property), defending their maleness in the only terms left—with knives. A knife and a broken bottle fuel a battle hardly resembling Faulkner's chivalric bout of honorable moves. Rather, the violence here is seeded in the economics of racial injustice; and, with statistically impeccable logic, all its players are black. Surviving this encounter, Milkman starts to enter upon race, class, and gender territory he has not even known existed to support him: camaraderie with his impoverished male peers, common bonding with the piece of earth they share. In a scenario increasingly dedicated to shoring up the black male ego—to grounding it in a natural world whose material properties (flora and fauna, landscape and wildlife) are shimmeringly themselves rather than alienated commodities symbolizing only their owner's power of purchase—Morrison ushers Milkman into the wilderness surrounding Shalimar, where deeper recognitions yet await him.

Faulkner represents Ike's route toward his own deeper recognitions as tortuous and time-steeped, not the casual events of a single day. Ike had to wait until he was ten before he could participate in his first hunt, and even then he was relegated to a minor position, unable to sight the bear. But the bear has sighted him—a textual gesture toward animal agency utterly foreign to Morrison's narrative interests. The bear is not an object but a subject in *Go Down, Moses*, as is the dog, Lion, that eventually tracks him. Wildness itself is a priceless value in Faulkner's text, and he produces nonhuman beings that embody that wildness, that let us register its dimensions. There are wild humans in "The Bear" as well—none of them mainly white—and through Boon Hogganbeck and Sam Fathers we measure (in two different keys) the physical empowerment, the psychic centering, and the social impotence that accompany an exit from cultural convention. All these textual moves are nourished by Faulkner's white male sensibility, betokening his extraordinary effort to envisage human resource outside the limits—alternately tarnished and exhausted—of white and male.[3]

Taught by Sam, Ike makes his way, after many failed efforts, to the totem figure itself, the bear, in the heart of the wilderness. He does this through a classic repetition of biblical injunction—you must lose your life if you would find it—for only in relinquishing the social orientation of watch, gun, and compass does Ike succeed in penetrating to the center and finding/getting found by the bear. It is a purification ritual, embodying the desire to escape the codings of his cultural estate, to be reborn as a creature of innocent nature rather than one of guilt-saturated culture, to become not-Ike McCaslin. When it succeeds, when he has his love encounter with Old Ben, he is marked forever as natural witness rather than social agent. He does not shoot. Faulkner represents Ike's identity as hunter in such a way as rarely to focus attention on the kill itself. His epiphany involves more a seeing of relations than a doing of deeds (in either the natural or the social sphere), and it lasts— through the private perusal of the ledgers at age sixteen, the scene of repudiation with Cass in the commissary at age twenty-one, the later hunts in the Delta (including the final one in "Delta Autumn" when he is well past seventy)—his whole life long.

All this is heady stuff for Morrison to reconfigure, yet reconfigure it she does. Milkman is invited by the same black males he had earlier fought—no longer antagonists but comrades now—to trade in the knife for a gun and to join them in a nighttime hunt of more intricate, more rewarding violence. He joins reluctantly, his body wounded and his mind fatigued. They move too swiftly for him through an unfamiliar landscape that Morrison does not sacralize—this could be any woods—and eventually he drops to the ground, exhausted, thinking he has done nothing to deserve such crazy treatment. At this point the epiphany begins:

> Deserve. Now it seemed to him that he was always saying or thinking that he didn't deserve some bad luck, or some bad treatment from others. He'd told Guitar that he didn't "deserve" his family's dependence, hatred, or whatever. That he didn't even "deserve" to hear all the misery and mutual accusations his parents unloaded on him. Nor did he "deserve" Hagar's vengeance. But why shouldn't his parents tell him their personal problems? If not him, then who? And if a stranger could try to kill him, surely Hagar, who knew him and whom he'd thrown away like a wad of chewing gum after the flavor was gone—she had a right to try to kill him too. (276–77)

If Ike's experience is of rebirth into a nonsocial self (one with enough distance upon his race-haunted estate to say no to it), Milkman's is the reverse. He sees that since childhood he has refused the ever-present social dimensions of his own life, his creaturely involvement with family and lover, his unerasable tissue of indebtedness. As Milkman recognizes his radical interdependency, he begins to abandon his first line of defense, his insistently masculine selfhood: "his self—the cocoon that was 'personality'—gave way" (277). Once free of the boundaries of this protective cocoon, in which his urban male "personality" acted as a lens to filter out the bulk of his experience, Milkman begins to register as his own all those calls upon his subjectivity that he had earlier read as a sort of foreign static. He abandons his desire to be "himself alone"—which is a (middle-class) desire to be unraced, unaccountable to his race—and starts to become a citizen of his racial commonwealth.

More urgently, this escape from middle-class goals allows him to come into his own body, to take on full somatic presence. He is wholly there in time and space, he is his lungs and legs and racing thoughts, "not his money, his car, his father's reputation, his suit, or his shoes" (277). Freed of such mediating ideological baggage—of objects intrinsically useless, of value only as they symbolized his privilege within a schema of invidious ownership—freed of this and attentive for the first time to the immediate activity of his senses, Milkman begins to register this nocturnal forest scene as a system of given and received signals. "The men and the dogs were talking to each other. In distinctive voices they were saying distinctive, complicated things" (277–78). Ike, we remember, learns to read the behavior of the little fyce that takes on Old Ben within his already established code of masculine honor—events may be unanticipated in the wilderness but the code for evaluating them remains fixed—whereas Milkman is pressing toward a larger and hitherto unknown semiotic system: "No, it was not language; it was what there was before language" (278).

It would be hard to exaggerate the implications of this claim. Milkman is beginning to access a discourse—one that proposes a primitive bond between the human and the natural—that his lifelong alienation as an urban black male has kept him from hearing. If Morrison intends to reimmerse him in his social conditions, she must first, like Faulkner, widen his grasp on those conditions. For this, a crisis is required, in which he loses himself totally, his local and class-limited language simply ceasing to orient. Only then can he begin to "hear" what has been sounded all along in Shalimar, the children in the lane, singing the Solomon jingle. Ten years later, Morrison will activate the same linguistic insight in Sethe's capacity to "hear" a language spoken in a code she no longer knows, the African language of her Ma'am, and to decipher its meaning. In both cases a beleaguered self that has used up the resources provided by the familiar language of a current ideology manages to access the resources that only the language of another—and unexhausted—ideology can bring. This change of the language of self-access is a change of the vocabulary that inflects identity.

Milkman yields the cocoon, gets out of his own way by slipping clear of the vocabulary of "deserve" that has paved that way, and steps unprotected into a social space that he now recognizes to have been all along occupied by others as well. Ike McCaslin may achieve an exquisitely solitary relation to the natural world when he learns to decipher its inhuman sounds—Faulkner's Romantic heritage announces itself here: the privileged epiphanies of the (male) wanderer within the natural scene—but Milkman's moment of self-recovery hurls him into racial contradictions that have never ceased to stalk his life.[4] Ike's epiphany in the wilderness permits him to enjoy an all-but-life-long innocence (it will end in "Delta Autumn"), requiring only the repudiation of what the wilderness itself has shown him he doesn't truly want: his race-haunted property. By contrast, Morrison immerses Milkman not in a wilderness cleansed of social complication but rather in a forest where, finally, he can hear the buzz and murmur (the call and response) of an incessant sort of speech. Not Faulkner's wilderness where things finally get quiet, but Morrison's forest where you finally start to hear. More, Morrison gives

Milkman considerably less time—only a few moments—to "live without absorbing the sins of his kind, the foul air of his innocence" (*TB*, 243). As he dilates into this newfound self-knowledge, he thinks he "understood Guitar now. Really understood him" (*SS*, 278). But really to understand Guitar may require something more difficult if not impossible: ceasing to be Milkman. A second later Guitar's cord encircles his neck; the epiphany is over, its solitary privilege ended.

The supreme moment of vision in "The Bear" hardly ends on such a restrictive note. Rather, it unfolds to Ike McCaslin as a pageant in which love and death come together unforgettably:

> This time the bear didn't strike him [Lion] down. It caught the dog in both arms, almost loverlike, and they both went down. . . . He saw the bear . . . rising and rising as though it would never stop, stand erect again and begin to rake at Lion's belly with its forepaws. Then Boon was running. The boy saw the gleam of the blade in his hand and watched him leap among the hounds . . . and fling himself astride the bear . . . his legs locked around the bear's belly, his left arm under the bear's throat where Lion clung, and the glint of the knife as it rose and fell. . . . For an instant they almost resembled a piece of statuary: the clinging dog, the bear, the man astride its back, working and probing the buried blade. Then they went down.   (*GDM*, 177)

A dance of love and death, a man and a dog and a bear in intolerable embrace: Ike absorbs this spectacle as a life-reshaping image of unspeakable male bondings. Neither his relation to the wilderness nor the wilderness itself is ever the same again after this moment: its unsocializable beauty, maleness, and doom coalesce as a searing recognition he will never get beyond. Sam Fathers's death occurs at the same time; the hunt enters its autumnal phase. But Ike has had his Keatsean moment—"Forever wilt thou love and she be fair"—and five years later, at age twenty-one, he faces Cass in the commissary and relinquishes his contaminating social heritage with the peaceful words: "Sam Fathers set me free" (222). Free now to hunt at his leisure on land no one can own, "in the communal anonymity of brotherhood" (190), Ike inaugurates his own widowhood and early retirement, acceding to a quasi-biblical vision of American history in which his preordained role is to exit from the racial and gendered violence that fills that history of tainted ownership. He would secede from the rosters of both race and gender, a dream—as Ike's trusty rifle shows us—that appeals especially to troubled males.

Morrison, for her part, terminates Milkman's liberating epiphany only to enclose him in Guitar's cord and then to immerse him in another epiphany starkly different in its resonance. There is no question of escape from social time, there is question only of the right way of reentering it. Just able to fire his weapon into the air, Milkman sends Guitar scurrying from detection as the other hunters draw near. The hunt continues, they close in on the bobcat, the creature is put to death. All this unfolds swiftly, with no sense of hallowed moves as the hunters encounter and dispatch their prey. Following the kill, however, there occurs perhaps the most mesmerizing ritual sequence in all of Morrison's fiction. The big cat is opened and eviscerated, and Milkman glimpses therein the condition not only of his life but of his race:

> Omar sliced through the rope that bound the bobcat's feet. He and Calvin turned it over on its back. The legs fell open. Such thin delicate ankles.
> *"Everybody wants a black man's life."*
> Calvin held the forefeet open and up while Omar pierced the curling hair at the point where the sternum lay. Then he sliced all the way down to the genitals. His knife pointed upward for a cleaner, neater incision.
> *"Not his dead life; I mean his living life."*
> When he reached the genitals he cut them off, but left the scrotum intact.
> *"It's the condition our condition is in."*
> Omar cut around the legs and the neck. Then he pulled the hide off.
> *"What good is a man's life if he can't even choose what to die for?"*
> The transparent underskin tore like gossamer under his fingers.
> *"Everybody wants the life of a black man."*
> Now Small Boy knelt down and slit the flesh from the scrotum to the jaw.
> *"Fair is one more thing I've given up."*
> Luther came back and, while the others rested, carved out the rectal tube with the deft motions of a man coring an apple.
> *"I hope I never have to ask myself that question."*
> Luther reached into the paunch and lifted the entrails. He dug under the rib cage to the diaphragm and carefully cut around it until it was free.
> *"It is about love. What else but love? Can't I love what I criticize?"*
> Then he grabbed the windpipe and the gullet, eased them back, and severed them with one stroke of his little knife.
> *"It is about love. What else?"*
> They turned to Milkman. "You want the heart?" they asked him. Quickly, before any thought could paralyze him, Milkman plunged both hands into the rib cage. "Don't get the lungs, now. Get the heart."
> *"What else?"*
> He found it and pulled. The heart fell away from the chest as easily as yolk slips out of its shell.
> *"What else? What else? What else?"*   (281–82)

Eva Peace reaching all the way into Plum's rectum to clear him out, Ruth Dead reflecting on her son Milkman's body as part of her own body and known to her as her own is: those two scenes herald the unbearable somatic inventory taking place in this one. All three scenes hypnotically enact not a (masculine) getting free but a creaturely getting caught, being touched. If Ike's indelible memory focuses upon a noble dance of living energies met in death, Milkman sees the dance of death as an utter invasion of the lifeless creature. As I read it, this ritual dismembering signals, prophetically, the death suspended over his entire race—its inescapable caughtness—the condition a black man's condition is in. The castration that operates in Faulkner's most moving figures of failed descent (Benjy, Joe Christmas) recurs here, as Milkman witnesses his own potential evisceration. He glimpses what the Sutpen/McCaslin dream of dynasty, like every dream of dynasty, is designed to avert: self-annihilation, the imposture at the heart of the male pretense of autonomy, an intact will. More, this is not a private undoing, for Milkman registers the death of the big cat as figuratively inflicted upon a race and a gender. Guitar, escaped for a while, returns in these remembered words that Milkman earlier shrugged away in his fantasies of flight. How easy, this terrifying scene shows us, it is to be killed and dismembered. How unresistingly the organs exit from the sheath, the "cocoon" that once coordinated and empowered them.

To witness this scene of undoing, of course, is to escape rather than undergo it. Morrison's art is marshaled to give beauty to the recognition of a suspended self-undoing, indeed to postpone (and perhaps eventually avert) that undoing by recognizing its constant menace. It is the bobcat that dies, not Milkman. In what Faulkner might call "strophe and antistrophe"—and what black culture would see as "call and response"—the animal's passive yielding of its organs is silhouetted against the human's tonic thinking of terrible thoughts.[5] Like the killing of Old Ben, this scene yokes love and death, yet in such a way as to produce not a lyrical celebration but a bodily exposure and invasion that would be unbearable were they not rhythmically paced. The opened and entered carcass of the big cat radiates an ever-threatening death as the inescapable racial frame within which love raises its ultimate questions. As the suspended death frame cannot be transcended, the questions can only be asked, not answered. Black and black inextricably bonded in racial trust and class betrayal, a bonding necessarily formed and deformed by the larger interpenetration of black and white in each other's hearts and minds: what can order this disorder, turn this mutual caughtness into mutual possibility? What else but love? What else? This is the deepest question of racial torment in both writers, testifying to their awareness of how much else than love does enter this death-ridden scene, yet conveying their knowledge that only love, if somehow kept alive, could confront and transform the carnage. They know that nothing else will.

Milkman is marked by this final vision, inscribed inexpungeably in the race, class, and gender turmoil to which Guitar has devoted his life and his death. The final reckoning with the fate that Guitar carries is unavoidable; no exit exists. "The condition our condition is in" emerges into view as a bedrock belying all the attempted flights that punctuate this text. Far from Faulkner's bittersweet portrayal of Ike's epiphany in the wilderness as a relinquishment both precious and unworkable, Morrison lodges her protagonist in his unshakable conditions—conditions that are beyond accommodating. There is simply no place she can take Milkman after such recognitions: his urban space is named Guitar and it remains blighted, however eloquently his rural epiphany has prepared him for return. Morrison ends *Song of Solomon* with Milkman literally in midair, less centered than halved, and hurling toward his killing twin.[6] If you would ride the air, you must first surrender to it: a descent in eloquent contrast to its Faulknerian counterpart, with no predictable landing in sight. In this diasporic novel of longing rather than arrival, the question of love remains terrifyingly open.

6

Miscegenation and Might-Have-Been
Absalom, Absalom! and *Jazz*

I approach this second pair of texts locally at first, as in the last chapter, by opening up the implications of a specific encounter and reshaping. There is a moment in *Jazz* where we virtually hear Faulkner's voice — the moment when an astonished Golden Gray learns of his departed black father and meditates upon the damage this lifelong paternal absence has inflicted upon him. Before citing the passage, I want to develop the *Absalom* context in sufficient detail to establish what it might mean to "hear Faulkner's voice."[1] Then it can become clear in what ways the racial dynamics of Morrison's rewriting differ from those of the Faulknerian narrative. After attending to this difference, we can then pursue some larger comparisons. For *Jazz* — which hardly resembles Morrison's other novels, let alone anyone else's — uncannily reprises several of *Absalom*'s most salient motifs.

Golden Gray recalls Charles Bon: abandoned sons in search of their paternal origins. In *Absalom*, the notion of absconded paternity takes on a mythic cast, Bon imagining his mother as "swooping down at those almost calculable moments out of some obscure ancient general affronting and outraging which the actual living articulate meat had not even suffered but merely inherited; all boy flesh that walked and breathed stemming from that one ambiguous eluded dark fatherhead" (AA, 246–47) — a fatherhead Bon later aligns with "the old infernal immortal male principle of all unbridled terror and darkness" (258). In this patriarchal schema, the father is essence, the mother accident.[2] The son's desire to recover his progenitor virtually shapes the plot of *Absalom, Absalom!*, as Shreve and Quentin spend page after page speculating on Bon's wounded psyche and ardent search.[3] The Bon they envisage is apparently in love with Judith, more credibly in love with Henry, but ultimately in love with his father, Sutpen. Looking at Henry's face, Bon thinks: *"There, just behind a little, obscured a little by that alien blood whose admixing was necessary in order that he exist is the face of the man who shaped us both . . . there . . . I shall penetrate and strip that alien leavening from it and look not on my brother's face . . . but my father's, out of the shadow of whose absence my spirit's posthumeity has never escaped"* (261–62).

An absent father, a posthumous son—this fatal equation commands Bon's quest, allows him to see Judith and Henry both as mere deviation from the patriarchal source, his mother, Eulalia, as mere contamination of it. The swooning, Latinate vocabulary fetishizes that "eluded dark fatherhead" as a phallic origin of immeasurable power, unamenable to domestic schemas of legitimacy and fidelity. As with all fetishes, the exaggerated plenitude of the prized object conceals the fetishizer's fear of his own insufficiency. Sonship registers here as a gaping wound in being itself, one that only the father's recognition can cure. Sutpen's force is imagined as a founding force, and Bon seeks only the merest nod of acknowledgment: "He would just have to write 'I am your father. Burn this' and I would do it. Or if not that, a sheet a scrap of paper with the one word 'Charles' in his hand, and I would know what he meant and he would not even have to ask me to burn it. Or a lock of his hair or a paring from his finger nail and I would know them because I believe now that I have known what his hair and his finger nails would look like all my life" (269). A lock of hair, a paring from a nail: these are the materials of a narrative of unrequited love.

Absalom diagnoses the reasons why Sutpen cannot requite his son's love in such a way as starkly to illuminate the racial injustice of antebellum Southern culture. In this pre-segregation time of slavery, whites live closer to blacks, and in these intimate conditions they abuse them more, but white fathers within a patriarchal economy neither marry the black women they impregnate nor permit their offspring to inherit. The text brilliantly explores the inhumanity of this repudiation, but it never doubts the motive force shaping it. It never escapes its own patriarchal alignment in such a way as not just to diagnose the father's damaging power, but actually to rethink his emotional and conceptual primacy. The drama that unfolds therefore takes on its salient traits: authority as white and male and paternal, the crime as the father's dishonorable refusal to acknowledge his own miscegenated offspring, the wound as the black son's incurable longing to be recognized—followed by a gathering outrage that, in erupting, brings down the dynasty.

Morrison employs this trajectory in order to revise it. First, the father is dethroned, appearing here initially in the guise of the startled white figure who learns that his daughter has been impregnated by a black man: "Realizing the terrible thing that had happened to his daughter made him sweat, for there were seven mulatto children on his land" (*J*, 141). He sweats because he perceives obscurely a poetic justice swelling in his daughter's womb, and he disowns her. (The fundamental act of *Absalom*—the father's miscegenous begetting that Faulkner shrouds until the final pages and thereby charges with all but intolerable implication—is here deflated by being casually narrated at the beginning. It hardly embodies "an immortal male principle" dictating fatally everything that follows.) Vera Louise moves to Baltimore with her house servant True Belle, and together they dote upon the beautiful fatherless boy they call Golden Gray. At age eighteen, this coddled young man learns from his mother that his father is black.

Morrison's novelistic mode for expressing racial astonishment here shifts briefly from one of her literary resources—Faulkner—to another resource: Twain. Golden Gray, she writes, "had always thought there was only one kind [of nigger]—True Belle's kind. Black and nothing. Like Henry LesTroy. Like the filthy woman [Wild] snoring on the cot. But there was another kind—like himself" (149). This could be Twain's Tom Driscoll learning (to his unappeasable amazement) from his mother, Roxy, that it is he, not Chambers, who is the "nigger." The new racial identity registers as pure disaster. But the writer being rewritten in this scene of revealed miscegenation is only for a moment Twain. Morrison's deeper frame, as the following passage announces, is Faulknerian:

> Only now, he thought, now that I know that I have a father, do I feel his absence: the place where he should have been and was not. Before I thought everybody was one-armed, like me. Now I feel the surgery. The crunch of bone when it is sundered, the sliced flesh and the tubes of blood cut through, shocking the bloodrun and disturbing the nerves. They dangle and writhe. Singing pain. Waking me with the sound of itself, thrumming when I sleep so deeply it strangles my dreams away. There is nothing for it but to go away from where he is not to where he used to be and might be still. Let the dangle and the writhe see what is missing; let the pain sing to the dirt where he stepped in the place where he used to be and might be still. I am not going to be healed, or to find the arm that was removed from me. I am going to freshen the pain, point it, so we both know what it is for. . . . What do I care what the color of his skin is, or his contact with my

mother? When I see him, or what is left of him, I will tell him all about the missing part of me and listen for his crying shame. I will exchange then; let him have mine and take his as my own and we will both be free, arm-tangled and whole.   (158–59)

If you hear Charles Bon in this passage, you are in a position to know what "Faulkner's voice" means. It means (not always, of course, but recurrently) a certain kind of rhetoric: a highly wrought, poetic discourse of interiority, circulating about the motifs of pain inflicted and gravely registered, of a wound culturally mandated and nobly endured within, and of an inexpressible longing that is beyond articulation. In this representative instance, the source of the wound is the absent father, the locus is the unintact son, the motive is race. It is all saturated in the priorities of honor and self-respect, and it comes together as a sort of patriarchal male romance. Twain gives Morrison a form for writing the corrosive irony of racism, but only Faulkner can bequeath to her the story of racial turmoil as the heartbreaking poetry of filial outrage. Morrison makes the father black, however, and that changes everything. Faulkner's wounded son looking for the authority of the white origin becomes Morrison's wounded son missing the authority of the black origin. In place of Bon's eroticized paternal investment—which drains his relationships with others of substance, which leads (when balked) to suicidal immolation—Golden Gray's commitment to the father is schizoid: hatred of the racial contamination, longing for the paternal blessing. In other words, paternity without patriarchy.

Jazz sets up this conflict without resolving it, giving us nothing more between father and son than the following:

"Look here [says the father]. What you want? I mean, now; what you want now? Want to stay here? You welcome. Want to chastize me? Throw it out your mind. I won't take a contrary word. . . . If she told you I was your daddy, then she told you more than she told me. Get a hold of yourself. A son ain't what a woman say. A son is what a man do. You want to act like you mine, then do it, else get the devil out my house!"

Golden Gray groans that, if revealed, he might have grown up a slave. His father replies that he might have been a "free nigger," to which he responds: "I don't want to be a free nigger; I want to be a free man." At this the father lets him have it straight:

"Don't we all. Look. Be what you want—white or black. Choose. But if you choose black, you got to act black, meaning draw your manhood up— quicklike, and don't bring me no whiteboy sass."   (172–73)

In the patriarchal poetics of *Absalom*, black is an uninhabitable subject position for a mulatto son—a proposition borne out by three generations of Bons.
The first and the second are openly suicidal when confronting the insult
embodied in their black blood, the third (Jim Bond) is mentally defective.
Faulkner imagines the survival of this descent with grim conviction—they
will be still there (however bleached out) when all others have succumbed—
but he can grant them no significance other than their humiliation of the
dynastic pretensions of the progenitor. Morrison's black father not only inhab-
its viable subjective space, but he puts to his son a clean choice. Freedom—
that will-o'-the-wisp that draws Faulkner's Sutpen to his fatal design—emerges
here as a chimera that all men, black and white, long for. Both of these racial
paths permit its pursuit (this father—Hunter's Hunter—appears no more and
no less free than anyone else). If Golden Gray is to pursue it as a black man,
however, it is time to cut out the "whiteboy sass." Listening to the "singing
pain" of Faulkner's Bon, Morrison seems to have heard in such outraged innocence a certain note, finally, of adolescent complaint. Get on with it, this
father says to his son, we all make our way radically impeded. Absorbing the
sins of their kind, realizing that everyone wants a piece of their life and that
they are already indebted beyond repaying, black youths become men—
when they do become men—by outgrowing the Faulknerian syndrome of
outraged innocence.

The foregoing comparison between *Absalom, Absalom!* and *Jazz* has been as
specific as the following one is diffuse. Both texts, I want to argue, announce
their authors' voices as henceforth unmistakable rhetorical performances.
Absalom is the purest instance of what we retrospectively recognize as
Faulknerian vocabulary and syntax, and *Jazz* is the novel in which we seem
most clearly to hear Morrison speaking. In each case, a writer is reaccenting
a larger culture's expressive resources with unheralded power. *Absalom* tells
us Faulkner is Southern white as openly as *Jazz* tells us Morrison is urban
black. To believe that we now hear the writer's own voice is therefore to say
that we now align with greater confidence the writer's ways of saying "I" with
the larger culture's forms for saying "We." (In *Beloved* Morrison had little use
for this insistent communal voice. As she said in a televison interview, her
need was to speak as quietly—almost anonymously—as possible, so that the
drama in the materials themselves could compel the reader's attention. In
related manner, no reader of early Faulkner has the sense of a governing
rhetorical strategy deriving from a tradition of Southern oratory.) In the pages

that follow I pursue—with an eye toward differences attributable to racial positioning—both texts' extensive relation to their larger culture's norms.

Here is Mr. Compson painting the portrait ostensibly of Henry in New Orleans but actually of the larger culture that makes Henry who he is:

> I can imagine Henry in New Orleans, who had not yet even been to Memphis, whose entire worldly experience consisted of sojourns at other houses, plantations, almost interchangeable with his own . . . the same hunting and cockfighting . . . the same square dancing with identical and also interchangeable provincial virgins, to music exactly like that at home, the same champagne . . . I can imagine him, with his puritan heritage . . . in that city foreign and paradoxical, with its atmosphere at once fatal and languorous, at once feminine and steel-hard—this grim humorless yokel out of a granite heritage where even the houses, let alone clothing and conduct, are built in the image of a jealous and sadistic Jehovah, put suddenly down in a place whose denizens had created their All-Powerful and His supporting hierarchy-chorus . . . in the image of their houses and personal ornaments and voluptuous lives.   (AA, 89–90)

This portrait registers a finished take upon antebellum Southern culture. Henry's mind-set is puritanical, sexually naive, violently hard-edged yet body-shy, and locked inalterably in racial categories. He will move, in the crisis, as his culture has instructed him; he is his culture's child. *Absalom* delights in set pieces like the above, culturally laden friezes (rural Mississippi versus New Orleans) in which the aggregate tropes that articulate a society's norms are assembled, deployed, and opposed.[4] Take the tragic octoroon, for example: Faulkner's attention to her clothes (elegant), her habits (picturesque), her setting (New Orleans), her painter (Beardsley)—in a word, her aura—puts before us less a unique figure than a set of cultural alignments. To fall afoul of these alignments (to encounter those of an opposing culture that is equally finished, inalterable) is to enter that state of vertigo—of outrage caused by the failure of one's cultural assumptions—that occasions every male crisis (Sutpen's, Henry's, Bon's, Bon's son's) of this text and functions virtually as Faulkner's signature.

So deeply is this novel attentive to cultural texture and assumptions that not only its characters but even its narrators tend to lose their vocal uniqueness. We access them all as both individuals and appendages to a larger social drama whose unfolding is unstoppable and ultimately impersonal. After, for example, Shreve says, "No, you wait. Let me play a while now," and he takes over the narrative of Sutpen and Wash Jones for a half page, we next read that "there was no harm intended by Shreve and no harm taken, since Quentin did not even stop. He did not even falter, taking Shreve up in stride without comma or colon or paragraph: '—no reserve to risk a spotting shot with now so he [Sutpen] started this one [pursuit of Wash's granddaughter] like you start a rabbit out of a brier patch' " (231–32). But Quentin doesn't take up Shreve inasmuch as Shreve hadn't been talking about Sutpen's courtship, he had been talking about Sutpen and Wash. It was Mr. Compson (speaking "through" Quentin) who had a page earlier characterized Sutpen's failed courtship with Rosa as *"just a spotting shot with a light charge"* (231).[5] My point is neither that Faulkner is sloppy nor that the reader fails to spot an error in transmission. Rather, the error is in effect no error, for we read it as we are meant to: as a single epic narrative told in more or less the same voice no matter who speaks, with its own irresistible impetus, delivering a culture's story — not simply an individual's.

The novel thus lavishes upon its imagined alternatives to the culture's irreversible patriarchal norms the tenderness that one musters for the impossible. "A might-have-been which is more true than truth" (118), Rosa insists when her own aspirations collapse: more true, but cut off from the real. *Absalom's* dreams of love, of escape from Thomas Sutpen's undoing of them all — its desire to accede to a realm of race and gender acknowledgment — all this can be figured only in the form of peripheral designs that collapse before the central patriarchal design of the antebellum South. Inevitability is this novel's abiding theme, an inevitability that even seventy years later, in 1935 when Faulkner is writing *Absalom*, seems beyond revision. From Sutpen and Eulalia, through Bon and the octoroon, through his son and the "coal black and ape-like woman" (170): miscegenation breeds further miscegenation, leaving at the end a howling Jim Bond bleached out unrecognizably but black nevertheless, incarnating for Quentin — in Bond's body, his mind, and his genealogy — the epitaph of a culture. Quentin may or may not manage not to hate that culture (the text ends in perfect suspense), but the one thing he cannot do is change its racial politics.

Jazz accesses its urban 1920s culture with similar attention to the inertial power of communal norms. "Alice Manfred had worked hard," Morrison writes, "to privatize her niece, but she was no match for a City seeping music that begged and challenged each and every day. 'Come,' it said. 'Come and do wrong' " (67). Doing wrong is what you do in this city when you succumb to its shaping force, and Dorcas (the niece) remains open to the call of that music, unprivatizable just as *Absalom's* characters are unprivatized, steeped in a public atmosphere of calls and responses. When Violet does her wrong, attacking the dead body of Dorcas with her knife, in front of a host of Dorcas's horrified friends and family gathered together for the funeral, Morrison describes the scene as follows:

> It [the knife] bounced off, making a little dent under her earlobe, like a fold in the skin that was hardly a disfigurement at all. She could have left it at that . . . but . . . Violet, unsatisfied, fought with the hard-handed usher boys and was time enough for them, almost. They had to forget right away that this was a fifty-year-old woman in a fur-collared coat and a hat pulled down so far over her right eye it was a wonder she saw the door to the church not to speak of the right place to aim her knife. They had to abandon the teachings they had had all their lives about the respect due their elders. Lessons learned from the old folks whose milky-light eyes watched everything they did, commented on it, and told each other what it was. Lessons they had learned from the younger old folks (like her) who could be their auntie, their grandmother . . . [and who] could stop them cold with a word, with a 'Cut that mess out!' shouted from any window, doorway or street curb in a two-block radius. And they would cut it out, or take it downstairs behind the trunks, or off in a neglected park, or better still, in the shadow of the El where no lights lit what these women did not allow, don't care whose child it was. But they did it nevertheless. Forgot the lessons of a lifetime, and concentrated on the wide, shining blade, because who knew? Maybe she had more than one cutting in mind. Or maybe they could see themselves hang-dog at the dinner table trying to explain to these same women or even, Jesus! the men, the father and uncles, and grown cousins, friends and neighbors, why they had just stood there like streetlights and let this woman in a fur-collared coat make fools of them and ruin the honorable job they had worn white gloves for. They had to wrestle her to the floor before she let go.   (J, 91–92)

I have quoted at length to give the flavor of this unhurried narrative. The personal moment of violence is absorbed within a network of communal norms, the text "unprivatizing" Violet and her act as it delivers the multifaceted cultural resonance of the event. Violet's deed becomes neighborhood story—we gather how it will be told in larger groups later that day and in time to come—and Violet's person is equally extended into familial networks. She could be the boys' auntie or grandmother, the one who prevents such outbreaks rather than causes them. When she is wrestled to the ground, therefore, we see something richer than a local act: we see a communal event. The local gesture has taken on the other meanings it culturally possesses, and the actors are glimpsed within the invisible weave of expectations and consequences shaping their moves (how difficult it is for the boys to go against one kind of training, yet how—if they don't—they will have gone against another and will have infuriated their disbelieving menfolk). We get as well the larger backdrop of doings and misdoings, the El where these things take place most satisfactorily. We hear it all, finally, within a wry and unshockable vernacular voice far removed from Faulknerian outrage: "don't care whose child it was . . . Jesus!" The novel builds, in other words, toward an open-eyed accommodation of aberration as gradually as *Absalom* builds toward a tragic repudiation of the nonnormative. In *Jazz*, there is no place the subject could be situated that is outside the normative reach of this capacious black cultural weave.

The voice that carries such capaciousness is new in Morrison, and its distinction as a voice overpowers any particular thing it may say. "What was meant came from the drums" (53), Morrison writes of the black protest parade in 1917, in which no written banner or headline could convey, as the drums convey, the emotional core of black pride and a race's refusal to be cowed. So with *Jazz*; the stunning thing is the voice itself, the unceasing music of the drums framing and dwarfing all specific characters' doings and sayings.[6] Like *Absalom*, this text's supreme insistence is rhetorical rather than predicative, a gesture rather than a declaration. But whereas *Absalom*'s gorgeous rhetorical periods insist upon the monumentality of the culture that has been lost (however well lost), *Jazz*'s fluid vernacular unfoldings—alternately nonchalant and moving, street-smart and lyrical—signal loss as an unbearable phenomenon that yet occurs every day:

> "We born around the same time, me and you," said Violet [to Alice]. "We women, me and you. Tell me something real. Don't just say I'm grown and ought to know. I don't. I'm fifty and I don't know nothing. What about it? Do I stay with him? I want to, I think. I want . . . well, I didn't always . . . now I want. I want some fat in this life."
>
> "Wake up. Fat or lean, you got just one. This is it."
>
> "You don't know either, do you?"
>
> "I know enough to know how to behave."
>
> "Is that it? Is that all it is?"
>
> "Is that all what is?"
>
> "Oh shoot! Where the grown people? Is it us?"
>
> "Oh, Mama." Alice Manfred blurted it out and then covered her mouth.
>
> Violet had the same thought: Mama. Mama? Is this where you got to and couldn't do it no more? The place of shade without trees where you know you are not and never again will be loved by anybody who can choose to do it? Where everything is over but the talking?   (110)

Perhaps the hunger this novel best expresses is old age's longing for the emotional intensity of youth. Not Faulkner's postmenopausal dignity, but an awareness—even keener in age—that life promises more "fat" than is ever made good on, that the shape a life ends by taking is radically inadequate to the heart's ceaseless demands. "Mama," both these older women think, "Mama" as an involuntary call upon the original figure of plenitude who might help them accept (or at least understand) this permanent gap between desire's reach and reality's yield. *Jazz* aches with this sense of yearnings unacted: not in the Faulknerian register of might-have-beens that come crashing down against the inalterable racial and gender protocols of the South, but rather in the form of open-ended vignettes that delineate the multiple scenarios of desire itself. Here is Violet wondering what Dorcas really saw, what they all truly felt, within the orphanhood and incompleteness, the game of substitutions, that shadowed their lives:

> Could she have looked at him and seen that [i.e., Joe Trace not as a fifty-year-old but as the radiant young man Violet had first seen in the field]? . . . That and other things, things I should have known and didn't? . . . What did she see, young girl like that, barely out of high school? . . . And also what did he? A young me with high-yellow skin instead of black? A young me with long wavy hair instead of short? . . . A me he was loving in Virginia because that girl Dorcas wasn't around there anywhere. Was that it? . . . Who was he thinking of when he ran in the dark to meet me in the cane field? Somebody golden, like my own golden boy, who I never saw but who tore up my girl-hood as surely as if we'd been the best of lovers? . . . Is that what happened? Standing in the cane, he was trying to catch a girl he was yet to see, but his heart knew all about, and me, holding on to him but wishing he was the golden boy I never saw either. Which means from the very beginning I was a substitute and so was he.   (97)

When Faulkner represents Rosa Coldfield in the field of balked desire, he produces a discourse of vicarious longings and substitute fulfillments, concluding in frustration and anger. We follow her all the way to her incandescent death in the house that embodies that implacable patriarchal culture she could never accommodate. Morrison, by contrast, produces Violet's life as flaring into these extraordinary recognitions, then subsiding into domestic rituals that make for survival. The novel enters and exits from her with equal ease, moving from subject to subject, time period to time period, shaping its vignettes as provocative echoes of each other, none of them finished. "I have to alter things," Morrison writes (161), and the altering is accomplished most through *Jazz*'s form, not its story line. Thus Joe Trace's fruitless search for his mother—"All she had to do was give him a sign, her hand thrust through the leaves, the white flowers, would be enough to say that she knew him to be the one, the son she had fourteen years ago" (38)—is textually pressed against his finding, forty years later, a girl named Dorcas who had been orphaned even worse than he:

> Maybe her nothing was worse since she knew her mother, and had even been slapped in the face by her for some sass she could not remember. . . . And of all the slaps she got, that one was the one she remembered best because it was the last. She leaned out the window of her best girlfriend's house because the shouts were not part of what she was dreaming. They were outside her head, across the street. Like the running. Everybody running. For water? Buckets? The fire engine, polished and poised in another part of town? There was no getting in that house where her clothespin dolls lay in a row. . . . But she tried anyway to get them. Barefoot, in the dress she had slept in, she ran to get them, and yelled to her mother that the box of dolls, the box of dolls was up there on the dresser can we get them? Mama?
>
> (38)

Orphans meeting though thirty-five years apart, he mothers this girl, fathers her, loves her as the Violet he has lost, as the woman for whom Violet was the substitute. The roles blend into each other, all of them related under the sign of loss represented by the missing Mama. "I have to alter things": Morrison intervenes unpredictably throughout this musical text, yoking vignettes suggestively, incompletely, letting us glimpse the penumbra of desire and possibility that hovers unacted on the edge of the impoverished real. She mothers her text's orphaned options, intimating a wider schema of communal implication and potential. Thus even Faulkner's "coal black and ape-like woman"—a mere humiliating cipher in *Absalom*'s patriarchal drama of miscegenated descent—beckons to her in *Jazz* as a throwaway she can maternally recuperate.[7] Reconceived, this black woman becomes Joe Trace's mother, Wild, resonating with the same identity-confirming importance that Faulkner's Bon sought from the white father: "Give me a sign then [Joe Trace begs her]. . . . Let me see your hand . . . and I'll go; I promise" (178). In her very refusal to answer, Wild seems to figure forth the priceless African mother that Morrison's twentieth-century orphans have lost, the Mama they therefore half remember, half invent in their damaged and indestructible lives.

7

The Circulation of Social Energy
Race, Gender, and Value in *Light in August* and *Beloved*

The previous chapters of part 3 have each staged a local encounter between a pair of texts. This one likewise focuses on a single pair of texts, but the frame of reference widens to address explicitly the larger questions raised in my introduction. What roles do race and gender play in the shaping (and, secondarily, the receiving) of fiction? Insofar as they do play a role, what kinds of value, in today's ideologically charged climate, can literary practice possess? What light does the practice of the white male Faulkner and the black female Morrison shed upon their cultures' ways of understanding self and other?[1]

I begin with the issue of artistic form, the central tenet in traditional Western paradigms of aesthetic value, as well as a tenet that both writers share. ("The language, only the language," Morrison claimed, is what makes literature "good" [*TM*, 373]. Faulkner's rapture at having written, in *The Sound and the Fury*, "something to which the shabby term of Art not only can, but must, be applied" [*SF*, 226] is no less telling.) To this insistence on form I would add, however cautiously, the criterion of content. The topics engaged by the writer's ordered language matter as well. "The language" tells most when it serves as the medium in which the culture's most disturbing questions get formally raised in the most provocative ways. As my chapter title indicates, to propose aesthetic value as a function of both form and content involves a modest attempt to revise traditional Western notions of the literary itself: seeing it as less a domain of disinterested form than one of successfully represented social energies in conflict. In seeking to demonstrate this proposition, I must depart from Faulkner and Morrison in order to rehearse briefly the centrality of form in Western aesthetic norms since the

Enlightenment, as a background for discussing challenges recently mounted against those norms. (My commentary becomes, for the next several pages, unavoidably dense, as it characterizes the aesthetic norms that I am seeking to revise. The specific reading of Faulkner's and Morrison's texts resumes thereafter.) The source figure in this discussion—the thinker whose arguments most current aesthetics seeks directly or indirectly to revise—is the eighteenth-century German philosopher Immanuel Kant.[2]

Kant's *Critique of Judgment* assumes throughout that art is not cognitive. In thus dismissing the Aristotelian tradition of mimesis—of art as a sort of mirror of the social that carries invaluable knowledge—Kant opens the way for a formalist definition of art as a nonreferential activity divorced from issues of correspondence with the outer world. Kant's revolutionary epistemology had already decreed an unbridgeable gap between things as they are in themselves and things as they appear to the human mind. The mind unavoidably imposes as it accesses, and the lawfulness of its findings reveals the lawfulness of the mind (which Kant will universalize) rather than anything reliable about the objects themselves. If the work of art is to have value, that value must be located subjectively rather than objectively: as a function of the work's relation to its audience rather than of the work's grasp upon its object. Only the work that fully achieves this relation to its audience validates its claim to be *aesthetic*.

How does a work of art justify its aesthetic claim? The answer, Kant proposed, is through a form so achieved that its appeal is universal. The work of art embodies a perfected formal purpose—all of its parts interrelated so as to compose that purpose—without being grounded in any cognitive purpose. Purposefulness without purpose (Kant's famous phrase) occurs at the level of form. This formal purpose is said to be achieved—the work attains its beauty and value—when the work is universally accessible and uncontaminated by any deforming personal interest. "Every one has to admit that if a judgment about beauty is mingled with the least interest," Kant writes, "then it is very partial and not a pure judgment of taste" (46). Only when "someone likes something and is conscious that he himself does so without any interest" can he be "justified in requiring a similar liking from everyone" (54).

The territory of Kantian aesthetics takes shape as an exquisitely organized realm detached from any cognitive grasp upon the world, freed from any deforming appetite or interest on the part of either creator or audience. The work of art's coherence is both universal and unique unto itself. Unlike the Kantian realm of pure reason, in which particulars are brought under universal laws, and unlike the Kantian realm of practical reason, in which particulars are subordinated to universal maxims, the Kantian realm of aesthetics gives us (as Terry Eagleton puts it in *The Ideology of the Aesthetic*), "the curious sense of a lawful totality indissociable from our intuition of the immediate form of the thing" (85). The recognition propelled by this sense of "lawful totality" is at the heart of aesthetic experience, yet what the enchanted respondent recognizes involves no true relation to the world outside. Rather, through the mastery of disinterested form, the respondent grasps in the work of art an ideal self-recognition. The subjective experience that the work of art makes possible gives us back ourselves with a fullness that our daily commerce with the appetitive outer world perpetually keeps from our grasp. No wonder the work of art seems precious.

This preciousness comes at a high price. First, the sense of self being reflected back—the seemingly intuitive fit between the reader's imaginative capacity and the subjective unfoldings deployed in the work—is itself uncritical. Thanks to the work's formal framing, we imagine while engaging it our own lived and apparently unmediated relation to its materials. This is far from any critical and cognitive deepening—or questioning—of our relation to our world. Second, aesthetic form is mystified into an all-transforming capacity. Kantian aesthetics posits form as a force that masters its materials, reinscribing them into a schema in which nothing impinges upon anything else—each element enjoying exactly its proper space, interrelated perfectly with every other element. Appetite and interest and prior referentiality have been removed from this scene.[3] There is none of the exploitation, deformation, and coercion that characterize secular (and increasingly industrial) life outside the aesthetic frame. The mastery thereby obtained lifts us into a privileged space of contemplation, one in which we feel our own interiority to be attuned to the rhythms of the work's formal resolution.

The artist who would achieve such formal balance (who would, in generating a work of perfected identity, enable the respondent's recognition of his or her own latent identity) takes on a formidable task. The task involves nothing less than a purification of all the materials that go into the work of art, such that the contaminating network of implication—within which the materials are necessarily lodged—is gradually erased by the artist's formal labors, permitting the work to assume an achieved identity wrought (only and entirely) by its aesthetic form. Cleansed of reference, the materials become innocent again, submitting to a strange lobotomy in which their previous ideological charge dissolves under the artist's transforming purpose. This is a scenario, I have argued at length elsewhere, in which achieved individuality—that of the creator, that of the work, that of the respondent during aesthetic engagement with the work—is being sacralized.[4] Only in such a way can we be led to forget the following capital fact: that the materials out of which creator, work, and audience summon forth their distinctive identity are themselves steeped inexpungeably in larger social networks. Behind the sacralized scenario of sublime detachment, there is the secular reality of unceasing attachment—biases affected by alignments of race, gender, class, and other social demarcations—within whose jostling and pressure the creative and responsive acts take place if they are to take place at all. *Ex nihil nihil fiat.* Yet, from Kant through the dominant Western critics of art of the next century and a half, the nonaesthetic context that enables the text has been more or less treated as that which the formal splendor of the aesthetic itself transcends.

For the past three decades this model of formal transcendence—however it may continue to shape the general public's understanding of masterpieces—has become deeply suspect within the academy itself. The Kantian claim that the work of art displays purposefulness without purpose reached its apogee in the New Criticism of midcentury and has been in decline ever since. Who will argue in 1996 that, although the rhetorician deceives his neighbor and the sentimentalist himself, "art is but a vision of reality"?

Yeats did argue it, famously, drawing on the Kantian aesthetic as a realm of achieved disinterest, a notion he (along with Joyce and Eliot) developed by way of Schopenhauer. For it was Schopenhauer who wrote that "genius is the power of leaving one's own interest, wishes, and aims entirely out of sight, thus of entirely renouncing one's own personality for a time, so as to remain *pure knowing subject*, clear vision of the world" (108). Yeats's term—"a vision of reality"—may seem to reintroduce the cognitive factor that Kant had relinquished, and certainly Schopenhauer's revision of Kant insists upon art as the privileged activity of a "knowing" subject. But the twentieth-century history of this aesthetic (from Yeats through Cleanth Brooks) has emphasized the disinterestedness of art's universal truths, not the work's capacity to provide accurate social testimony.

How compelling these notions were to my generation in graduate school, drunk on modernism and delighted to be confirmed that the art we loved was also untainted by bias. Today, drawing on any number of cultural theorists who argue that we access the social in necessarily angled and group-interested ways, we can no longer accept the innocence of that term—"a vision of reality." What goes in its place?

Any credible answer must make room for bias by taking into account the ideological alignments that inhere in the construction of subjectivity itself. What we see—artist or critic—is inseparable from what we miss. All perception is perspectival, socially angled, and Bakhtin (among others) has shown us the astonishing clash of interested perspectives clamoring for attention in fiction. If utterance is inherently ideological—announcing group-inflected (though not therefore predictable) alignments, rather than a purely personal or disinterested take upon the real—then fiction delights in the encounter of ideological positions. Fleshed out in the coil and recoil of human dramas, this encounter rehearses the circulation, precisely, of a social energy propelled by race, gender, and other primary social factors. The "reality" that art would give "vision" to is itself fissured, lived differently by different groups (by different individuals within those groups), and the art that would give vision to it is projected differentially, received differentially: all of this ideological to the hilt.

Deconstruction emerged in the 1970s to argue that language is never disinterestedly available to the artist to shape magisterially as his or her own, it is always someone's—some group's—coming to the writer with certain cultural imprints already wrought into its usages. To unmasterable language we may add the equally unmasterable pressures of race and gender upon the act of expression. We access the world not as universal subjects but as racial and gendered persons. Therefore we write, a current argument goes, from within ideological perspectives proposed by these larger alignments, not in mastery of them. As Morrison herself puts it, "in a wholly racialized society, there is no escape from racially inflected language" (*PD*, 12–13). We write as men and women, as whites and blacks: ideologically, differentially, not disinterestedly. How, given the biases that now seem to affect literary form, can we speak of aesthetic value here?

The claim for the aesthetic as a realm of universal and disinterested value, however vulnerable to this critique, has long served to justify the canonical status of a writer's work. Not surprisingly, application of the claim (the business of canonizing) has rarely been innocent of "political" dimensions. Indeed, every element connected with the work—its linguistic medium, its social content, the subjectivity of both its producer and its audience—retains cultural inscription, notwithstanding the aesthetic claim of rarefaction and removal. As Jane Tompkins has argued, the defensive question raised against many nineteenth-century women writers' noncanonical texts—"but is it any good?"—serves often to conceal a range of nonformal reasons for continuing to exclude those texts from the canon.[5] Tompkins's remark takes me, then, to my above-mentioned questions. What roles do race and gender play in the shaping (and, secondarily, the receiving) of fiction? Insofar as the factors of race and gender do count, what kind of value can fiction claim? On what basis can we say that it is any good?

So long as our frame of assumptions remains Kantian, questions of race and gender simply do not enter to complicate the issue of value. But Kant is in serious trouble; and we come, therefore, to the point of contention inspiring this book. In much of today's climate, to move from male to female, from white to black, is to cross a chasm in which any common measure of aesthetic achievement ceases to be argued, leaving us with a balkanized literary landscape of subgroups championing their own. Aesthetic value (that dimension of the work that "survives" differences registered by race, gender, and other group orientations) is becoming a casualty of the academy's current civil wars. Faulkner starts to disappear into his white maleness, Morrison into her black femaleness. At the extreme, we move in the arts toward a version of identity politics in which the only valuable representation of a given race or gender or ethnicity is that produced by a writer of the race or gender or ethnicity in question. Others do not really understand; their representations are perforce marred by stereotypical assumptions. I want to say at once that I would not be writing this book if the current position (in its less extreme form) seemed to me simply right or simply wrong. Instead, I find it, in different ways, both perceptive and untenable: to open up its insight and mark its limitations are the motives underlying the local comparison that follows and the larger comparison that is my book as a whole.

What do whites know of blacks, men of women, and vice versa? What of sharable value remains in Faulkner's and Morrison's representations of the self-other dynamic if we grant that race and gender keep them from universality, predisposing them toward alignment within ideological arrangements too intricate to be fully mastered, seen beyond? For unless something does remain, unless we can replace the criterion of formally achieved disinterest with a more credible one, unless we learn to pose better the question "but is it any good?," then we are severely impoverished in our discussion of literary production. Unlike creative writers who remain inextricably invested in questions of value, of the degree of achievement in works of art, contemporary critics often judge this issue as mystified, in bad faith, off-limits. Yet can we read at all (not to mention justify syllabi, conceptualize courses, or write books) without some working sense of the dimensions that bespeak value in a literary text—dimensions lacking which one text is weaker than another text that possesses them? Can we afford to believe that, if race and gender are uncrossable indices of a text's importance, questions of canon evaluation amount to nothing more than a power debate among contending subgroups' claims?

I have argued that an aesthetics based upon purely formal tenets is untenable. I have claimed as well that an evaluative frame deliberately dismissive of the role of form—its aspiration toward achieved utterance, completed vision—risks reducing to nothing more than name-calling and power plays. I seek now to sketch out the middle position to which this book is devoted: a reconfiguring of the constellation of race, gender, and value. The Kantian insistence on disinterest seems to me a beacon we can hold to only on condition that we recognize its fictitiousness. Race and gender do play in the production and reception of art, for they are frames—both shaping and unforeclosed—that affect artistic practice. Only an occulted God model has permitted us to fetishize the artist as unmoved mover, universal voice. The ways in which race and gender play in the scene of writing are not only unforeclosed, however, they are invaluable. They enable insight even as they delimit it. Writing from within their distinctive racial and gender positioning, Faulkner and Morrison do not fail their potential, they achieve it, becoming Faulkner and Morrison. This positioning does not allow them to know everything, or indeed to know anything with perfect disinterest, but it is a constituent dimension of their range and their power.

No one is likely to object that Faulkner misunderstands his white males or Morrison her black females; the quarrel comes in the representation of the other, where the barriers of race and gender intervene. I claim, therefore, that great writers differ not least from lesser ones in their capacity to make these barriers permeable, turning them into membranes across which vision proceeds (but not in an unaltered fashion). As opposed to the liberal humanist position (that masterpieces get it all right—seeing steady and whole into the race- and gender-transcended human condition), and as opposed to the identity-politics position (that there are no masterpieces—each group possessing unique insights into its own that no other group can possess), I propose that Faulkner and Morrison (like other great writers) give us truths of relational seeing. Let me briefly explore this proposition through two representative examples: the black Dilsey from *The Sound and the Fury* and the white Bodwin from *Beloved*. These portraits, neither universally true nor mere self-projections, possess a limited yet precious truth.

Dilsey is a Southern white male's creation; the strengths and limitations of the portrait flow equally from that relation. Faulkner sees her with the generous eye of gratitude, compassion, and guilt. He portrays in the most minute ways how, unrewarded yet far from desolate, hemmed in yet resourceful, she has made (continues to make) her own life viable, indirectly, while keeping life viable, directly, for Benjy, his mother, and his niece. He registers her heavy body toiling up and down those Compson stairs, but he equally cites her shrewd and unsubmitting responses to Jason's vindictive moves. She is victimized but not victim. Above all, she is not duped. This is not *Gone with the Wind's* "Mammy," for Dilsey is in the "big house" without being of it, caught up in a white patriarchal economy without being complicit with the system. She may not complain, but she does suffer and she knows it; her wit is sharpened and directed by such suffering. The portrait is limited but genuine. The writer has seen, meditated on, and shaped into words something relationally available to him.

We turn now to what he has missed — all seeing is perspectival — and here we must proceed with care. To name only the cardinal omissions: he has missed her anger and her desire. He has scanted her relation to her own family, giving us, indeed, almost nothing of Dilsey's life that happens outside the Compson sphere. How Dilsey experiences from within her racial and gender identity is absent, which means that she is silent about the systemic oppressions within which she finds the operative terms for her life. How, given these omissions, can the portrait be said to succeed? My response is twofold. First, all portraits omit more than they contain, and they succeed by virtue of their creator's capacity to make compelling the elements they do contain. Second, and perhaps more painful to our contemporary sensibility, the writer shows her *making* a life within conditions that we find repellent: not by endorsing those conditions but by sustaining her integrity despite them. Neither brainwashed nor in rebellion, she is *there* in the Compson household: a daily presence (which means, *present daily*), a person of parts, someone the Compsons exploit but must also reckon with. The portrait contains Faulkner's extraordinary (and far from innocent) consciousness of race as it broods upon a black woman within conditions he is familiar with. He has infused into the lineaments of this character his power of relational seeing — a seeing that proceeds from his own race and gender position toward engagement with hers, producing (at the point of imaginative encounter) the figure we know as Dilsey. For this reason the portrait of Dilsey possesses a truth I used to believe to be universal and that I now see as complexly enabled and disabled by its setting in culture: it is a truth of history.

Bodwin looms less large in Morrison's canvas, but he is no less acutely understood from within a racial lens. Heading (at the end of the novel) toward

124 Bluestone Road in order to pick up Denver, he muses over his long history and this return to the house he was born in but has not seen for thirty years. Morrison gives us the sweetness of his attachment to the place as well as his memories of items buried there long ago—his box of tin soldiers, his old watch chain. We become aware of his physical beauty when younger, juxtaposed by his failing body today as he remembers "the wars he had lived through but not fought in (against the Miami, the Spaniards, the Secessionists)" (B, 260). As he turns toward 124, he thinks: "Now he just wanted to know where his soldiers were and his watchless chain. That would be enough for this day of unbearable heat: bring back the new girl and recall exactly where his treasure lay" (260–61). Within seconds (and we never see this from his perspective: the text departs from him) he is attacked by Sethe with an ice pick (she thinks he is schoolteacher come back to steal once more her Beloved, her "best thing"), and were it not for the intervention of Ella and Denver, these would be his last moments on earth. Why has Morrison chosen to enter this white man's subjectivity, and what is the value of the portrait?

Its value is wrought into its raced perspective. Relational seeing helps Morrison find in Bodwin the buried white child going back for his toys, the protected white man who could live through three wars without having to fight in any of them, the abolitionist who could defend Sethe's family without registering their individual differences, the white landowner who has the luxury of pleasure-laden memories and who remembers 124 as ancestral property rather than a life-and-death space that Sethe and her children hold to/almost tear apart. A few pages earlier the text visited (with Denver) his other house, and there the reader was required to linger over the only object dilated upon in this novel: a figurine of a "blackboy" with his "mouth full of money" and his head "thrown back farther than a head could go" (255). The figurine is on its knees; its purpose is to hold coins for small transactions; on the pedestal are written the words "At Yo Service" (255). We have seen blacks in Beloved with their heads bent back inhumanly, with bits and penises inserted into their mouths: the figurine all but explodes with implication. But it is lost on Bodwin, showing him to be not hypocritical but innocent—he never did those terrible things to slaves and so doesn't grasp the resonance of his "toy" and the ways in which, despite his benevolence, blacks remain in his "service."

The innocence that Faulkner exposes registers white male consciousness blind to its own offenses (Hightower, McEachern, Sutpen, McCaslin, among others), but the innocence that Morrison exposes registers less the ignorance of specific deeds committed than the unawareness of a systemic brutality in which one is—as white—complicit. In ways he will never understand, Bodwin evades "the foul air" of his own innocence, misses the meaning of his racial privilege, is spectator to a drama that Sethe and Paul D experience on their bodies and in their souls. His toys show us that, at some level of immunity, he is free to play with life, treating its materials as objects. Therefore Morrison unerringly has Sethe (mis)identify him as schoolteacher, and the text renders this (mis)identification as simultaneously aberration and prophecy. Of course he is not schoolteacher; he aids rather than damages blacks, he will be the financial support behind Denver's going to Oberlin. It is not for nothing that Sethe is wrestled to the ground, joked about by Paul D and Stamp Paid. (" 'Every time a whiteman come to the door she got to kill somebody?' 'For all she know, the man could be coming for the rent.' 'Good thing they don't deliver mail out that way.' 'Wouldn't nobody get no letter.' 'Except the post-man.' 'Be a mighty hard message.' 'And his last' " [265].) At the same time, the faint but pervasive "foul air" that Bodwin gives off is insidiously damaging to his self-righteousness. For Morrison to register all this—to keep perfectly clear both the distinctions and their collapse—is for a black writer to exercise rela-tional seeing. Her vision of Bodwin makes his otherwise invisible whiteness salient; she sees him through the color-sensitive optic of racial experience. This is not all there is to Bodwin—it is certainly not how he or his white friends and family see him, and it scants his genuine goodness—but it is a true seeing, indebted to the reality of race for its value.

As these examples reveal, Faulkner's and Morrison's achievement is insep-arable from their own raced and gendered positioning and from their (always contestable) grasp upon the ferment of their times: what Stephen Greenblatt has called "the circulation of social energy."[6] For a spectacular example of a text that registers this circulation, consider one of Greenblatt's own choices, Shakespeare's *Othello*. Whatever else Shakespeare saw in his source materials (Cinthio's 1566 Venetian story), he saw a clash of race and gender, of the civil and the primordial, that illuminated the conflicts of his own culture. His play maximally dramatizes these conflicts, it is in the business less of resolving or correcting them than of getting us to register them. Value in the arts, I want to argue, derives (not only but not least) from an artist's capacity to draw on his or her own orientations in such a way as to pass into the mind and heart of an audience the oppositional currents of energy that shape a social scene and ori-ent its constituent members. Value resides in a text's ability to seize upon (to find imaginative form for) the subjective engagement of individuals with their larger culture's most significant certainties and doubts. That the seeing enacted in such texts is positioned—relational—keeps it from being innocent, making it simultaneously right, wrong, and precious.

On this model the value of a text is incompatible with either universality or disinterest. The text is willy-nilly launched into a representation coming from somewhere: committed to the view that its angle of access provides, producing insight out of its necessary blindness. Everything human is marked by interest and no less valuable for that. Even in the realm of epistemology (let alone art), we have passed the point of believing in universally valid forms of cognition. Of this stained state of affairs the philosopher Hilary Putnam writes in *Realism with a Human Face*:

> If "values" seem a bit suspect from a narrowly scientific point of view, they have, at the very least, a lot of "companions in the guilt": justification, coherence, simplicity, reference, truth, and so on, all exhibit the *same* problems that goodness and kindness do, from an epistemological point of view. None of them is reducible to physical notions; none of them is governed by systematically precise rules. Rather than give up all of them (which would be to abandon the ideas of thinking and talking) . . . we should recognize that all values, including the cognitive ones, derive their authority from our idea of human flourishing and our idea of reason. . . . What the universe of physics leaves out is the very thing that makes that universe possible for us, or that makes it possible for us to construct that universe from our "sensory stimulations"—the intentional, valuational, referential work of "synthesis." I claim, in short, that without *values* we would not have a *world*. (141)

The raced and gendered practice of Faulkner and Morrison produces worlds of value. These worlds are differential, irreducible to each other, and— inasmuch as they bear the imprint of race and gender—capable of awakening us to the telling role of race and gender in the lineaments of any cultural representation. More, they allow us to access, as we read them, the orientational pressure of race and gender in our own subjective alignments. (This is, of course, not all that Faulkner and Morrison give us, but it is a great deal, already more than this study can fully compass.) The insight that their work conveys, finally, is cognitive—not in the sense that Kant longed for yet could not justify (a knowledge of things in themselves) but in the sense that Putnam describes: the experience of a representational ordering that—energized by relational seeing—is intentional, finite, and uninnocent.

This claim of cognitive content significance qualifies the Kantian reliance upon form, it does not jettison it. All texts may symbolically encode the social—display representational features—yet not all texts are equally imbued

with value. The differences have everything to do with a writer's formal powers, but form no longer understood as universal or disinterested. Rather, novelistic form embodies, I wish to argue, the desire of the artist to represent the
social as a scene of *encounter*: to dramatize (within the clash of subjective projects) a society's compelling circuits of energy. Kant's insistence on the disinterestedness of such representation may be an illusion, but the aim it encodes
is not. For a writer to be traversed by race and gender is to be marked, not fore-
told, to be inflected, not preshaped. For a writer to be inscribed within by ideology is not to be ideology's puppet. Form registers a writer's speculative and
unpredictable negotiations with the ideological schemas that shape both self
and social. Seeking humanly to interrelate, form does not manage divinely to
integrate. It reveals not mastery and disinterest but the desire for relational
accuracy, a desire shaped by a specific cultural positioning, yet striving to
communicate both within and across that positioning. In surrendering
Kantian universality, we need not surrender generosity toward the insights
that the orientations of race and gender—raised by formal energy into
resource and not just limitation—may bring to the verbal worlds we encounter in fiction and (through that encounter) to the nonverbal world we reaccess
in our lives. These are the larger concerns that operate as I turn to *Light in
August* and *Beloved*.

Citing a single lengthy passage from each text, I want to explore as fully as possible the implications of the passage, in order to generalize the writer's practice with respect to the representation of race and gender. I begin with *Light
in August*. The scene is the orphanage where the infant Joe Christmas has
sneaked into the dietitian's room, intent on stealing some toothpaste. The
dietitian suddenly enters with an intern named Charley. Joe hides, and this is
what follows:

> He was safe now, behind the curtain. When they went away, he would
> replace the toothpaste and also leave. So he squatted behind the curtain,
> hearing without listening to it the woman's tense whispering voice: "No!
> No! Not here. Not now. They'll catch us. Somebody will—No, Charley!
> Please!" The man's words he could not understand at all. The voice was
> lowered too. It had a ruthless sound, as the voices of all men did to him yet.
> . . . He heard other sounds which he did know: a scuffing as of feet, the turn
> of the key in the door. "No, Charley! Charley, please! Please, Charley!" the
> woman's whisper said. He heard other sounds, rustlings, whisperings, not
> voices. He was not listening; he was just waiting, thinking without particu-

lar interest or attention that it was a strange hour to be going to bed. Again the woman's fainting whisper came through the thin curtain: "I'm scared! Hurry! Hurry!"

He squatted among the soft womansmelling garments and the shoes. He saw by feel alone now the ruined, once cylindrical tube. By taste and not seeing he contemplated the cool invisible worm as it coiled onto his finger and smeared sharp, automatonlike and sweet, into his mouth. By ordinary he would have taken a single mouthful and then replaced the tube and left the room. Even at five, he knew that he must not take more than that. Perhaps it was the animal warning him that more would make him sick; perhaps the human being warning him that if he took more than that, she would miss it. This was the first time he had taken more. By now, hiding and waiting, he had taken a good deal more. By feel he could see the diminishing tube. He began to sweat. Then he found that he had been sweating for some time, that for some time now he had been doing nothing else but sweating. He was not hearing anything at all now. Very likely he would not have heard a gunshot beyond the curtain. He seemed to be turned in upon himself, watching himself sweating, watching himself smear another worm of paste into his mouth which his stomach did not want. Sure enough, it refused to go down. Motionless now, utterly contemplative, he seemed to stoop above himself like a chemist in his laboratory, waiting. He didn't have to wait long. At once the paste which he had already swallowed lifted inside him, trying to get back out, into the air where it was cool. It was no longer sweet. In the rife, pinkwomansmelling obscurity behind the curtain he squatted, pinkfoamed, listening to his insides, waiting with astonished fatalism for what was about to happen to him. Then it happened. He said to himself with complete and passive surrrender: "Well, here I am."

When the curtain fled back he did not look up. When hands dragged him violently out of his vomit he did not resist. He hung from the hands, limp, looking with slackjawed and glassy idiocy into a face no longer smooth pink-and-white, surrounded now by wild and dishevelled hair whose smooth bands once made him think of candy. "You little rat!" the thin, furious voice hissed; "you little rat! Spying on me! You little nigger bastard!"   (*LA*, 488–89)

So much is at work in this passage, locally and more largely; it bears Faulkner's signature. First we see how creatively invested he is in the mentality of a boy child, still innocent of sexuality even though present at its enactment. Typically Faulkner's point of entry will be the boy child, and from this vantage point the sexed woman figure necessarily becomes strange. She acts while he watches: a little paradigm of Faulknerian plot. What she acts is her sexuality. Though abusively called "Jezebel" by the janitor, the dietitian has no name (little attention is bestowed on her interiority, her relation to herself). It is the child's attention to her that Faulkner renders hypnotically. The child's attention, yes, but an attention long since forgotten. That chapter opens a page earlier with the haunting words, "Memory believes before knowing remembers. Believes longer than recollects, longer than knowing even wonders" (486). The grown-up Joe Christmas will have no clue that he witnessed this earlier scene as a child, which only makes his bondage to it the more inescapable. Like Calvinist predestination the event "predates" Joe himself, shapes his belief system at a level deeper than knowing, and disposes him toward a lifetime of deforming encounters whose motivation he will never catch up to.[7]

The child in that scene is passive, ignorant, caught in woman territory: her room, her bed, her toothpaste, her suffocating, candylike pinkness. The sex act registers here as joyless, male-enforced, overseen, incomprehensible. Throughout not only Joe's life but Faulkner's work, the grown-up male—Horace, Quentin, Ike, Gavin, among others—will have trouble accommodating the act of sex. The risks entailed in it, the bodily exposure, the emotional ecstasy, are beyond his management. Here the sex act on the bed is replaced by a kind of sex act within Joe Christmas himself: male and female, squeezer of the tube and swallower of what is squeezed, doing it and watching himself do it, his mind alienated from his body, remote from his moving hands and soon-to-be-moving stomach. Eating and intercourse fuse in this passage, and Joe will never be good at either of these acts of the body. Nausea haunts this text, a nausea rooted in the male mind's fascinated repulsion toward the body's behavior when under the spell of sexual desire, in the realm of the female.

The female is being othered in this scene of infancy, made strange, and we grasp the stakes of her strangeness—we see this as a primal scene—when we probe further her function. As dietitian at the orphanage she supervises Joe's feeding. This is a feeding scene gone awry: his substitute-mother fornicating on the bed, him attending in horror. The act of intercourse changes her from maternal to vicious. The hair that made him once think of candy is now wild, disheveled: Medusa, seemingly nurturant once, but now about to undo/castrate him for gazing upon her.

The form of that undoing is revealed in her curse: "You little rat! . . . You little rat! Spying on me! You little nigger bastard!" How does she know he is black? He doesn't look black. (Faulkner describes his skin as "parchment colored," inviting us to see that it is skin others write upon, and the writing becomes prophecy.) It turns out that we never do know if he is black, and by the end it hardly matters whether he "is" black. That verb "is" has been turned on its head. Subjective assent has little to do with it, melanin even less. To "be" black in *Light in August* is to be seen as, treated as, black. By that standard he qualifies. She thinks he is black, it turns out, because a crazed janitor (later revealed as his hate-filled grandfather) has been present on the orphanage playground and staring continuously at Joe, encouraging the other children to see him as different, in a culture where the worst difference you can be is black. The dietitian has heard him called this, and under pressure herself—at risk for betraying her own professional identity—she eludes self-censure by projecting censure upon another and scapegoating him. Threatened by this moment of exposure, she must make the child pay for her distress. He must be a "little nigger bastard."

The surface view of Faulkner's world is that you are who you are by virtue of inherited blood, but the deeper view is that you are who you are by virtue of how you have been called: what calls upon you you have internalized as you. Identity may be founded most primitively on this dynamic. We are called long before we ever answer—called as infants before we can even talk—and our answer to these calls is our reflexive way of knowing who we are. Identity is reflexive in just this way—responsive, reciprocal, a negotiation with societal interpellations—and Joe Christmas becomes (it takes all of *Light in August* to tell this story) a "little nigger bastard." It is stared and punished into him. He is not born one, and he will never manage to live as one. Faulkner has extraordinary sympathy for this act of fatal becoming. He shows us just how complicit it is, how many damage-dealing others it takes, how relentless is the social engine that turns Joe Christmas into a "little nigger bastard."

If we step back from the scene, we can register its larger racial and gender alignments.[8] First, there is the poetics of (white, male) innocence that I have described in earlier chapters and that is enacted here with exemplary fullness. Innocence unfolds as a not-knowing of one's own surroundings, a radical subjective incapacity to read and adapt to their otherness. Though Joe is in the same room with two other people, he may as well be on another planet. Few of their cultural assumptions are available to him. Faulkner has immersed him in a suffocating space of barriers at once uncrossable (he understands nothing of what he has witnessed) and transgressed (he is where he has no business being). As though naked, deprived of all cultural accommodation and legacy, Joe can only be headed toward outrage, though it will take many years and the spectacular failure with Bobbie Allen to crystallize this outrage.

The outrage is specifically Oedipal.[9] Faulkner presents Joe's career as a series of failed white-male becomings. Orphaned at birth, deprived by his maniacal grandfather of maternal substitutes, kept by this same man and the complicity of others from any of the fellowship that comes from a secure racial identity, Joe Christmas cannot achieve male individuation, cannot bring into focus either his body or his mind. Liquids terrify him; Mrs. McEachern "was trying to make me cry," he thinks. "Then she thinks that they would have had me" (523). The entry of another into his emotional economy threatens him altogether, and Faulkner all but fiendishly exploits this situation by injecting everyone into that economy. Doc Hines, McEachern, Bobbie, Joanna, Percy Grimm: everyone gets a piece of Joe Christmas, an entire town seems to gaze upon his crucifixion. If the male child is meant to resolve his Oedipal crisis by achieving a satisfactory relation of self to other—a separating from the mother, an internalizing of the father, an entry into the awaiting cultural territories of speech, norms, law, and inheritance—then Joe is incapable of socialization.[10] His relation to the otherness inside and outside him registers as pain either turned into routine or still unbearable.

A racial term that might help us understand the structure of Joe's outraged innocence is "segregation." This text written during one of the most virulently racist periods of the South explores the nightmare of a figure immersed in a culture that would fetishize all boundary definitions so as to keep them immaculately preserved. White is so opposed to black that one drop can denature you. Male is so opposed to female that homosexual fantasies circulate as a sort of cultural unconscious. Saved is so opposed to damned that only castration and murder of the evil one allow the virtuous to safeguard their virtue. In *Light in August* men and women tend to live in separate camps. (If they live together like Tulls and McEacherns and Hineses, they share neither bodies nor minds. If they live together like Joe and Bobbie, Joe and Joanna, they abuse both bodies and minds.) Whites and blacks live in crisply segregated neighborhoods, Freedman's Town being a sort of nighttime space that can suffocate a white man caught in it at the wrong hour, threatening to make him disappear again into the female womb he never securely exited from in the first place. The text is mapped like a war zone filled with armed camps, each group ratifying itself through its abjection of the other. So pronounced is this culture's masculine need of purity that it worships a Protestant music dedicated to its two principal deities: violence and death. "Pleasure, ecstasy, they

cannot seem to bear: their escape from it is in violence, in drinking and fighting and praying; catastrophe too, the violence identical and apparently
inescapable *And so why should not their religion drive them to crucifixion of
themselves and one another?"* (671). *Light in August* carries this insight to its
ultimate scenario: a world of white male will dedicated to registering the
range of human difference as mortal insult, and therefore committed to anni-
hilating self and other in the service of its unlivable ideal.

Only at the level of form does *Light in August* transcend conceptually the
suicidal insistences of its plot. European modernism gave Faulkner the artistic tools for diagnosing a sort of regional insanity. The confidence of his culture's binary racist narratives is revisited, called into question, by the layered
and nonchronological sequencing of events.[11] Shifting from perspective to
perspective, time frame to time frame, the text denies any innocent unfolding or single meaning to its events. An essentialist Southern culture encounters in Faulkner's European modernist form a structure that de-essentializes,
that turns assertions into questions, claims into echoing doubts, common
sense into absurdity. If Faulknerian form casts Joe Christmas as alternately
brutalizing adult, brutalized child, idealistic lover, abusive man on the run,
"nigger murderer" and exile from human community who wants only peace,
then each of these incompatible takes possesses its limited (and abused)
authority. To read the book is to descend into and exit out of stances that are
not so much true or false as partial. It is also to undergo, through exposure to
those whose single-mindedness nothing can surprise or alter, an education in
racism. *Light in August* is the most brilliant novel Faulkner wrote to make us
not only realize but register, in the act of reading, how men invent and
enforce authority in the absence of reliable knowledge. To tell this story, he
needed no black characters, only white ones in an obsessive mode. We move
now to Morrison's *Beloved.*[12]

In Morrison's novels one is rarely turned into a black person. Most are born
that way, and the trouble they encounter in her work derives from others abusing that obvious difference of skin color.[13] The supreme abuse of blacks is, of
course, that inflicted by the institution of slavery. The passage I'm going to cite
from *Beloved* begins in the post-emancipation year of 1873. Paul D has unex-
pectedly returned from that infernal 1855 past and showed up on Sethe's
doorstep. They have talked about those old days—her disappeared husband
Halle, Sixo and the other Pauls, the Garners—and they have slept together.
Paul D had been desiring her ever since Sethe first appeared at Sweet Home,

especially after she chose Halle among the Garner slaves to be her mate, so this intercourse has long been building. It is too swiftly over, though, physically completed before the emotions get even halfway started. Sethe lies in bed, Paul D next to her, and she muses:

Although her eyes were closed, Sethe knew his gaze was on her face, and a paper picture of just how bad she must look raised itself up before her mind's eye. Still, there was no mockery coming from his gaze. Soft. It felt soft in a waiting kind of way. He was not judging her—or rather he was judging but not comparing her. Not since Halle had a man looked at her that way: not loving or passionate, but interested, as though he were examining an ear of corn for quality. Halle was more like a brother than a husband. His care suggested a family relationship rather than a man's laying claim. For years they saw each other in full daylight only on Sundays. The rest of the time they spoke or touched or ate in darkness. Predawn darkness and the afterlight of sunset. So looking at each other intently was a Sunday-morning pleasure and Halle examined her as though storing up what he saw in sunlight for the shadow he saw the rest of the week. And he had so little time. After his Sweet Home work and on Sunday afternoons was the debt work he owed for his mother. When he asked her to be his wife, Sethe happily agreed and then was stuck not knowing the next step. There should be a ceremony, shouldn't there? A preacher, some dancing, a party, a something. She and Mrs. Garner were the only women there, so she decided to ask her.

"Halle and me want to be married, Mrs. Garner."

"So I heard." She smiled. "He talked to Mr. Garner about it. Are you already expecting?"

"No, ma'am."

"Well, you will be. You know that, don't you?"

"Yes, ma'am."

"Halle's nice, Sethe. He'll be good to you."

"But I mean we want to get married."

"You just said so. And I said all right."

"Is there a wedding?"

Mrs. Garner put down her cooking spoon. Laughing a little, she touched Sethe on the head, saying, "You are one sweet child." And then no more.

Sethe made a dress on the sly and Halle hung his hitching rope from a nail on the wall of her cabin. And there on top of a mattress on top of the dirt floor of the cabin they coupled for the third time, the first two having been in the tiny cornfield Mr. Garner kept because it was a crop animals could use as well as humans. Both Halle and Sethe were under the impres-

sion that they were hidden. Scrunched down among the stalks they could-
n't see anything, including the corn tops waving over their heads and visible to everyone else.

Sethe smiled at her and Halle's stupidity. Even the crows knew and came
to look. Uncrossing her ankles, she managed not to laugh aloud.

The jump, thought Paul D, from a calf to a girl wasn't all that mighty.
Not the leap Halle believed it would be. And taking her in the corn rather
than her quarters, a yard away from the cabins of the others who had lost
out, was a gesture of tenderness. Halle wanted privacy for her and got public display. Who could miss a ripple in a cornfield on a quiet cloudless day?
He, Sixo and both of the Pauls sat under Brother pouring water from a
gourd over their heads, and through eyes streaming with well water, they
watched the confusion of tassels in the field below. It had been hard, hard,
hard sitting there erect as dogs, watching corn stalks dance at noon. The
water running over their heads made it worse.

Paul D sighed and turned over. Sethe took the opportunity afforded by
his movement to shift as well. Looking at Paul D's back, she remembered
that some of the corn stalks broke, folded down over Halle's back, and
among the things her fingers clutched were husk and cornsilk hair.

How loose the silk. How jailed down the juice.

The jealous admiration of the watching men melted with the feast of
new corn they allowed themselves that night. Plucked from the broken
stalks that Mr. Garner could not doubt was the fault of the raccoon. Paul F
wanted his roasted; Paul A wanted his boiled and now Paul D couldn't
remember how finally they'd cooked those ears too young to eat. What he
did remember was parting the hair to get to the tip, the edge of his finger-
nail just under, so as not to graze a single kernel.

The pulling down of the tight sheath, the ripping sound always convinced her it hurt.

As soon as one strip of husk was down, the rest obeyed and the ear
yielded up to him its shy rows, exposed at last. How loose the silk. How
quick the jailed-up flavor ran free.

No matter what all your teeth and wet fingers anticipated, there was no
accounting for the way that simple joy could shake you.

How loose the silk. How fine and loose and free.   (*Beloved*, 25–27)

One of the sublime scenes in *Beloved*, this passage moves fluidly back and
forth in time, across different subjects and genders, in contrast to *Light in
August*'s focus upon a private, frozen, unrememberable moment of traumatic
encounter.[14] Beginning in the present time of 1873, Sethe, knowing Paul D's
gaze is upon her—gently—moves back into memory, recalling Halle's earlier

gaze and the 1855 slavery-shaped patterns of their lovemaking. This takes her into the request for a marriage ceremony, followed by a narrative transfer to Paul D—beside her in bed in 1873 but also reminiscing to himself—remembering that same intercourse in the cornfield from his horny spectator's point of view. Each of these perspectives is entered and legitimized, making the scene intersubjective. The fluidity operative here is not just an ease across times and perspectives, it is also an ease across identities. Halle's being more like a brother than a husband would surface in *The Sound and the Fury* or *Absalom, Absalom!* as the taboo threat of incest. Brothers must not be lovers of their sisters—the patriarchal imperative is clear about this—yet it happens all the time in Faulknerian narrative, usually with disastrous results. In *Beloved* the patriarchal imperative is absent, allowing the young black men deprived of inheritance responsibilities to escape a cluster of repressive norms. Halle's unpossessive stance toward Sethe prepares for Paul D's stress-free replacement of him, at once a brother substituting for a brother, a lover for a lover. Even the relationship between races, terrible though it be in *Beloved*, lacks the hysterical fear of being touched/contaminated that never ceases to energize *Light in August*'s psychic life. Mrs. Garner is almost a friend of Sethe's (the two women alternately mother each other), and Mr. Garner thinks he has offered to all his slaves the same model of manhood he enjoys. Of course these relations and models collapse under pressure—they do not successfully bridge racial difference in a time of slavery—but they are nevertheless tokens of a presegregated world.

The narrative then moves into the feast of new corn, and it likewise accesses this event from both Sethe's and Paul D's perspectives. *Beloved* generates the scene by dancing its many facets through its several players—what Satya Mohanty calls "the braiding and fusing of voices and emotions" (61)—enacting the interconnectedness of past and present, lover and lover and lover (how refreshingly unpossessive this trio of lovers is, what a generous—or at least forgiving—erotic economy it implies). It all comes to conclusion in the ceremony of corn-feasting that beautifully conveys the release of sexual climax itself.

As much as the scene in the dietitian's room, this one circulates about the mystery of the body, the commerce that its orifices invite. Whereas the male Faulknerian body is an object of interest insofar as it can be controlled by the will—and the female Faulknerian body, when young, an object of obsession that must be policed by male guardians—the Morrisonian body (male and female, at all ages) is in *Beloved* simultaneously a hostage to fortune and a priceless resource. Hostage to fortune because of the institution of slavery: Baby Suggs wonders repeatedly about the texture and markings of the hands and feet and foreheads of her disappeared children; Paul D works hard to love as cautiously as possible others whose embodied lives he cannot safekeep. "We are all trying to leave our bodies behind" (210), Beloved reveals. The slave body is wholly exposed, invaded and operated by others, the locus of an entire people's humiliating nonownership. Yet the slave body is inexhaustibly precious: however much milk those white boys take, Sethe has more to give to her waiting baby girl.

"Here, in this place here, we flesh" (88), Baby Suggs tells her congregation in the Clearing. It is somehow a clarification that no Faulknerian white or black can attain, perhaps because the physical appropriation of one's black body by a white owner reaches Morrison's imagination in such a way as to reduce the drama to its simplest stakes: either claim that body as one's own or lose it altogether. Thus the ceremony of corn-feasting joins other ceremonies in this sly and supple text of black repossession of black bodies. Not just the textual attention bestowed upon tired feet and scarred backs and ruined legs and caked breasts, but the care Morrison devotes to the making of a meal or the preparation of a feast. The sensuous world vibrates in Beloved—sometimes unbearably, as when Sethe remembers those beautiful Sweet Home trees with black corpses hanging from them—and this vibration reaches and enchants black bodies still open to the possibilities of pleasure, regardless of the stoicism they impose upon themselves in order to survive at all. Or not regardless: pleasure stolen within the very precincts of the white owner's decree against it—this is the joy that Sixo feels as he slips out in search of his Thirty-Mile Woman, and that Sethe remembers in the feast of lovemaking followed by the feast of the corn.

Such black release is exactly what the institution of slavery was constructed to repress or reroute. Faulkner's institution of slavery produces above all, in the pained brooding of white Southerners, the feelings of guilt and shame. Their anguish is his focus, just as, in Light in August, their racism is his focus. Morrison has no time for these peripheral responses; her focus is on the deliberate assault upon black human beings living within the system. Thus this scene passes on to us the casual yet horrifying economy of slavery, its temporal regulations for when a black man may see and linger over his black wife (only on Sundays), its refusal to recognize black marriage as ceremonial, the reason being that the offspring of such coupling belong to the white master, not the black parents. Beloved conducts perhaps the most powerful investigation in American literature of the subjective response to slavery as an impersonal institution with its specific rules for organizing family, offspring, labor, and amusement. Not Faulkner's focus on the anguished white inheritance but rather a sustained exploration of what your life would be like—how your body would be treated, your mind and heart assaulted—if you were black and enslaved.

This is why the writing of ceremony into a scene in which it was officially denied is, in its way, a revolutionary act. Morrison shows how the calls imposed by the institution were both absorbed and resisted. The wedding does takes place, surreptitiously, and the condescending white conviction that this union will be merely physical and produce offspring, that its actors are less than fully human ("You are one sweet child")—these are quietly refuted by the feeling, wit, and subtle agency (not victimization) that suffuse the scene. The black refusal to be simply enslaved by slavery, their refusal to internalize as their own the boundary conditions enforced by slavery, emerges most succinctly in that richly mobile, "unenslaved" figure of the "ear of corn." A figure of assessment (Paul D judging the ear of corn), a crop that cheaply feeds both animals and humans, a bed that serves to release black desire, and finally an item to be savored—lingered over, undressed with exquisite care and rising expectation—the ear of corn is male and female (the organ that enters, the sheath that receives), and its consummation is simultaneously quotidian (a meal eaten), sexual (a climax achieved), and political (a people released). For the deepest logic of the passage is inscribed in its movement from "jailed down . . . jailed up" to "free." "How fine and loose and free."

As in Faulkner, identity is written on the body; Sethe's history is a history of her body. But Morrison also understands the body as sacred despite the damage done to it, and she finds her way into the daily ceremonies that somehow survive and outlast degradation. Outlast degradation, not avoid it.[15] This text is full of bodily humiliation, and it rises to terrifying heights as it envisages—through Sethe's murder of her own child—what blacks will do to themselves rather than let whites do it in their place. More, Morrison focuses upon the career of the body outside the discipline of the will (a focus that attracts Faulkner's patriarchal gaze only in the guise of taboo). Urine and feces are the abjected objects commanding her attention, returned to the scene of representation. Sethe's "breaking" urine reveals that the return of her child Beloved is going to affect her entire living economy at a level deeper than the will. What we are like before we become (or when we cannot remain) ourselves, what marks our bodies are susceptible to outside the discipline we ourselves impose in order to make that body our own (that is, culturally recognizable): this is the non-Oedipal realm that Morrison opens up in *Beloved*. This is the subjective experience of slavery that she supremely conveys.

I have already characterized *Beloved*'s remarkable departures from the techniques of Western realism. Indebted, instead, to modernist plotting (and, equally, to Faulknerian temporal layering), *Beloved* yet uses these resources to its own purposes. Drawing on García Marquéz–like magic realism and upon African notions of nonchronological time, Morrison unfolds not the Oedipal plot of conflict overcome, followed by a proper inheritance, but the pre-Oedipal plot of primordial connections broken off and now renewed. This drama is enacted beneath the level of identity, outside the territory of law, as mother and daughter elementally embrace and assault each other with increasing intensity. The narrative trajectory is circular, a call and response of hints and repetitions in a different key, building toward recognitions that would be unbearable if proposed earlier. "How much is a nigger supposed to take?" (235), a weary Paul D asks Stamp Paid. "All he can," Stamp replies, and this is the formal wager of the book: to pass it on to you surreptitiously, indirectly, in parcels, the aggregate becoming all but intolerable as the burden of American slavery comes to rest upon the mind and heart of the entranced reader.[16]

These modernist moves granted, Morrison nevertheless refuses the plot of tragic impasse to which modernist forms tend to lead Faulkner. She is not interested in the narrative of cultural exhaustion, the doing to death of the scapegoated figure, the diagnosis of a cultural malaise that strikes the reader more as assault than therapy. In the same vein, she reconfigures one of the recurrent separations of Faulkner's segregated canvas: the vocal chasm between poetic and private voice, on the one hand, and vernacular and public voice, on the other. Morrison turns this vocal chasm into a vocal continuum:

> Paul D laughed. "True, true. She's right, Sethe. It wasn't sweet and it sure wasn't home." He shook his head.
> "But it's where we were," said Sethe. "All together. Comes back whether we want it to or not." She shivered a little. A light ripple of skin on her skin, which she caressed back into sleep. "Denver," she said, "start up that stove. Can't have a friend stop by and don't feed him."   (14)

This modest example will stand for countless others, the elegance of "caressed back into sleep" casually placed next to the vernacular of "Can't have a friend stop by and don't feed him." Vocal range in *Beloved* seems limitless, and the sense of unfolding black community owes everything to this single voice that, even more than the character Stamp Paid, unites the different elements of the canvas.

In *Light in August* vernacular voice and poetic voice less often coincide, making for a community whose shared and spoken utterance can make little contact with its isolated and poetic understanding. To put it too simply, one could say that in *Light in August* agency is shortsighted and vernacular, while awareness is speechless and poetic.[17] *Beloved*, by contrast, imagines a disowned community moving through the painful process of reclaiming itself, recovering its agency. The language they draw on for these purposes, as I indicated in my chapter on slavery, is forged from an experience unknown to whites and therefore communicable among the blacks even in the midst of a white presence that fails to hear it. *Beloved* closes on survival—an unpredictable future that will pass through the white-authored institution of Oberlin—abandoning its half-African ghost yet again if there is to be any future at all. This resolution is tentative and far from innocent, but it does show the principal black characters we met at the beginning to be stronger, more intact, for the confrontations they have encountered. They plan on staying alive.

I can now return to my opening theoretical question: how to make the separating parameters of race and gender compatible with the unifying question of value. Faulkner's grasp of blacks and women, we have seen, is inseparable from his own cultural positioning. He writes as a sensitive white male immersed within an early twentieth-century setting of acute racial turmoil—a turmoil he registers but cannot escape. The dynastic project of the antebellum South remains the myth most cherished by his belated generation, and his work narrates the imposition and collapse of this project with increasing power. His culture's manipulation of women (its refusal of female roles other than those prescribed by patriarchy) and his culture's exploitation of blacks (its postbellum brutality, its continuing economic bondage, its insistence on "nigger" as the intolerable other of white)—these materials join together to fuel his narrative designs. *Light in August* attends to, understands, and diagnoses racism as the circulation of a social energy empowering white men at a level deeper than thought. Increasingly, tragic failure emerges as Faulkner's artistic signature, for his immersion in his culture's ideologies means not that he is blind to the pain of blacks and women (as opposed to that of white males) but that their pain—whose resonance and consequences he unerringly grasps—is simply beyond his power to assuage. He cannot envisage what only another ideological orientation could propose: genuine cultural redress of that pain.

Morrison's purchase upon her characters is likewise culturally shaped. Though her moment may be too near our own for us to see all that this implies, we can at least note that she has her eye upon a community's survival. Her slaves have cultural roots, and their bodies remember these roots—which go all the way back to Africa—even when their minds do not. Wounded, they move not into outrage but into suppler communal strategies of self-sustaining. White pain compels Morrison's attention only in *Tar Baby*—and there more as diagnostic case than compassionate dilemma—but there is so much other pain (both male and female) demanding understanding. Although Mrs. Garner, and even more Mr. Bodwin, are entered and gravely presented in *Beloved*, they have no subjective possibilities that Morrison cares to pursue. Rather, she has her eye on a racial structure within which white benevolence and malevolence uncannily collapse into doubles of each other (Bodwin structurally inseparable from schoolteacher, however different psychologically), leaving the liminal Amy Denver as the only white figure unambiguously to enable black ones. The trajectory of that enabling, like the bleaker trajectories of black disabling, is Morrison's true focus, and I know of no critic white or black who has faulted her for such selective attention.[18] The stories she does tell seem desperately to need telling and hearing, for they allow us to grasp as never before the raced and gendered dimensions of our larger national history. What do these different strategies tell us about value?

Both texts negotiate, I have tried to show, an extraordinary investment in the torments and possibilities of their lived social scene—an investment accented decisively by race and gender. These two novels are valuable insofar as they dramatize their culture's "circulation of social energy" within the frame of clashing subjective designs. If such dramatization—issuing from an authorial seeing that is relational rather than objective—is therefore biased, it is no less for that informative. A certain blindness conditions seeing, it does not disqualify it. (*Beloved* is Morrison's strongest text, on this argument, because, from its post-1960s African-enlarged angle of vision, it articulates in the language of human interiority so much of her country's unspeakable social turmoil.) The social energy circulating—in the text's materials, in its perspective on those materials—is palpably raced and gendered, and "the words to say it," to draw on Morrison's phrase from *Playing in the Dark*, register these ramifications of race and gender.

Aesthetic value inheres in a text's formal power to interrelate (not integrate: that is beyond human power) its society's ideological clashes. It resides as well in a text's capacity to subjectify—through character—those clashes: subjectify them and pass them into the permeable subjectivity of the reader. Despite Kant and the reprisal of his aesthetics in New Criticism, neither the work nor its reader can be disinterested. Art appeals to us as a complex call, an inter-pellation that invokes no specific action but somehow alters our interior sys-tem of accents. We see things a little differently. This fissured confrontation that great texts stage within us, in which we take on imaginatively the race and gender of others and in so doing momentarily realign our own, is never merely private. We live our culture's categories of race and gender from within, in a labile rather than fixed fashion, and an arrangement as apparently modest as the wording of a mere text can momentarily make our whole world turn strange.

It follows that the brutality of Faulkner's language is indispensable to his achievement. On the issue of race he has a disastrous story to convey—a story shaped by his troubled membership within his own race and gender—and if that story is to make its way in and wound, it must retain its wounding accents. "Nigger" is the indisputable password of American racism for the past two cen-turies, and Faulkner's task is less to judge that racism overtly than to pass the virulence of racism into the subjectivity of his reader: *as* confrontation, *as* vir-ulence. The racist writer is the one who passes *off* racism as normal, its effects as self-evident, rooted in nature, how things are, maybe even so obvious as to be invisible—the writer who lets us watch these things and remain unin-volved. By contrast, Faulkner generates a uniquely disturbing diagnosis of racism, an extensive mapping of an ill that he has suffered from, sought to understand, managed to communicate, but cannot resolve, cannot escape. It is because racism is so offensively alive in his texts—neither endorsed nor "corrected" but shown as embedded (even when resisted) within the weave of his community's subjective norms—that we measure its intractability, if you will, its seriousness.

His are narratives that women and blacks may be less likely than white males to take pleasure in—given the intensity of his investment in white male subjectivity—yet his work reaches beyond this single category of readers. Kafka once said that art exists to thaw the frozen deep within us, to remind us of our irremediable lack of grounding, the motleyness of our being, the makeshift-ness of our social identity. Kafka's subject-haunted angst is not Faulkner's race-saturated diagnosis, but they share, so to speak, a sense of human plasma unspeakably exposed to the markings that culture must inflict. Faulkner's art interrogates his culture's markings in such a way as to reach into that frozen territory inside—through the vehicle of his white male protagonists mainly but not only—and to thaw it. His drama is the agon of human plasma receiving and enacting its cultural alignment. Why would he invent such a tortured rhetoric of selfhood—his Benjys and Quentins and Joe Christmases—if not to generate in us, while reading him, the turmoil of cultural injunctions seething within the individual? *Individual*: the word reveals our fantasy of undivided-ness, wholeness, and Faulkner shows us—beneath that fantasy and in the nor-mal/abnormal that is Benjy, the white/black that is Joe—the cluster of others whose orientations share our mind and shape our body.

I've stressed "our" throughout that last paragraph, but of course not all of us are equally "called upon" by Faulkner's fiction. "Our" can be an insuffer-ably selective pronoun. The women in his novels function mainly within the optic of their anxious and adoring brothers, fathers, uncles, and lovers. And the blacks tend to function as the irrepressible sign of white male abuse. Coming from elsewhere—another race, another gender—Morrison beauti-fully reconfigures that word "our" and lets us see so much else—how the social positioning of even well-intentioned whites may blind them to the intri-cacies of black feeling, how black interiority succumbs to or survives the sys-temic assaults of white racism, how African folklore traditions still nourish black American life (how, to take the tiniest example, that verb *pass* is not a euphemism for *die* but a different cultural vision of death, in which the dead are not extinguished, but pass elsewhere, a source still of strength and align-ment to the living), how women sustain homes that men have understandably fled from, how women feel desires as elusive and potentially taboo as the men's desires in Faulkner. The different emphases fueled by her different race and gender are major, not minor. We seem to be in a different world, with white and black, male and female starkly reconfigured. And we are: not because hers is true and his is false but because the cultural alignments that both of them exploited to become Faulkner and Morrison oriented them to such different dimensions of an ongoing drama.

A courageous black woman in a seminar I taught a few years ago insisted on rejecting Faulkner's finest effects, arguing that he participated in the racist ills he addressed and that his use of racist language to describe blacks was intolerable. His participation in racism I can largely counter (if not make palatable), and his use of those foul words I can justify. Yet I came away from these encounters knowing that Faulkner was writing more for me than for her.

And I realized that he inhabited a social world in which blacks would function as scripted objects of his compassion, not as reading subjects of his work. By contrast, this 1930s and 1940s social frame does not apply to Morrison's practice during the past twenty-five years. However we will eventually assess the value of her work, its capacity to speak to white and black at the same time remains remarkable: a difference irreducible to merely personal factors. The larger point is that even the greatest writers have their selective audiences (the "us" they call to is not universal), and that selection often operates—however unconsciously—on the basis of ideological alignments shaped by race and gender. If I were black or female, what would it be like to read Faulkner? How would I hear his call?

I cannot answer that question abstractly without falling into stereotype. Yet race and gender, this entire book has sought to show, position us differently, often decisively. It is as foolish to dismiss this differential positioning as it is to foreclose in advance its effects. Finite ourselves, we do not answer all finite calls. The ones we do answer put us differently in touch with ourselves—not as finished beings but as beings in process, marked by this encounter with other subjectivities. It may be especially the calls of another race or gender that we manage to answer that show us something more disconcerting but no less necessary: how we (our group) register in the subjective optic of the other, how constructed (rather than "natural") we appear when seen outside the familiar gaze of a shared perspective, how—uncannily—we glimpse a portion of ourselves figured in situations that we find intolerable. We need to know this too, for the self-other axis we daily draw on to orient our interior world is in continuous danger of lopsidedness. Value resides, therefore, in the text that creatively disturbs such axes, making us realize afresh—as though we had never suspected this—that we carry our culture's raced and gendered arrangements (the most brutal as well as the most beneficent) inside ourselves. The text that unleashes/manages these disturbances in both its materials and its reader achieves its value neither by ignoring nor by mastering the parameters of race and gender. Instead, it negotiates them, tapping our identificatory energies and revealing the outrageous orientations to which these energies may lead us, thus locating us in a remapped world that is ours yet no longer our own.

Conclusion

Conclusions are delicate matters, especially when one of the two careers I have followed has not concluded. Morrison's work, moreover, defies augury; each of her texts seems to rewrite the givens of her previous one. *Sula* cleanly refuses *The Bluest Eye*'s abiding sadness; *Song of Solomon* dilates upon a spatial and temporal panorama all but absent from *Sula*; *Tar Baby* moves suddenly to the Caribbean and devotes a microscopic attention to black and white domestic relations; *Beloved* returns with unprecedented power to American shores to take on nineteenth-century slavery; *Jazz* flaunts a vernacular and vibrantly self-delighting voice unheralded by *Beloved*'s grave and self-occulting meditations. In my experience, the worst way to read her latest text is to expect it to operate according to the conventions of the preceding one. But this sketch tells us little of the larger traditions she draws on, the formal stakes of her practice, and, above all, the race and gender dimensions of her developing career.

Faulkner's career, given its temporal distance, is easier to characterize with respect to its larger allegiances. Many critics have already given us book-length summaries of his developmental path, and I supply here only the briefest outline: first, the early forays into modernist form, then the full-blown modernist masterpieces (*The Sound and the Fury* and *As I Lay Dying*), followed by the remarkable experiments of the 1930s and early 1940s in which modernist technique increasingly accommodates social upheaval (*Light in August, Absalom, Absalom!, Go Down, Moses*). If we add to these a sustained interest in Southern class dynamics (the Snopes trilogy) and an increasing tendency—whatever the theme—toward apocalyptic utterance (the overwhelming syntactical performances in *Intruder in the Dust, Requiem for a Nun,* and *A Fable*), we arrive at a reductive but not misleading summary of the paths he took and the major stops along the way.[1]

What are the broader race and gender dimensions of each career? How do the formal traditions they draw on and reaccent intimate race and gender orientations lodged at the level of form? What audiences, for what reasons, do these formal procedures tend to invite? More concretely, as Faulkner and Morrison succeed in becoming "Faulkner" and "Morrison"—enterprises launched collectively in the public domain, figures serving as icons in the politics of literature—what audiences actually emerge to do battle and establish for them canonicity?[2] These questions deserve more consideration than I can give, and the last one is beyond my capacity to answer with authority. But I would conclude by at least gesturing toward the race and gender aspects of two sustained careers and the orientations that enable them. Gesture, not assert: the speculations that follow, however aggressively they seem to generalize careers and movements, are offered speculatively. Rather than trying to lay down the law, I am deliberately overshooting my target— to bring it into visibility—trusting my reader, on recognizing the configuration, to modify accordingly.

Faulkner's early engagement (1920s–1930s) with modernist techniques and assumptions is, in my reading, decisive. It enacts his coming of age as a writer within a cosmopolitan and European worldview utterly alienated from his native culture's convictions. These latter, when healthy, enter a writer's fictional practice as natural, reasonable stances: the materials of daily commerce. In Faulkner, from the beginning, they appear constructed, under pressure, heartbreaking. Freud and Joyce (and through them Sherwood Anderson) help him to register his knowledge of something awry in his native scene, his developing sense of its irreparable fractures.[3] Familiarity with their paradigms informs his repertory of novelistic modes and deepens his take upon the psychopathology of everyday life. A young man whom every biography shows to have been distant, uncomfortable, uselessly perceptive: this figure encounters the deracinated brilliance of modernist techniques—their capacity to break experience down into opposing and incompatible takes, to register subjectivity as a mental and emotional energy no longer harnessed to conventional social projects, to undo the promise of time by showing effects before causes—and finds in them a perfect set of diagnostic tools. With these he returns home, exploring the ways in which the premises of his own life and of the larger culture that bequeathed them (premises not least about normative racial and gender identity) have unraveled and become unworkable. He is America's greatest novelist of the unworkable.[4]

At the heart of such a career is the drama of an innocent boy child outraged at his disinheritance. The stories of cultural disabling he tells involve ferociously experimental ways of producing the interior pain of this orphaned boy. As Faulkner's gaze widened, he saw, by the time of *Light in August* and *Absalom, Absalom!*, that an entire culture's arrangements—and the widest cast of supporting characters—conspired unknowingly in the child's undoing. This undoing, the failure of traditional culture to pass on to its sensitive young men (the writers, their protagonists) the materials out of which they might compose identity, project, and destiny, suggests the dysfunction of patriarchy itself—a dysfunction whose primary damage to white male sons, and secondarily to women and blacks, commands Faulkner's attention. In this primary focus he was not alone. Other major novelists of Western modernism—Joyce, Mann, Proust, Kafka—tell in their vastly different ways a related white male story of patriarchy undone.[5]

This germinal story is both raced and gendered, and so perhaps, indirectly, is the formal experimentation that delivered it. Modernism is famous for its willful difficulty—Joyce is the obvious case, but Kafka is no less inaccessible to a traditional hermeneutic—and Faulkner proudly ran the full modernist risk of not being understood. The stance here is Stephen Dedalus's "all or not at all," a refusal (or ironizing) of forms of narrative coherence fueled by assent to social norms. Familiar unfoldings are to be avoided. Lukács and the Marxists long ago read such modernist intransigence as the artist's withdrawal from a vulgar world of marketplace commodity-consumption, and that reading remains as cogent as ever.[6] To it we might add a missing gender component: an artistic practice so obsessed with interrupted sequences and erudite allusion (Pound and Eliot come to mind) that the common reader—the only reader in the first half of the twentieth century as likely to be female as male—is all but systematically excluded.

The audience, in other words, to which modernism makes its most compelling invitations is university-trained, which is to say (until well into the twentieth century), almost always white and mainly male: an audience of elaborately educated sons who saw themselves cut off from the certainties of an earlier time. To a readership "specializing" in hyperactive and underresolved sensibility—a readership for which not just the career patterns but the very fabric of thought and feeling of the parental generation was distinctly less viable—Faulkner's modernist text was hard to resist. (Not so for much of today's university audience, as any number of contemporary professors of literature could attest. The Faulknerian enterprise has its preferential audiences, and black and women students—along with others committed to the idea of noncanonical literature—are less likely to be among them. As I mentioned in the last chapter, he never envisaged a substantial black audience, and one can only wonder what, if any, difference the emergence of that possibility might have made with respect to the brutality of his language, the word *nigger* that rhythmically punctuates his diagnostic citation of racist practice. I say this neither to excuse his language nor to wish it were different, but to ponder—as a "might-have-been"—how he might have met that further complication.)

Faulkner speaks as obsessively as Beckett of failure, of the incapacity of words to capture experience. Flaubert stands behind them both, and they are drawn (Beckett throughout his career, Faulkner for a portion of his career) to Flaubert's vision of writing as ordeal for reasons related to his: how to write accurately when conventional language itself belongs to the bourgeoisie, is in fact its greatest tool? Normal ways of saying things, on this model, are stale and biased: hence art's heroic mandate to purify language from its philistine moorings, to erase its recognizable referentiality within the nonaesthetic realm of daily transactions. To insist on failure, to prefer failed communication to traditional communication, to envisage writing as priestly torment standing in for the discourse of an earlier period's genuine priests, to encounter the culture's repertory of projects as so many ways of betraying the spirit, to dilate on the outrage that follows from this humiliating impasse: this is a generic description of both the modernist writer's plight and his protagonist's characteristic stance. Both figures, defiantly unamenable to social norms, display the attributes of sensitive white sons deprived of their cultural inheritance. How would the novels they write and figure in not be deliberately, magnificently difficult?[7]

Early twentieth-century existentialism—with its refusal of traditional forms of coherence and value—is arguably the philosophy that underwrote the modernist literature of authenticity. Anglo-American New Criticism emerged shortly thereafter as a technique of choice for reading that same literature. The former orientation invited one to ponder the vast field of assumptions that such literature was refusing, and the reasons why. The latter provided ways of attending to this new fiction with a care earlier devoted to poetry—ways of seeking out and organizing imagistic and allusive patterns controlling a narrative that, while superficially local, was actually unique and universal: "a cosmos of my own."[8] During the 1930s and 1940s Faulkner was a supreme writer for the major French existentialists (Sartre, Malraux, Camus). During the 1950s and 1960s he became a darling of the American New Critics. Under the aegis of both sets of endorsement he took on canonical status. As one who entered the university scene during the 1960s and found Faulkner's practice irresistible, I did not then and do not now seek to revoke that status. But I do want to note its race and gender dimensions. His topics (isolation, heartbreak, failed inheritance, wounds that do not heal) and his methods (allusiveness; refusal—or ironic citation—of conventional formulae of thought, feeling, and behavior) point clearly enough—though of course not exclusively—to white male values cherished by the philosophy that launched him and the critical school that enshrined him. Faulkner does not reduce to these traits, but his work displays them in ways that are neither random nor purely individual. It took many structures to be in place for Faulkner to become "Faulkner," and these are some of them.

Morrison encountered the forms and themes of modernism forty years later than Faulkner. The movement had passed its state of generative ferment and entered a sort of monumental repose. The major texts of the canonical writers (including Faulkner and Woolf, the subjects of her master's thesis) were securely in place, awaiting and receiving study.[9] Thus distanced, she draws from modernism detachedly and selectively throughout her career, avoiding the extremes of Faulkner's early devotion and later repudiation. Modernism is but one of a range of fictional practices—including Latin American "magic realism" and various strands of black American literature from the Harlem Renaissance up to the outpouring of black fiction (alternately naturalist and absurd, soberly referential and wittily self-mocking) in the 1960s—that Morrison deploys in her own fashion. Even more than these fictional practices, she draws from and reshapes an inherited culture of folkloric sayings and doings that resonate all the way back to Africa.[10]

Morrison's never assenting to modernism in Faulkner's all-risking way translates, I believe, into her writing a less experimental, more broadly accessible fiction. His coterie in the 1930s and 1940s—sophisticated male readers, for the most part, already attuned to modernist techniques and fascinated by the struggle needed to put together the Faulknerian text—has only a modest counterpart in Morrison's steadily growing audience. If his very technique "announces" that you must learn how to read him (you cannot assume that your culture's traditional reading practices will function here), her work, from the beginning, invites "the participation of the other" (*TM*, 418).[11] Indeed, in contrast to Faulkner, she would make sense to the black people she writes about: "I write what I have recently begun to call village literature, fiction that is really for the village, for the tribe" (*TM*, 370). With the possible exception of *Jazz*, though—and there only with respect to a recognizable narrative voice, not to the complex emplotment of episodes—her texts are always on the edge of escaping general readability (white or black). She remains formally demanding, not least in ways that she learned from modernism. Even *The Bluest Eye* (her first and "easiest" novel) organizes its canvas spatially, moving without warning from focus to focus, from present to past to present again. The result is something closer to a many-stranded weave than to "the mirror in the roadway" that is realism's deceptive promise.

Sula registers Morrison's rewriting of some of the most brilliant devices of Latin American "magic realism."[12] Not García Marquéz's non-Newtonian events—in which the "scientificity" of the represented world is suspended— but rather a deployment of events that are possible yet simultaneously fabulous: the appearance of the indistinguishable Deweys, the drowning of Chicken Little, the burnings of Plum and Hannah, all of these in a deadpan manner. Her practice begins in this second novel to depart from realist norms in ways that Faulkner's never does (his characters' weirdest behavior, like that of the Bundrens throughout *As I Lay Dying*, is always, so to speak, statistically credible, if only because they pass through a human landscape of normal and scandalized others). Morrison's departures take us cleanly somewhere else, past individual or family eccentricity. That elsewhere is a vividly delineated, nonbourgeois black folk culture that she draws on with increasing power: "My own use of enchantment simply comes because that's the way the world was for me and for the black people that I knew"—producing what in the same interview she calls a black "cosmology" (*TM*, 414). As she put it in another essay, "We are very practical people, very down-to-earth, even shrewd people. But within that practicality we also accepted what I suppose could be called superstition and magic, which is another way of knowing things" ("Rootedness," 342).[13]

Another way of knowing things: one reason for her enormous popularity today is her refreshing capacity to narrate human behavior calibrated upon something other than a capitalist model of consumption, exchange, and individual empowerment. In different ways all of her texts after *Sula* testify to the task that, at its grandest, Morrison calls "the reclamation of the history of black people in this country" (*TM*, 418). Her interviews return to the differences between this history and that of the whites: "There is a confrontation between old values of the tribe and new urban values. It's confusing. There has to be a mode to do what the music did for blacks, what we used to be able to do with each other in private and in that civilization that existed underneath the white civilization. I think this accounts for the address of my books" (TM, 371). Spoken nine years before the publication of *Jazz*, these words are prescient. Tribe, enchantment, music, a civilization beneath a civilization: Morrison's formal inventions seek as strenuously to access earlier traditions of thought, feeling, and behavior as Faulkner's great work so often seeks, through the immediate illegibility that accompanies fierce formal experiment, to disown them.[14] The traditions she would make contact with are black: the staying power of the matriarchal black family and the tissue of shared beliefs and behaviors that make up a community; the dignity-enabling roots of black families as these go back to nineteenth-century records and then further back to folk myths of flying men and swamp women; the survival of black people even during the depredations of slavery, thanks to their mutual dependencies and inventiveness, their fragmented yet still viable grasp upon an African heritage that predated the Middle Voyage; and finally the irresistible music with which they colonized New York of the 1920s into a series of interlocking neighborhoods at once intimate and dangerous.

Any of Morrison's later texts is capable of producing this mental/emotional texture of a black folk culture different from the secular norms of her white readership. The ghost who occupies 124 Bluestone Road occasions trouble but not surprise: "Paul D scratched the hair under his jaw. 'Reminds me of that headless bride back behind Sweet Home. Remember that, Sethe? Used to roam them woods regular.' 'How could I forget? Worrisome . . .' " (B, 13). The "reclamation" of this culture may be difficult, and the experience of reading her texts far from cozy; but an abiding aim of her formal experiments is to increase human capacity. At a price often terrible (corpses fill her novels, there is no innocence to be regained), the texts seek, through their intricate weaving, to enable a survival of the ordeals they represent: "She gather me, man," Paul D remembers Sixo telling him about his Thirty-Mile Woman, "The pieces I am, she gather them and give them back to me in all the right order" (B, 272–73). To read her, to respond to the interpellative energy of her form, to knit together the fragmented yet implicitly interrelated pieces of her narrative, is to experience one's own taxed coherence come into focus again. We are far from the tonic devastation that accompanies an embrace of Faulknerian tragedy.

Morrison assembles, then, formal tenets from Western modernism, African folktales, and black American cultural traditions, producing a plot line that moves when necessary from realism to the fantastic, speaking in a narrative voice at once vernacular and elegant, able to enter any character's subjectivity, capable of stitching these subjectivities together into the semblance of a community: "An artist, for me, a black artist for me, is not a solitary person who has no responsibility to the community. It's a totally communal experience where I would feel unhappy if there were no controversy or no debate or no anything—no *passion* that accompanied the experience of the work. I want somebody to say amen!" (*TM*, 419) What is remarkable is how many different groups have fervently said amen. However Morrison's work draws formally on black traditions and stresses female endurance, its audience is demonstrably black and white, male and female.[15] At the time of this writing, 1996, no living American writer enjoys more canonical status among university critics than Morrison. (Gauging the makeup and stance of her broader general audience is more difficult.) The awarding of the Nobel Prize of 1993 to Morrison surprised the community of university scholars and literary critics not by its choice—they had already enshrined her—but by the swiftness with which their local admiration was echoed in this global accolade.

The past few pages have speculated on the race and gender dimensions of each writer's career, the differential currents that each of them half created, half responded to. I would close by rehearsing even more briefly the race and gender dimensions of their value. Faulkner tells the story, in myriad ways, of the lost homeland, the disenfranchised white son. The ordeal of innocence wounded and transformed to outrage is his signature event. In finding fresh ways to write that pain, to allow us to access the pain without subscribing to conventional formulae that would in rendering it betray it, he became America's supremely experimental novelist. In figuring out the ramifications of that young man's pain—the cultural dysfunction that underlay it, the women and blacks that necessarily suffered its fallout—he became one of America's most provocatively diagnostic novelists. The drama he narrates is at once patriarchal and Oedipal, and Faulkner emerges as the American writer who best sees through, without pretending to see past, the twentieth-century unworkability of this drama.

Morrison understands, as a woman writer well might—and a black woman writer virtually must—that the most artful sorts of survival start on the other side of innocence. Her canvas never tolerates "the foul air of innocence"; it has no investment in figures who live "without absorbing the sins of [their] kind" (*TB*, 243). In Morrison's world, thanks to a frame of variable but irremovable racial injustice, you are put under such pressure that sooner or later you will be wrong, very wrong, but that is not necessarily a lethal mistake. The culture she brings to life in her pages has had to find the terms of its survival—and its dignity—outside the syndrome of the proper, propriety, and property. Seasoned by centuries of slavery, it has absorbed too much white abuse to envisage its own will as immaculately intact. Flexibility and a contingent, redefinable identity tend to replace Compson paralysis, Sutpen monumentality. She has no interest in mourning the collapse of a system of inheritances that never acknowledged her people in the first place. She focuses less on the trauma caused by a closed door than on the kinds of motion made possible by the closing of a door. Her diaspora goes further back than the Lost Cause.

Each of these writers develops a remarkable sense of the other race and gender, though Faulkner's need to make sense of the damage whites inflicted on blacks weighs more imperiously on his practice than Morrison's interest in figuring out why the whites might have done it. She is wise enough to focus on the resources that remain, or better yet, have always been there but were rarely visible to the white eye. The texts of both writers explore, with unequaled power yet in such different ways, the range of human cost and possibilities occasioned by the two races' mutual caughtness, their inextricable interpenetration. This is why I have chosen them as the figures of my book.

There has been, for me, little question of preferring one writer to the other or of finding one writer's representation of race or gender superior to the other's. There has been even less question of wishing one writer's insight to obtain in the other's practice. Enmeshed within the cultural orientations that they seek to understand and render, both write as they can and must. There has been least of all, in this book, any question of "getting it right." Whatever one gets right, one also gets wrong—a fortiori in matters of race and gender. If it were otherwise, literary criticism would have dried up centuries ago. Morrison shows us, moreover, that getting it right and getting it wrong are inseparable processes—witness Sethe's killing of her baby—and that we can survive these deformations. Rather than getting it right, I prefer to understand the writing of this book within the frame of a giving and taking whose mutual name is acknowledgment. The textual dimension of acknowledgment is the phenomenon of inheritance that so affects the capacity of Faulkner's and

Morrison's children black and white, male and female, to mature. The personal dimension of acknowledgment is that I was given much at the start of my own life by two women, one white and the other black. The complexity of that giving exceeds my capacity for analysis but not for gratitude. Whatever this book bequeaths to anyone else is beyond my power to guess, but I could not have written it without a sustaining gift of love that crossed the lines of race and gender.

Notes

Introduction

1. The caveats registered in this paragraph center upon race, but in essentials (if perhaps more subtly) they operate as well in the functioning of gender. Men and women are positioned differently—again, not so much biologically as culturally—and these differences play in the shaping and responding to literature. It seems to me as naive to deny them as it is prejudicial to define, legislate, or foreclose in advance the consequences that follow from them.

2. For a recent collection of essays committed to exploring Faulkner as participating in a range of cultural structures of thought and feeling, see *The Cambridge Companion to William Faulkner*. As for Morrison, the most recent commentary on her work has valuably attended to its relation to larger black cultural resources. See, for example, the criticism of Kimberly Benston, Barbara Christian, Trudier Harris, Denise Heinze, Karla Holloway, Valerie Smith, and Hortense Spillers. I want to acknowledge at the outset that this work—most of it by black critics—supplies a cultural context that I am unfamiliar with and grateful for. I draw where pertinent on this context but do not seek here to enlarge it. Rather, both novelists create verbal worlds so richly organized, resonant, and related to each other in their concern with race (and secondarily gender) that this comparative study—with its own pertinent questions—has seemed to me a necessary project.

3. It is worth noting that the anxiety fueling this paragraph—is it possible to do justice to a writer's aesthetic achievement while attending to the politics of race and gender?—attaches to a specific cultural formation. Western Eurocentric culture has for more than two hundred years proclaimed the ideal of universality. Put less charitably, such culture has refused to see itself as *a* culture. Black culture, at least in some respects, lacks this universalizing urge, and Morrison has no problem reconciling the cultural imprint upon her work with that work's aesthetic aims: "It seems to me that the best art is political and you ought to be able to make it unquestionably political and irrevocably beautiful at the same time" ("Rootedness," 345).

4. Appiah and Gates are less opposed than these quotes indicate. Both begin by exposing the biological fallacy of racism, and both go on to explore the ways in which black culture (for Gates, American culture; for Appiah, a range of African cultures) exhibits a rich diversity of intellectual and emotional resources. Yet Gates seems committed, in several of his texts, to the nonbiological reconstruction of blackness as a meaningful group term for the diasporic experience of black people within the United States. By contrast, Appiah (whose meditation on his own Ghanaian background is determining) remains forthrightly critical of attempts to organize human experience significantly within racial categories. I have learned much about "race matters" from them both, as well as from Eugene Genovese, Herbert Gutman, Andrew Hacker, Jacqueline Jones, Nicholas Lemann, Lawrence Levine, Werner Sollers, Eric Sundquist, Cornel West, Joel Williamson, and C. Vann Woodward.

5. Not surprisingly, the issue of whether race as a category for understanding the individual is full or empty, enabling or limiting, is fiercely contested among many critics in today's postdeconstructive climate. Appiah writes: "What blacks in the West . . . have mostly in common is the fact that they are perceived—both by themselves and by others—as belonging together in the same race, and this common race is used by others as the basis for discriminating against them" (*In My Father's House*, 17). In the same negative vein, Aldon Nielsen claims that "the fact that race is a consummately empty signifier, that it is constituted out of a people's desire for power over others, out of their desire to name themselves as not-other, that it is a reification with no material ground, does not mean that it no longer has material consequences" (*Writing Between the Lines*, 16). A considerable number of other critics assent to the nonbiological basis of race yet insist that blackness as a common frame for identity is something more than a white-imposed illusion. Rather, they define race positively, as the primary element in a diverse yet organic black culture that teems with human problems and possibilities. See the work of Barbara Christian, Deborah McDowell, and Hortense Spillers, among others.

6. For a devastating account of the differences between the first and the third audiences—the avant-garde and the general public—see Pierre Bourdieu's *Field of Cultural Production*, 112–40. Bourdieu argues that the avant-garde systematically reverses the criteria of general readers—formal accessibility and coherence, familiarity of content—when evaluating the merit of "original" work. To the extent that his argument of extremes guides American cultural norms, this book's ambition to appeal to a range of audiences is placed under considerable pressure.

PART 1. BEGINNINGS

1. *Plessy v. Ferguson* has received ample attention as a landmark decision in the history of U.S. race relations. For discussion of its ramifications within literary practice (black and white) in the 1890s, see Eric Sundquist, *Wake*, 1–24, 225–70. For a further account of the historical context of *Plessy*—the period from Reconstruction to the beginning of the twentieth century—see Joel Williamson, *Crucible*, 224–58. The most eloquent book-length treatment of the context and reverberations of *Plessy v. Ferguson* remains C. Vann Woodward's *Strange Career of Jim Crow*.

2. The most salient contemporary statement of ideology is Louis Althusser's. He defines ideology not as the illusions of false consciousness but as those class-shaped

forms of coherent subjectivity, issuing in specific practices, that organize for each of us the texture of lived experience. Terry Eagleton's commentary on Althusser, as indeed his larger exploration of ideology itself, is continuously brilliant, though not always judicious. See his *Ideology: An Introduction*, 136–58.

1. Personal Beginnings

1. Going to a Memphis hospital was, even in 1971, a race-coded activity. My Swedish sister-in-law was instrumental in this sequence, insisting on taking Vannie to the best hospital she knew of (the one my father had used often), which was essentially white. They admitted Vannie with great reluctance. As she gradually gave up her life during that afternoon, they permitted my brother and his wife to visit her at will, but allowed Vannie's own family to come into the room only one by one and only as ushered in by my brother or his wife. A few days later, the racial setting was reversed; at the burial ceremony in Somerville, my brother and his wife were the only whites present. As one of Vannie's male relatives sought to get my brother to back off—not to serve as one of the four men who lowered her coffin into the ground—my brother insisted on his place in her life and in her death. As he said to me later, she had been neither mammy nor mother (she had no children of her own) to anyone else there. He knew that, so did I, but it is not difficult to understand the offense that grieving black family members might take at a claim once more being made on Vannie, this time in her death as earlier in her life, by the white family she spent thirty-five years working for. This moment of racial friction demonstrates with perfect clarity the relationship at once deep and constructed, private and public, between white child and black mammy.

2. This paragraph and the next four are indebted in general and specific ways to Lawrence Levine's work on nineteenth- and twentieth-century black culture, Nicholas Lemann's exploration of black migration from the South, Jacqueline Jones's studies of black female workers, and Stephen Steinberg's work on post–Civil War black bondage.

3. Domestic work in white homes put pressure upon the black maid's identity in ways that go beyond the clothes that "other" her: "Once the black woman leaves the black community, she will encounter cultural differences which suggest that she can no longer be completely, comfortably, at home. She must make some kind of change in the way she acts. . . . Even if she 'loves the white folks to death,' the possibility is that she is different in her affection from that she shows when she is at home in her own community" (Harris, *Mammies*, 14).

4. I want here to register my gratitude to Hattie Mae Bond for her willingness to talk with me so openly about her family history. This essay would have been inconceivable without her cooperation.

5. See Levine (*Black Culture*, 39) for these lines from the nineteenth-century spiritual. His study of black folklore provides innumerable instances of the resources of wit, poetry, and wisdom with which American blacks survived white abuse from the period of slavery well into the twentieth century.

6. To my knowledge, little has yet been written about Mammy Callie, though I understand that Judith Sensibar's work-in-progress will attend to the role that Callie (as

well as three other women) played in Faulkner's life and work. I draw my sense of her from the Faulkner biographies by Joseph Blotner and Joel Williamson, as well as from the published reminiscences of Faulkner's two brothers. I am also indebted, in my last revisions of this book, to Diane Roberts's *Faulkner and Southern Womanhood*.

7. For the full text of Faulkner's funeral oration, see Cox, *Faulkner*, 73–74.

8. Roberts reads Dilsey persuasively as a departure from (yet covert return to) the stereotype of the "mammy," relating Faulkner's "exterior" rendering of this figure not to the modernist interiority of the Compson brothers but rather to the larger cultural expectation of "mammy" selflessness: "Dilsey is valued not for what she might reveal of herself but for what she represses of herself in giving to the Compsons" (62). For other representative readings of Dilsey, see (among the secondary readings collected in Minter's revised Norton edition of the novel) the essays by Irving Howe, Ralph Ellison, Olga Vickery, Myra Jehlen, John Matthews, and Thadious Davis. See also André Bleikasten (*Ink of Melancholy*), James Snead, Eric Sundquist (*House Divided*), and Philip Weinstein (*Faulkner's Subject*).

9. The otherness of Dilsey that I here explore derives from a white child's differential access to his black mammy. It also derives from Faulkner's recurrent flirtation with the racial stereotype of the mammy. For further commentary on this stereotype, see Roberts and Harris, *Mammies*.

10. I have explored the cultural basis of Mrs. Compson's dysfunction more fully in *Faulkner's Subject* (29–41). Roberts comments at length on the "Confederate woman" and the "mammy" as structurally defined by their opposition to each other.

11. The text is confusing on this point. All three of the blacks a generation younger than Dilsey and Roskus—Versh, T.P., and Frony—are members of their family and seem to be their children. (They appear too young in the early scenes of the novel to be anything but siblings, with Versh the elder brother.) Luster, the youngest black on the Compson estate, is, moreover, clearly identified as Dilsey's grandson. Yet the text later identifies Versh as Luster's "pappy" (38) and Frony as "his mother" (180). If this is so, then Versh and Frony seem to be married and only one of them would be Dilsey's child. The confusion is so unobtrusive that most critics ignore the crux, which further supports my claim that Faulkner's focus is not upon Dilsey's own offspring. The point is pertinent because the more the text represents Dilsey as mothering white children in place of her own, the nearer it flirts with the stereotype of the "loyal" black mammy.

12. For provocative readings of "That Evening Sun" that respect its resistance to decoding, see Laurence Perrine, " 'That Evening Sun' "; and Dirk Kuyk Jr., "Black Culture." Noel Polk's book-length revisionary reading of *Requiem for a Nun* centers upon the rehabilitation of Temple in ways that, unfortunately, further inculpate Nancy. For suggestive readings of Nancy in *Requiem*, see Moreland, *Faulkner and Modernism*, 194–238, and Roberts, 218–23.

13. Cf. Denise Heinze: "She [Morrison] scrambles the structure, locus, ideology, and value system of the family, dramatically illustrating that the home is not necessarily housed in a two-parent nuclear family but where the heart is" (*Dilemma*, 66).

14. Harris's study of Morrison focuses on the shaping role of folklore in her fiction, and she eloquently notes this abandonment of black mores for white ones: "It is unfortunate when people who do not have the economic means aspire to the pattern, but it

is more unfortunate when that straitjacketing pattern has been presented to them as normal and desirable. For black people to attain such status, to escape the colorfulness, as Jean Toomer would say, as well as the spontaneity of black life styles, reflects a self-hatred that manifests itself in Pecola Breedlove's desire for the bluest eyes of all" (*Folklore* 28–29).

15. Sydney and Ondine employ this same prejudicial usage, we might note, for Morrison is as attuned in this novel to black class distinctions as she is attentive to (grosser) racial ones.

16. But see Cedric Bryant's persuasive discussion of Quentin and the Deacon as racial portraits that surprisingly mirror each other ("Mirroring the Racial 'Other' ").

17. It is a close call as to whether Morrison's deployment of white stereotyping does not itself border on stereotype. Jadine's generalization about Margaret is acute but perhaps a bit facile. Yet the very power of Faulkner's texts shows that, while Morrison may seem to overgeneralize, she is certainly not inventing. In any event, the comment comes not from the author but from a character who has reason at this point to be annoyed.

18. Addie Bundren and Charlotte Rittenmeyer are provocative exceptions to these generalizations, inasmuch as both flaunt patriarchal injunctions. Yet their deaths (Addie's late and Charlotte's early) testify to an incapacity to enjoy the fruits of their transgression. For further discussion of Faulkner's implicit gender categories, see my *Faulkner's Subject* (11–41) and Roberts (186–223).

19. The pathology of Southern race and gender norms has, ever since W. J. Cash's *Mind of the South* (1941) if not earlier, occasioned critical commentary. See Joel Kovel's *White Racism* for an intricately Freudian account of the imaginary roles projected by white males upon black males and females as well as upon their own white wives. For more restrained and historically framed analyses of the intersection of race and gender fantasies, see Winthrop Jordan for the period up to the Civil War. Williamson (*Crucible*, 306–10) construes more fancifully the post–Civil War white male imaginary as it envisages the differences between black male and white male intercourse with white women: "The black beast rapist was the only man on earth who had sex with Southern white women without inhibition, and, *mirabile dictu*, without guilt. Black men had achieved what white men, in the Victorian infatuation, had lost—'no-fault' sex. Simple death, clearly, was too good for them" (308). Three of Roberts's chapters (the first two and the last) explore, as well, the interpenetration of Southern paradigms of race and gender.

20. No one is likely soon to surpass Harris's definition of a dewey: "A dewey is an individual who exists on the borderline between tolerable behavior and reform school. A dewey is contained lawlessness just as Shadrack is contained insanity. A dewey is rootless and uncommitted, existing from day to day with no knowledge of past or future. . . . A dewey is the physical manifestation of Eva's power to control the environment around her" (*Folklore*, 65).

21. *Jazz* refigures the maid/mammy as well. Far from Pauline's victimization and Ondine's radiant anger, True Belle serves more or less painlessly (but not sentimentally) as Vera Louise's all-purpose maid, their gender bond making manageable their racial difference. She not only adores the infant Golden Gray but will be remembered

by him, years later, as (dearer than his own mother) "his first and major love" (150). Through reflection on this intermediary black maid/mammy/mother Golden Gray finds his way, it seems, to the erotic/prolific promise embodied in the "liquid black woman" (149) that is Wild.

2. Historical Beginnings

1. Patterson's global treatment of slavery has served as an invaluable resource in this discussion. The texts on American slavery from which I have learned the most are, first, the historic texts of Frederick Douglass and Harriet Jacobs (Linda Brent), then the scholarly ones of Stanley Elkins, Eugene Genovese, Herbert Gutman, Winthrop Jordan, Lawrence Levine, Hortense Spillers, Eric Sundquist, and Joel Williamson. Elkins, following on Franklin Frazier and Kenneth Stampp, may be said to have consolidated the position that Daniel Patrick Moynihan drew on in his famous Moynihan Report of 1965. Moynihan saw the current black family as dysfunctional, and he traced this distress back to a fundamental undoing of black family values under the aegis of slavery. This view of black incapacity is one that most of the other scholars noted above have sought to overturn. Whatever their differences, these more contemporary scholars question the traditional view of slavery as an institution in which all the shaping was white and all the receiving black. Instead, and in various ways, they argue for the resourcefulness of black men and women despite the impositions of a dehumanizing system. For example, Gutman finds little supporting evidence for the claim that slavery succeeded in its aim of undermining the black family: "Adult slaves in long marriages were direct 'models,' making it possible to pass on *slave* conceptions of marital, familial, and kin obligation from generation to generation" (*Black Family*, 17). Finally, another text associated with Morrison—*The Black Book*—has been a suggestive guide. I owe to Patterson the sense of irony that attaches to the American phrase—"the peculiar institution"—for a practice common to mankind throughout history.

2. Bernard Bailyn (*Ideological Origins*, 232–46) and Williamson (*Crucible*, 5–15) both discuss the recurrently spirited American disapproval of slavery that accompanied its arrival on these shores without successfully abolishing it for over two centuries.

3. The cited phrase—"the circulation of social energy"—belongs to Stephen Greenblatt and appears as subtitle of his *Shakespearean Negotiations*. It aptly describes one of the crucial dimensions of great texts that lesser texts lack: the capacity to dramatize the larger culture's deepest convictions and (at the same time) its deepest quarrels with itself. In part 3 I return to this phrase as the keynote of an aesthetics that might replace the (mystified) Kantian criteria of universality and disinterest.

4. "Social death" is Patterson's phrase—it serves as half the title of his major work on slavery—and it means the nullification of a slave's symbolic extension in space and time (one's family, one's history) that constitutes a birthright of free men and women. Faulkner can grant Joe Christmas no place within a black community that might have served to normalize and socialize him. The extinguishing of such social identity is a definitive move of slavery itself.

5. Patterson (*Slavery and Social Death*, 94–97) and Williamson (*Crucible*, 24–35) both offer shrewd readings of the race and gender pathology attaching to an exagger-

ated ethics of honor. The main text on Southern honor is Bertram Wyatt-Brown's *Southern Honor*. Warwick Wadlington's *Reading Faulknerian Tragedy* draws extensively on Wyatt-Brown to produce a sustained reading of Faulkner's work within an honor-shame frame of values.

6. Louvinia comes perhaps closest of all Faulkner's "mammies" to the Aunt Jemima stereotype of the black woman so faithful to her white family that she will (when necessary) sacrifice her own (Louvinia does not hesitate to spy on her own rebellious son, Loosh.) Of this generic figure James Baldwin writes: "There was no one more forbearing than Aunt Jemima, no one stronger or more pious or more loyal or more wise; there was, at the same time, no one weaker or more faithless or more vicious and certainly no one more immoral" (*Notes*, 28). I am indebted to Roberts for a better sense of the resonance of this character.

7. For a suggestive reading of Drusilla's unsettling implications as scattered, so to speak, throughout the text rather than concentrated in a set of focused iconoclastic gestures, see Patricia Yaeger's forthcoming essay *The Unvanquished*. See also Anne Goodwyn Jones's briefer but shrewd commentary on this text, "Male Fantasies?"

8. For exposure of the masculine authority lurking beneath Bayard's apparent discarding of masculine authority, see Jones, "Male Fantasies?"

9. *Absalom's* insistence on revising the rules of the game—on increasing the number not only of details we must keep in mind but also of the interpretive schemas within which those details have their resonance—poses an extraordinary challenge to its reader. As Wadlington says, "If Quentin's brooding over the open book can be thought of as emblematic, we can begin with a reader's choice no less important for being obvious: to continue confronting the novel's outrageous style and structure or to close the book unfinished. Many readers have not only closed the book but slammed it shut as an affront to reading. And more than one reader—no doubt including many eventually sympathetic to the novel—can appreciate the vengeful riposte (unwittingly celebratory) by Clifton Fadiman that in *Absalom, Absalom!* Faulkner had invented a new form, the life sentence" (*Tragedy*, 216).

10. For a remarkable meditation on the repercussions of patriarchy—its fallout as experienced by women and blacks—see Carolyn Porter's two essays on *Absalom, Absalom!*—"Symbolic Fathers and Dead Mothers" and "(Un)making the Father."

11. The claim is stark, and it ignores the power of other foci in this novel, especially Rosa's account, which is fueled from start to finish by gender insults wrought into the very fabric of antebellum norms. My point is that Sutpen's class wound is the inaugurating trauma in a (near endless) sequence of repercussive wounds. I am indebted to Warwick Wadlington for further speculation on this point.

12. This chapter's focus on slavery mandates a primary concern with race. But even as I have stressed the importance of class in Sutpen's humiliation, so here I should emphasize *Absalom's* attentiveness to the gendering of inequality. It is Sutpen's sisters who reveal to him (as soon as he can decipher what is before his eyes) the demeaning roles his kind are meant to fulfill—a demeaning that he himself will continue to inflict in his relations with women, leading to his execution at the hands of the outraged Wash Jones. Women in this novel, however, are not mere victims: Rosa seeks out indirect paths of fulfillment with an imaginative energy that no male Sutpen can summon,

and Judith (in complex ways) cares for (as her own) the offspring of Charles Bon that she was kept from bearing. Both women choose impure life projects over no project at all—both refuse the all-or-nothing procedures of Sutpen and his sons—and their demise shows less their incapacity for the real (Mr. Compson steadfastly gets this wrong) than the imposition upon them of an unrevisable patriarchal design that they can neither endorse nor escape. Even Clytie goes to her death maintaining (for as long as possible) life and dignity within the returned and unsavable Henry Sutpen. Quentin may, at the novel's close, rock back and forth between hatred and nonhatred of the South; the women are busy seeking positions in between. I am indebted, in this note, to the work of Kathy Vanderhook, Swarthmore class of 1997. For further, suggestive commentary on women's possibilities in *Absalom*, see Minrose Gwin, *The Feminine and Faulkner*; Deborah Clarke, *Robbing the Mother*; Diane Roberts, *Faulkner and Southern Womanhood*; and Porter's essays "Symbolic Fathers and Dead Mothers" and "(Un)making the Father."

13. For a reading of Charles Bon's exotic/erotic appeal, see my *Faulkner's Subject*, 53–57.

14. Ramón Saldívar's essay in *The Cambridge Companion to William Faulkner* has recently supplied some of the Caribbean context of gradated racial thinking (a wide spectrum of race and ethnic identities) within which the Southern code of either-or (all white or all black) reveals its inhuman brittleness. It is possible to read *Absalom* as a prolonged lamentation that this more humane understanding of racial permutation (which functioned sporadically for centuries in the Deep South, notably in Charleston and New Orleans) has been replaced by a Jim Crow virulence that spurns all mediated positions between black and white. See also Williamson, *New People*.

15. This is one of the rare instances in Faulkner where the difference between the master's and the slave's understandings of the slave's name is pertinent. Gutman argues at length that white owners were usually unaware that their slaves typically went (among themselves) by a name different from that of the most recent owner.

16. David Cowart's comparative study of Faulkner and Morrison focuses on this episode as Faulknerian in its wry sense of dislocated parents and abused children in the grip of an inescapable historical dynamic. The problematic of naming is a commonplace in criticism of this novel. Joyce Middleton acutely notes that the text's later privileging of orality over writing casts an ironic light upon this early belittling of Macon Dead's illiteracy.

17. See John Duvall, "Doe Hunting and Masculinity," for a reading of the patriarchal insistences of the Seven Days.

18. See *Faulkner's Subject*, 29–41, for further reflection on the narrow polar options that Faulkner proposes for his female characters.

19. Cf. Valerie Smith: "Of course, however evocatively Morrison renders human suffering in *Beloved*, finally the reader experiences only narrative representations of human suffering and pain. To speak of what is necessarily and essentially and inescapably unspoken is not to speak the unspoken; it is rather only to speak a narrative or speakable version of that event or thing" ("Circling the Subject," 349).

20. Gutman writes: "Obligation toward nonslave kin was most powerfully expressed during and just after the Civil War in the attention ex-slaves gave to black children

orphaned by the sale and death of their parents, by parental desertion, and by wartime dislocation" (*Black Family*, 226).

21. For a range of speculations on Beloved's identity and role in this novel, see Stephanie Demetrakopoulos, Deborah Horwitz, Karla Holloway, Elizabeth House, Ashraf Rushdy, Barbara Schapiro, Carol Schmudde, and Arnold Weinstein. For suggestive readings of Beloved's "notlanguage," see Horwitz, Holloway, Lorraine Liscio, Schapiro, and Jean Wyatt.

22. *Ideologeme* is Fredric Jameson's useful term for understanding how ideology registers at the microscopic level of narrative movement: "As a construct it [the ideologeme] must be susceptible to both a conceptual description and a narrative manifestation all at once" (*Political Unconscious*, 87).

23. "Go slow now" is the key phrase in Faulkner's famous 1956 "letter to the North," urging Northern liberals to restrain themselves and allow the white South to work out (what he could only see as) the white South's problem. Charles Peavy's *Go Slow Now: Faulkner and the Race Question* seeks carefully to supply context and a cumulative coherence to Faulkner's extranovelistic utterances during this period. One may wonder, though, whether Joel Williamson is not nearer the mark in pointing out Faulkner's contradictory statements and decreasing interest in racial problems in the later 1950s: "In matters of race and class, obviously Faulkner simply decided to cut himself loose from previous alliances. When Paul Pollard, a black man who had worked for him in Charlottesville, wrote to ask Faulkner to buy a lifetime membership in the NAACP for him, Faulkner curtly refused. He thought that the NAACP, seeking to join all black people together in the demand for full civil rights, was in error. 'As I see it, if the people of your race are to have full equality and justice as human beings in our culture, the majority of them have got to be changed completely from the way they now act,' he declared. 'Since they are a minority, they must behave better than white people. . . . If the individual Negro does not do this by getting himself educated and trained in responsibility and morality, there will be more and more trouble between the races' " (Williamson, *Faulkner*, 336).

24. For biographical information about Morrison, see Wilfred Samuels and Clenora Hudson-Weems, *Toni Morrison*. The interviews collected in Gates and Appiah (*TM*) are also extraordinarily informative.

25. The impress of *The Black Book* (1974) on Morrison's writing was to be considerable. In addition to being a compendium of writings, clippings, and photographs charting more than three hundred years of black suffering and achievement in America, this text cited (on p. 10) a contemporary version of the Margaret Garner story. The passage, though long, is so central to the genesis of *Beloved* as to be worth quoting in full:

From the American Baptist
A VISIT TO THE SLAVE MOTHER WHO KILLED HER CHILD

Last Sabbath, after preaching in the city prison, Cincinnati, through the kindness of the Deputy Sheriff, I was permitted to visit the apartment of that unfortunate woman, concerning whom there has been so much excitement during the last two weeks.

I found her with an infant in her arms only a few months old, and observed that it had a large *bunch* on its forehead. I inquired the cause of the injury. She then proceeded to give me a detailed account of her attempt to kill her children.

She said, that when the officers and slave-hunters came to the house in which they were concealed, she caught a shovel and struck two of her children on the head, and then took a knife and cut the throat of the third, and tried to kill the other, — that if they had given her time, she would have killed them all — that with regard to herself, she cared but little; but she was unwilling to have her children suffer as she had done.

I inquired if she was not excited almost to madness when she committed the act. No, she replied, I was as cool as I now am; and would much rather kill them at once, and thus end their sufferings, than have them taken back to slavery, and be murdered by piece-meal. She then told the story of her wrongs. She spoke of her days of suffering, of her nights of unmitigated toil, while the bitter tears coursed their way down her cheeks, and fell in the face of the innocent child as it looked smiling up, little conscious of the danger and probable suffering that awaited it.

As I listened to the facts, and witnessed the agony depicted in her countenance, I could not but exclaim, Oh, how terrible is irresponsible power, when exercised over intelligent beings! She alludes to the child that she killed as being free from all trouble and sorrow, with a degree of satisfaction that almost chills the blood in one's veins; yet she evidently possesses all the passionate tenderness of a mother's love. She is about twenty-five years of age, and apparently possesses an average amount of kindness, with a vigorous intellect, and much energy of character.

The two men and the two other children were in another apartment, but her mother-in-law was in the same room. She says she is the mother of eight children, most of whom have been separated from her; that her husband was once separated from her twenty-five years, during which time she did not see him; that could she have prevented it, she would never have permitted him to return, as she did not wish him to witness her sufferings, or be exposed to the brutal treatment that he would receive.

She states that she has been a faithful servant, and in her old age she would not have attempted to obtain her liberty; but as she became feeble, and less capable of performing labor, her master became more and more exacting and brutal in his treatment, until she could stand it no longer; that the effort could result only in death, at most—she therefore made the attempt.

She witnessed the killing of the child, but said she neither encouraged nor discouraged her daughter-in-law,—for under similar circumstances she should probably have done the same. The old woman is from sixty to seventy years of age, has been a professor of religion about twenty years, and speaks with much feeling of the time when she shall be delivered from the power of the oppressor, and dwell with the Savior, "where the wicked cease from troubling, and the weary are at rest."

These slaves (as far as I am informed) have resided all their lives within sixteen miles of Cincinnati. We are frequently told that Kentucky slavery is very innocent. If these are its fruits, where it exists in a mild form, will some one tell us what we may expect from its more objectionable features? But comments are unnecessary. *P.S.BASSETT*. Fairmount Theological Seminary, Cincinatti, (Ohio,) Feb. 12, 1856.

One could write at great length on the ways in which this piece "worked" in Morrison's imagination. I mention only the following: the essential character of Sethe and Baby Suggs, as well as the nature of their relationship, are already established; the drama of murder and love scandalously cohabiting is under way; and the most eloquent rebuke of slavery is administered — for if this is the fruit of mild treatment, what does more brutal treatment bring forth? For a fuller account of Morrison's use of this historical vignette, see Wolff, "Margaret Garner"; and Sale, "Call and Response."

26. I owe this tracing of the antelope to Deborah Horwitz's essay on *Beloved*.

PART 2. LEGACIES

1. The phrase *Jim Crow* seems to have emerged in 1832 to describe a shuffling sort of song-and-dance routine thought to be "characteristic" of blacks and performed at that time by a black-faced white man. The performance was notoriously successful, and the phrase remained available for further demeaning service. A half century later it took on its political meaning as a general rubric for the cluster of laws passed in the South in the 1880s, 1890s, and 1900s that laid out (with increasingly maniacal precision) the boundaries separating black and white. For a cogent summary of the emergence and demise of the Jim Crow laws, see Woodward. For further commentary, see Williamson, *Crucible*, 50–78.

2. Cited in Williamson, *New People*, 18.

3. *Light in August* (1932) provides eloquent testimony to the anxiety with which Southern white segregationists, in a period of unraveling social coherence, contemplated the possibility that light-skinned blacks might move invisibly within their midst. "Towns that had been relatively stable suddenly experienced a sizable influx of strangers whose origins were wholly unknown. Where once it had been highly unlikely for a resident to have 'black blood' without the town knowing of it, the system of community genealogy was now doomed" (Singal, *The War Within*, 182).

4. Cited in Woodward, *The Strange Career of Jim Crow*, 81.

3. "Mister"

1. This chapter revises a paper delivered at the Faulkner and Yoknapatawpha Conference in 1994, which will be published by the University Press of Mississippi among the conference papers for that year.

2. In chapter 7 of *Group Psychology and Analysis of the Ego*, Freud undertakes his fullest exploration of the dynamic of "identification," which he generalizes as "the earliest expression of an emotional tie with another person" (105). This tie may or may

not be libidinal, and it can later occur significantly among members of a group who share "an important emotional common quality . . . [which] lies in the nature of the tie with the leader" (108). This last description seems clearly to implicate the odd bonding—affectional and rivalrous—that unites scholars mutually attached to a single author: like Faulknerians or Morrisonians.

Laplanche and Pontalis characterize Freudian "Identification" as the "psychological process whereby the subject assimilates an aspect, property, or attitude of the other and is transformed, wholly or partially, after the model the other provides. It is by means of a series of identifications that the personality is constituted and specified" (*The Language of Psycho-Analysis*, 205). Such transformative dynamics may well be the core psychic resource enabling subject-other interaction. It is therefore fascinating that Freud has, on the whole, so little to say about "identification," and one may speculate that Freud's own anxiety about "identification"—e.g., his sustained silence about Nietzsche's influence, his neurotic response to Jung's brilliance, his insistence on his own priority—is pertinent to his reticence. Freud's insistence on the successful negotiation of the Oedipal complex as achieved individuation may shed light on why he waited until late in his career before considering the radically "unindividuated" condition of the pre-Oedipal. Jim Swan speculates that, for Freud, "Maturity (that is, *masculine* maturity) means being well-defended against one's past, which amounts to the same thing as having a strong capacity for resisting identification. . . . In effect, Freud's picture of maturity is of a man driven to outrun . . . identification with the body of his mother, the original unity of mother and infant" ("Mater and Nanny," 9–10).

Transference may seem to be a rough synonym for *identification*, but Freudian analysis differentiates sharply between them. Rather than relating transference to that larger and continuing intersubjective process whereby one invests another with one's own psychic structures—or becomes oneself reshaped by the perceived structures of the other—Freudians understand transference as primitive, neurotically charged, and more narrowly enacted within the psychoanalytic encounter itself. "For psycho-analysis," Laplanche and Pontalis write, transference is blindly projective, "a process of actualization of unconscious wishes. Transference uses specific objects and operates in the framework of a specific relationship established with these objects. Its context *par excellence* is the analytic situation. . . . Classically, the transference is acknowledged to be the terrain on which all the basic problems of a given analysis play themselves out" (455). Since the interactive model of identity that I am pursuing in this essay is potentially reciprocal and enabling, I shall speak more of *identification* than of *transference*.

3. The *OED* gives twenty-three different definitions for *master* as a noun. Most of them circulate around the notion of control over something (or someone) else, and the seventh definition is typical: "One who has the power to control, use, or dispose of something at will" (2:1738). As early as the sixteenth century, British children in well-off families were addressed by servants as "master" or "young master." (The *OED*'s twenty-second definition identifies *master* as "the usual prefix to the name of a young gentleman not considered old enough to be entitled to be called Mr" [2:1738].) Remove the constitutive relation between possessor and person/thing/concept being possessed, and the term loses its conceptual core.

4. It should be clear that I am describing in an ideal or normative fashion the frame of assumptions that attach to *mister*. Actual usage varies enormously, yet the normative frame (diminished since the civil rights activity of the 1950s and 1960s but not eradicated) affects that usage.

5. Commentary on Locke is legion. For useful discussion of Locke's importance to the Founding Fathers' notions of American politics and appropriate norms, see Bailyn, Louis Hartz, Richard Hofstadter, Thomas Pangle, David Schultz, James Tully, and Gary Wills.

6. Hartz, *Liberal Tradition*, 60.

7. Webster, "A Citizen of America," 157–58.

8. Pangle (among others) notes this problem: "Locke's conception of the natural law of property . . . imposes no effective, intrinsic restriction on acquisitiveness" (*Spirit*, 161). Indeed, this abuse remains unavoidable so long as inventive labor remains, in Locke's worldview, a primary good. Subscribing to an Enlightenment project that has its source paradoxically in both Bacon and Genesis, Locke sees the scientific progress of civilization as founded on a limitless transformation of the brute, natural world. In Pangle's words, "The sum of Locke's message, then, is this: so barren is nature, so difficult is it for mankind to wrest from nature's materials a comfortable existence, that there is no ascertainable limit to the necessary growth in the productivity of human labor" (166).

9. I have developed this argument more fully in *Faulkner's Subject*, 82–109. For a rigorous classification of the different registers of Faulknerian voice, see Stephen Ross, *Fiction's Inexhaustible Voice*.

10. In an impressive essay on the "sinister" language of claim and ownership in *Beloved*, Trudier Harris demands: "Is ownership, ostensibly with love as its basis, any different from ownership by designation as chattel?" ("Slavery," 339). I think it is different, for the identifications that characterize love always involve psychic investment in the other, an investment whose potential for both good and ill is visible in that tiny terrifying pair of words so crucial to this novel: "my" and "mine." "My love" is not the same as "my property," though the former has an equivalent potential for abuse. Morrison's courage as a writer registers in her taking on, unflinchingly, the mystery of love itself: its projection (at once precious and menacing) of self into other and other into self.

11. Locke writes: "But there is another sort of servants which by a peculiar name we call *slaves*, who being captives taken in a just war are, by the right of Nature, subjected to the absolute dominion and arbitrary power of their masters. These men having, as I say, forfeited their lives and, with it their liberties, and lost their estates, and being in the *state of slavery*, not capable of any property, cannot in that state be considered as any part of *civil society*, the chief end whereof is the preservation of property" (*Civil Government*, 322–23). Locke's justificatory phrase—"taken in a just war"—may have made sense within an Athenian frame, but its irrelevance to the American scene was not lost on eighteenth-century Americans. According to Bailyn, "The contrast between what political leaders in the colonies sought for themselves and what they imposed on, or at least tolerated in, others became too glaring to be ignored and could not be lightened by appeals to the Lockean justification of slavery as the favorable fate

of people who 'by some act that deserves death' had forfeited their lives and had been spared by the generosity of their captors. The reality of plantation life was too harsh for such fictions" (*Ideological Origins*, 235).

12. Gutman's study establishes in detail the cultural reality of black marriage during a period in which it did not legally exist. He warns against a confusion of the two realms of "law and culture" (*Black Family*, 52).

13. For a fuller reading of Lucas's overdetermined relationship to Old Carothers, see *Faulkner's Subject*, 64–81.

14. Cf. Harris: "As the rooster swaggers around the barnyard, strutting for the hens present, he has more freedom and control over his existence than Paul D. As that freedom and sexual play get interpreted, Mister is also more 'man' than Paul D, more human—in the sense of having a separate, independent identity—than human beings who are slaves. In popular definitions of maleness, Mister is ultimately the 'cock' that Paul D can never become" (*Folklore*, 181).

15. Deborah Sitter comments on Paul D's model of manhood in related terms: "Although Sixo is his [Paul D's] model of a manly man, the qualities Paul D associates with manliness originate in the dominant culture of the white slaveholder Mr. Garner. These qualities include strength, courage, and endurance—all of which Sixo possesses—but they are directed toward maximizing the power of the individual to dominate weaker beings" ("The Making of a Man," 24).

16. See Carolyn Porter's two readings of *Absalom, Absalom!*'s diagnostic engagement with the patriarchy/Oedipal. Porter claims that *Absalom* most disturbingly reveals what carnage occurs not when, as Bleikasten and others maintain, the father fails but rather when, in classic patriarchal fashion, he succeeds. By the time of *Intruder in the Dust*, I argue, Faulkner was seeking to dignify Lucas by immersing him within an Oedipal structure as phantasmally intact as it was materially nonexistent (no actual father: no land, no goods, no descent—except at the level of the spirit).

17. Probably no novelist in America today is the subject of more academic commentary than Morrison. For a useful introduction to Morrison studies, see the anthologies by Nellie McKay, Harold Bloom, and (especially) Gates and Appiah. For specific readings of *Beloved* that probe (through both form and theme) the idea of the masculine "proper," see Christian, "Fixing Methodologies"; Holloway, "*Beloved*"; Horwitz, Lawrence, Mohanty, and Wyatt.

18. Maggie Sale, having studied contemporary reactions to Margaret Garner's deed, reinforces this claim: "The abolitionist press . . . represented Margaret Garner's infanticide as in the heroic tradition of the American fight for liberty . . . [but] this polemical interpretation erases the emotional cost of Garner's decision" ("Call and Response," 44). The proslavery press predictably read Garner's behavior as simply monstrous.

19. This generalization may seem top-heavy and lacking in supportive examples. I pursue in the next chapter Morrison's developing meditation on manhood, from the disastrous Cholly Breedlove (incapable of escaping white norms of authority and thus doomed to despise himself) to the resourceful Joe Trace (at home, finally, with the orphanhood—the "trace"—that wounds black men's sense of their own proper). Paul D is at midpoint in the unfolding trajectory.

20. Drawing on Bailyn's *Voyagers to the West*, Morrison develops her most haunting vignette of American freedom enacted upon the body of black slaves. Silhouetted by figures of unfreedom over whom he has (and exercises) absolute control, William Dunbar of Scotland systematically beats his American slave and then thinks of himself as somehow magically transformed within this new American landscape: "Once he has moved into that [new] position, he is resurrected as a new man, a distinctive man— a different man. And whatever his social status in London, in the New World he is a gentleman. More gentle, more man. The site of his transformation is within rawness: he is backgrounded by savagery" (*PD*, 44).

21. It does not detract from Morrison's remarkable imagination to note that the mutuality she represents occurs less between whites and blacks than among blacks themselves—and most memorably among black women. Yet Paul D shows a similar resourcefulness in his capacity to enter the subjectivity of those other chain-bound slaves in Alfred, Georgia. Their effective mutuality transforms that chain from bind to bond, and they escape enslavement the only way they can: together.

4. David and Solomon

1. As mentioned earlier, Wyatt-Brown's is the central text on the honor-shame code of the Old South. Wadlington draws extensively on Wyatt-Brown's schema in developing his argument about Faulknerian tragedy.

2. Carolyn Porter's two recent essays develop the pertinence of this Oedipal argument to Faulkner's practice. Later in this chapter I seek to open up the terms and implications of Porter's argument.

3. For a collection of essays on the possibilities of a postpatriarchal father, see Patricia Yaeger and Beth Kowaleski-Wallace's *Refiguring the Father*. Yaeger seeks sympathetically to recover some of "the father" from the Lacanian abstractions that make him somatically invisible: "To read the father [only] as 'Law' or as 'the Symbolic' misses both the fracturable dimension of the father's role and the fact that the father problem is always a multiple tale: it is the product of divergent forces; not of a single, hegemonic structure or voice" (12).

4. Irwin's book-length Nietzschean-Freudian meditation on fathers and sons in the two Quentin novels is justly well known. Bleikasten's commentary on Compson weakness (*Ink*, 83–101) is more socially angled than Irwin's, while Moreland's critique of Compson irony (attentive mainly to his role in *Absalom, Absalom!*) is shaped by a larger critique of modernist irony itself.

5. Vanessa Dickerson suggestively explores Morrison's ways of representing the bodies of Claudia and Frieda's father and Pecola's father. The former is permitted to split into a concealed "lawgiver" on the one hand and an "exposed, spontaneous, physical" presence on the other—both phallus and penis. However, "unlike Claudia and Frieda's father, who survives, Morrison suggests, because he is able to be the obscured and the naked father, Pecola's father, even more the victim of unpropitious personal, social, and economic conditions, is cast out. He lives the life of the naked father" ("The Naked Father," 110). His nakedness is that of the paternal body shorn of its patriarchal/symbolic function.

6. It is becoming increasingly recognized that the organization of family roles in African-American culture, in Marianne Hirsch's words, "radically challenges the very bases on which the mythos of the patriarchal Oedipal family rests" ("Knowing Their Names," 70). See also Hortense Spillers, "Mama's Baby, Papa's Maybe."

7. Cited in Stockton, "Heaven's Bottom," 98.

8. It is a close call as to whether her refusal to ask of black males more authority than they can give represents a conceded wound (black failure to meet the patriarchal norm) or a provocative breakthrough (black rejection of the norm). Cf. Barbara Johnson: "One of the most revolutionary things Morrison does in *Sula* is to deconstruct the phallus as law, patriarchy, and cultural ground, while appreciating the penis for the trivial but exciting pleasures and fantasies it can provide for the female characters in the novel" (" 'Aesthetic,' " 168).

9. See Terry Otten for a book-length study of Morrison's treatment of innocence. Essentially, Otten places Morrison in the Romantic tradition: "Morrison does not so much reject as invert and amplify the Judeo-Christian tradition of Western thought, imitating something of the romantic interpretation of a fortunate fall" (*Crime of Innocence*, 96). In my reading, Morrison's rejection of innocence is more radical, implying a critique of the larger (white male) orientation guiding Western thinking (including Faulkner's thinking) about innocence, in order to imagine the conditions of a permanently postlapsarian world. I argue throughout these pages that an absorption of something of the experience of her race has positioned her to envisage and undertake this project.

10. See Porter, "Symbolic Fathers and Dead Mothers," 99–106.

11. Of course, the premise of free enterprise for blacks that lasted only one generation in the late nineteenth century may be said to have begun again in the mid-twentieth. One of the major cautionary implications of *Song of Solomon* is the racial denaturing that the unregulated black pursuit of property can entail. In the figure of Guitar, Morrison most profoundly probes the conjunction of propertylessness, insistent racial identification, and a politics that, however necessary, harbors more violence than redemption.

12. For a more negative reading of the Days as black exploiters of women hardly different from their white counterparts, see Duvall, "Doe Hunting and Masculinity."

13. Morrison recognizes this need to pursue her premises all the way: "All the books I have written deal with characters placed deliberately under enormous duress in order to see of what they are made" (*TM*, 400).

14. Commentary on *Song of Solomon* seems magnetically drawn to this (patriarchal) issue, though usually without mentioning Faulkner's prior example. Michael Awkward, among others, argues that Morrison subtly transforms the white male conventions she seems to be following ("Myth, Ideology, and Gender"). My own position is closer to Trudier Harris's: "The success of Milkman's journey depends in large part on the string of female bodies, figuratively and literally, that he leaves along his path" (*Folklore*, 107).

15. I have developed this argument more fully in *Faulkner's Subject*, 64–81.

16. Both Irwin's and Martin's essays appear in Kartiganer and Abadie's recently published *Faulkner and Psychology*.

17. Quote from Peavy (*Go Slow Now*, 81), citing (with apparent approval) Faulkner's sinister criterion for black equality. At the University of Virginia in 1958, Faulkner spoke of the "Negro" as prepared, as yet, for only "second-class citizenship. His tragedy may be that so far he is competent only in ratio of his white blood" (quoted in ibid., 81). The implication seems clear: American assimilation may well require racial erasure.

18. A suggestive visual contrast between Faulknerian and Morrisonian manhood emerges if we compare two males under duress: Mink Snopes bound to the sheriff's surrey in *The Hamlet* and Paul D bound to the slaveholder's chain in *Beloved*. Mink seeks his freedom through brute and self-damaging resistance to the instrument that thwarts his will, nearly breaking his neck in the process. Paul D eventually gets free by studying the regime of the chain and cooperating with its rhythms in order finally to outsmart it.

19. Alain Locke's introduction to the anthology of creative and critical writings that he published in 1925 proudly announced the advent of a New Negro: a figure finally emerging from the "protective social mimicry forced upon him by the adverse circumstances of dependence" (*The New Negro*, 3). Centered in Harlem, come together from all over America but predominantly migrating from the South, this new black community shared "a new vision of opportunity, of social and economic freedom" (6). Buoyed by his sense of the wealth of cultural resources embodied in the Harlem Renaissance, Locke envisaged liberated blacks rising from a centuries-long history of "social disillusionment to [a new] race pride" (11) which would fuel their contemporary role: that "of acting as the advance-guard of the African peoples in their contact with Twentieth-Century civilization" (14).

20. Or, if knowledge, then of the mysterious sort that Eusebio Rodrigues proclaims: "The text, vibrant with sound and rhythm, invites us, we slowly realize, to set aside Cartesian logic in order to enter a magic world that cries out for deeper modes of knowing" ("Experiencing *Jazz*," 734).

PART 3. ENCOUNTERS

1. Cited in Leclair, "The Language Must Not Sweat," 373.

2. Morrison has at different times affirmed and contested Faulkner's importance for her. "There was for me not only an academic interest in Faulkner, but in a very, very personal way as a reader, William Faulkner had an enormous effect on me, an enormous effect," she said in 1985 at the Oxford, Mississippi, conference on Faulkner (*Faulkner and Women*, 296). When asked that evening about his influence on her career, however, she answered: "Well, I'm not sure that he had any effect on my work" (296). In an interview two years earlier she had been more emphatic: "I am not *like* Faulkner. I am not *like* in that sense" (*TM*, 408). As should be clear by now, this study places Faulkner and Morrison side by side not to show that she is "like" him—and even less to demonstrate her indebtedness to him—but in order to highlight the racial and gender positioning of two major writers. I cannot prove, in the first two comparisons that follow, that Morrison is revising Faulkner. But I believe she is, and I try to show why, through close textual analysis. Of course, she does so in her own inimitable way, producing her texts in the act of encountering his.

5. "The Condition Our Condition Is In"

1. Many critics note in passing *Song of Solomon*'s investment in the (largely white male) genre of the Bildungsroman. To my knowledge only two scholars—David Cowart and John Duvall—have published essays on this text's specific relation to Faulkner's *Go Down, Moses*. Duvall's argument (which I came upon only after writing my piece) operates on the same terrain as I do, and we share at least two views. The first is that "Ike's family problem . . . is too much history . . . [whereas] Milkman's difficulty . . . is not enough" ("Doe Hunting and Masculinity," 96). The second emerges as a question that activates a great deal of my own study: "Is it possible for African-American men to reconceive their masculinity in a nonpatriarchal fashion, that is, in a way that does not reduce African-American women to objects to be possessed?" (110). We differ fundamentally, however. Duvall focuses on issues of gender, whereas I focus on ones of race. This leads him to read the question at the heart of my book— "What else but love?"—as heavily ironic, seeing Guitar's entire enterprise as about "male power and possession" (106), whereas I see it as about the anguishing interplay of love and violence. Cowart's commentary ("Faulkner and Joyce in Morrison's *Song of Solomon*") includes Joycean references as well as Faulknerian ones; he does not pursue a sustained comparison of the two texts.

2. For commentary on *Go Down, Moses* especially attentive to the representation of race and gender, see Richard Godden, Michael Grimwood, Myra Jehlen, John Matthews, Diane Roberts, James Snead, Eric Sundquist (*House Divided*), Philip Weinstein (*Faulkner's Subject*), and Craig Werner.

3. Earlier I treated Faulkner's urge to escape the constraints of gender, race, and culture as a fantasy common to male writers. Yet we might note as well the remarkable moves to which this urge gives rise. Old Ben and Lion are outside the range of Morrison's work, and not because they escape realist criteria (Morrison likewise transgresses those criteria whenever her aims require it). Rather—and in contrast to Faulkner—her energies are devoted to exploiting cultural narratives she has inherited, and these are more likely to give her Beloved and the deweys (nonrealist figures who encode communal realities) than a marvelous dog and bear who most cleanly embody escape from the cultural itself.

4. My reference to the Romantic tradition standing behind Ike's encounter with "nature" points to the dynamic operative as well in Milkman's encounter with "nature." That is, no human understanding of nature simply registers a given set of physical phenomena. The mind always arranges those phenomena—shapes them into something it knows as "nature"—through a culture's ideological paradigms. Morrison's culture has no use for the heroic (white, male) individual alone in a natural setting—the poetics of recovered innocence—that tends to be the generic stance of English Romanticism. Thus, her "natural world," while no less shaped to reveal truths beyond human bias, is invested differently and functions otherwise.

5. I owe this identification of the "ritual of skinning the cat" as a form of "call and response" to Linda Krumholz ("Dead Teachers," 562).

6. Although I recognize class as a major alignment in both writers, I have in general focused on race and gender. Yet—in the figure of Guitar—the balked resolution

of *Song of Solomon* virtually cries out the recalcitrance of class conflict. It is Guitar whose father was destroyed by a white capitalist economy, Guitar who gives Milkman a geography lesson by informing him of the reality of exploited workers both within and beyond the United States, Guitar who wouldn't go with Milkman to the middle-class sanctuary of Honoré ("that nigger heaven" [103], he calls it) except with dynamite to blow it up, Guitar who introduces Milkman to the politics of race and the need of his people to find their way into a first-person-plural pronoun. How sterile the book would be without him. Indeed, Morrison attaches so many intransigent realities to the figure of Guitar that her decision to figure his political ardor as both necessary and suicidal shows us, yet again, this text's focus on longing rather than arrival. I am indebted, in this note, to the seminar paper of Jeremiah Dittmar, Swarthmore Class of 1997.

6. Miscegenation and Might-Have-Been

1. The best book on Faulknerian voice is Stephen Ross's *Fiction's Inexhaustible Voice*. See also Warwick Wadlington (*Tragedy*) and Philip Weinstein (*Faulkner's Subject*) for a consideration of the provocations embodied by Faulknerian voice in this novel.

2. That the female is "accident" to the male's "essence" does not mean that Faulkner ignores the "general affronting and outraging" that she suffers. Addie, Joanna, Rosa, and Charlotte, among others, testify powerfully—in their own voices and bodies—to the constraints placed by a patriarchal culture upon women's desires. I attend less to their pain not because I find it insignificant but because male pain is both more prominent in Faulkner's work and more pertinent to the argument I pursue. In like manner, to identify "Faulkner's voice" as a way of articulating Bon's suffering does not imply that his voice never accesses female suffering. My larger dilemma here is one that all studies encounter: when does the marginalizing of one topic cease to be justified by the focus on another and become, instead, a critical blindness? I can only trust that this book has shown my alertness to issues I do not foreground. I know that if it has not, this note will not make up for it. For further commentary on the capacity of *Absalom*'s women to negotiate among their pinched patriarchal options, see note 12 of my earlier discussion of slavery (chapter 2).

3. It would be difficult to discuss *Absalom* without attending to the dynamics of paternity. John Irwin (*Doubling and Incest*), André Bleikasten ("Fathers in Faulkner"), Richard Moreland (*Modernism*), Joseph Boone, and Carolyn Porter provide richly intricate readings of the father. See my chapter above for a comparative account of fathering in Faulkner and Morrison.

4. For fuller treatment of Absalom's modes for representing antebellum Southern culture, see my *Faulkner's Subject*, 131–42.

5. I owe an elegant demonstration of this "confusion" to the seminar essay (1992) of my former Swarthmore student Andrew Perry.

6. The epigraph to *Jazz*—"I am the name of the sound/ and the sound of the name"—comes, Morrison tells us, from "Thunder, Perfect Mind." Eusebio Rodrigues explicates this epigraph in such as a way as to reveal the resonance of Morrison's use of black vernacular voice: " 'Thunder,' a short tractate in the Nag Hammadi collection,

is a revelation discourse uttered by a goddess figure whose name is Thunder, which in Greek is feminine. In this tractate, according to Douglas M. Parrott, 'Thunder is allegorized as Perfect Mind, meaning the extension of the divine into the world.' That it is the thunder goddess who narrates the story becomes clear at last in the first paragraph of the final section of *Jazz*, where the words 'thunder' and 'storm,' the phrase 'I the eye of the storm,' and the statement 'I break lives to prove I can mend them again' are heard" ("Experiencing *Jazz*," 748–49). Authority in *Jazz*, as these comments suggest, is embodied in the sounded power of black voice.

7. That this "coal black" woman appears to whites as "ape-like" is of course the reason Charles Etienne St. Valery Bon married her in the first place. In an impeccably self-destructive move he has chosen a woman who incarnates, point for point, his white culture's racist stereotypes, thus throwing down the gauntlet to his white "audience" by staging, in the drama of his own life, the material enactment of their most offensive clichés. The tormented brilliance of Bon's strategy in no way mitigates the textual reification of the black "gargoyle": Faulkner is as alert to this stereotype's functional resonance—its power to wound white sensibilities—as his narrator (Mr. Compson) seems blind to its status *as* stereotype.

7. *The Circulation of Social Energy*

1. I remind the reader of a point made in the introduction: anxiety over the power of a text's cultural frame to keep that text from achieving disinterested universality is itself culturally located. White Eurocentric culture has long resisted thinking of itself as *a* culture. Morrison's insistence—"It seems to me that the best art is political and you ought to be able to make it unquestionably political and irrevocably beautiful at the same time" ("Rootedness," 345)—is welcome acknowledgment that a text's political orientation and aesthetic value do not mutually exclude each other. Nor do they self-evidently accommodate each other. This chapter seeks to theorize a model for their interrelation.

2. Commentary on Kantian aesthetics is legion; the pertinent text is, of course, Kant's *Critique of Judgment*. My argument draws extensively on Terry Eagleton's work, but it is also indebted to Arthur Danto, Murray Krieger, and Richard Schusterman.

3. Rare is the contemporary critic of the arts who does not, directly or indirectly, rail against Kant, but I will keep this final note about the aesthetics of disinterest manageable. Arthur Danto opens his book on aesthetics by speculating on the two-thousand-year philosophical assertion (dating from Plato) that art (in Auden's words) makes nothing happen. Danto wonders, precisely, about the power of art to affect its audience, given this urgent insistence that nothing (in the "real world") is taking place. In a different vein, Pierre Bourdieu critiques the avant-garde definition of the art realm as a disinterested realm scrupulously opposed to the economic realm: one where form reigns and function (the key motif of the economic) has been banished, one where reference to the commonplace world has been purified out of existence and where art objects are said to have their value not as items in a schema of exchange (once again the contaminating market) but as objects of intrinsic formal preciousness. All materialist theories of culture seek, of course, to reinsert the art object within its

social context. The most supple of these arguments, to my knowledge, are Bourdieu's and Pierre Macherey's.

4. For the general pertinence of these New Critical commonplaces to the politics of Faulkner's canonization during the 1940s and 1950s, see Lawrence Schwartz, *Creating Faulkner's Reputation*. For specific application to the way in which we read his texts, see *Faulkner's Subject*, 82–89, 156–62.

5. Jane Tompkins's last chapter of *Sensational Designs* elaborates the resonance of this question. While on the lecture circuit and seeking to rehabilitate American women novelists who had passed from enormous popularity in the nineteenth century to oblivion in the twentieth century, she encountered this skeptical question from virtually everyone critical of her rehabilitation project.

6. As I discussed above, in note 3 to my chapter on slavery, Greenblatt uses this term in his introduction to *Shakespearean Negotiations*. He goes on to examine the Shakespearean theater as necessarily engaged with the widest range of activities, economic and symbolic, that made up the social practice of the English Renaissance. Greenblatt pursues his question, "how did so much life get into the textual traces" (2) of Shakespeare's plays, by exploring those collective social practices. My procedure here has drawn on his work, but of course he bears no responsibility for the use I make of his phrase.

7. "*On this day I became a man*" (507), Joe thinks later about his McEachern childhood. The phrasing shows the importance of a male calendar, a program entailing the mastery of time, for this confused young man in search of maturation. Given this orientation, the unconscious scene with the dietitian resonates all the more decisively.

8. James Snead (*Figures of Division*) and Eric Sundquist (*House Divided*) have produced the best full-length commentaries on Faulkner's representation of race, as well as suggestive readings of *Light in August*. See also the essays collected in Doreen Fowler and Ann Abadie, *Faulkner and Race*. The most adventurous (poststructuralist) readings of gender in Faulkner are Minrose Gwin's *Feminine and Faulkner* and Carolyn Porter's two essays; see also, for discussion of both race and gender, my *Faulkner's Subject* (11–81). For further commentary on the representation of race and gender in *Light in August*, see André Bleikasten (*Ink*, 275–351), Judith Wittenberg ("Women in *Light in August*" and "Race in *Light in August*"), and Diane Roberts (*Southern Womanhood*, 169–85).

9. Part 2 of this book probes more fully the ways in which Faulkner's and Morrison's texts engage the Oedipal paradigm. Porter's essays provocatively explore the intersection of patriarchal economics, the Oedipal model of maturation, and Faulkner's fiction.

10. I do not mean, of course, that he is unsocialized (or some "wild child"), but that his culture's insistences deform rather than form him.

11. Richard Moreland ("Modernism") acutely probes *Light in August*'s formal modernist structure in order to bring to light its ideological bearing.

12. Faulkner/Morrison comparisons are being pursued assiduously (at least four panelists at the 1994 ALA conference in San Diego spoke on this topic, and a collection of comparative essays is under way), but are just beginning to surface in the published literature. For specific consideration of *Song of Solomon*'s relation to *Go Down, Moses*, see Cowart and Duvall.

13. Golden Gray in *Jazz* (whom I explored earlier in part 3) is the obvious exception to this generalization. It remains to be seen whether this figure reminiscent of Faulknerian protagonists augurs a new direction in Morrison's work.

14. As I mentioned in part 2, probably no novelist in America today is the subject of more academic commentary than Morrison. For a useful introduction to Morrison studies, see the anthologies by Nellie McKay, Harold Bloom, and (especially) Gates and Appiah. For readings of *Beloved* that probe the relation of specific textual events to the larger context of black cultural resources, see Barbara Christian, Trudier Harris (*Fiction and Folklore*), Mae Henderson, Karla Holloway, Deborah Horwitz, David Lawrence, Marilyn Mobley, Satya Mohanty, Ashraf Rushdy, Maggie Sale, Deborah Sitter, and Valerie Smith.

15. Cf. Deborah Guth: "Frozen in a position of birth inseparable from the violation she submits to—'her knees wide apart as any grave'—Sethe herself posits womb and grave as mirror images, birth as life collapsed into its negation and the mother body as the desecrated locus of African-American history: its conception an act of violation, its unfolding a play of ghostly reflections, its remembering a testimony of tortured absence" ("A Blessing and a Burden," 588).

16. Maggie Sale characterizes Morrison's intricate reading strategy thus: "124 Bluestone Road, when it was a way station on the Underground Railroad, is described as a place 'where bits of news soaked like dried beans in spring water—until they were soft enough to digest' (*B*, 65). The text of *Beloved* functions in a similar way for contemporary readers: as a textual space in which the horrors of slavery and the sometimes equally horrific responses to it by the (formerly) enslaved are not simply denied or justified, or explained away, but are presented through an empowering use of oral tradition and language so that they become *digestible*" (44).

17. This formulation is too simple because Faulkner grants to Lena in the beginning, Mrs. Hines in the middle, and Byron toward the end some extraordinary reflections in the vernacular voice (reminiscent of Darl's stunning perceptions in *As I Lay Dying*). But I can think of no other exceptions in *Light in August*.

18. The fact that Faulkner, unlike Morrison, has been severely taken to task for selective attention is more interesting than might at first appear. (It might simply seem that Faulkner is being bullied or that Morrison is being coddled.) Rather, the stakes of selective racial and gender attention are not the same for the two writers. As a white male writer ineluctably participating in a hegemonic scheme, Faulkner acknowledges silenced voices less by citing them than by calling into question the authority of white male assertion. It was crucial for him to devise a mode of writing in which he could escape the tyranny of authorial insistence. *The Sound and the Fury*, followed by *As I Lay Dying*, successfully launched this enterprise of dialogic interplay among (mainly) white voices, each voice serving as a critical counterpart to the other voices. In his best work, voice is crafted against voice, begetting (as Flaubert urged in a different context) a fictional world that interrogates its own claims. If dismantling the platform of brutality from which the master class speaks (calling into question its vocal authority) emerged as one of his supreme tasks, Faulkner's memorable work did this by emphasizing the situatedness of both his speakers and what is spoken. Morrison, by contrast, inherits a different task: less to dismantle the authority of

hegemonic voices than to establish the authority of nonhegemonic ones. It matters greatly that she can enter Valerian and Margaret in *Tar Baby*, the Garners and Bodwins in *Beloved*, but it matters even more that she can create black voices we have not heard before. I am indebted to John Matthews for helping me work out the argument in this note.

Conclusion

1. The most suggestive reading of Faulkner's career as a series of interior imaginative crises is that of Gary Stonum (*Faulkner's Literary Career*). Eric Sundquist (*House Divided*) and Michael Grimwood (*Heart in Conflict*) both chart the altering capacity of Faulkner's texts to represent race, while Richard Moreland (*Modernism*) tracks Faulkner's entry into and exit from modernist premises. My *Faulkner's Subject* attends both to the representation of race in Faulkner's career and to the crucial impact of modernism upon him. Good criticism of Faulkner during the past two decades (e.g., that of Irwin, Bleikasten, Matthews, and Wadlington) always finds an appropriate way of taking into account his modernist orientation.

2. The most sustained exploration of Faulkner's success as intricately indebted to the hold of the New Critics (many of them Southerners) upon American cultural institutions during the 1940s and 1950s is Schwartz's *Creating Faulkner's Reputation*. For a briefer and more supple meditation on the same questions, see Wadlington's essay in *The Cambridge Companion to William Faulkner*. My *Faulkner's Subject* pursues the related drama of Faulkner's becoming "Faulkner": a social reality constructed by his words and others' responses to them. For a penetrating reading of Faulkner's work in terms of race and class, see Jehlen's *Class and Character in Faulkner's South*. The two sociologists of culture whose work has most enabled my sense of the writer's practice as nonreductively immersed in its cultural context are Macherey and Bourdieu.

As for Morrison, the response to her work since *Song of Solomon* (1977) has exponentially increased. That novel was a Book of the Month selection (the first black-authored text since Wright's *Native Son* in 1940). Major scholarly journals have recently devoted partial or entire (or even double) issues to her work. Her winning the Nobel Prize in 1993 probably guarantees a "Morrison industry" for many years to come. As Nancy Paterson writes in her introduction to the *Modern Fiction Studies* double issue on Morrison that appeared in late 1993: "Since the publication of *Beloved* . . . 'Toni Morrison' has become the name around which debates of considerable significance to American literature, culture, and ideology have amassed—these include debates about multicultural curricula; about the relation of slavery to freedom; about the possibility of creating literature that is both aesthetically beautiful and politically engaged . . . about the ability to construct meaningful dialogue across entrenched differences" (465). I read these remarks after I had conceived and mainly written this book, which only shows that the questions I am pursuing here are indeed part of a larger discourse on "Toni Morrison."

3. For brief commentary on the pressure of Freudian paradigms upon Faulkner's practice, see Zeitlin's and Kartiganer's essays in Kartiganer and Abadie, *Faulkner and Psychology*.

4. Matthews's *The Play of Faulkner's Language*, Wadlington's *Reading Faulknerian Tragedy*, and Bleikasten's *The Ink of Melancholy* provide perhaps our fullest readings of Faulknerian unworkability. The present study is especially attentive to the racial and gender coordinates of Faulkner's insistence on tragedy.

5. A good deal of work (following the breakthrough studies of Sandra Gilbert and Susan Gilbar) has been done on women modernist writers. My intent is not to ignore them but to generalize the concerns of their most salient male counterparts.

6. Lukács's classic essay on this topic is "The Ideology of Modernism," but see also his earlier studies of nineteenth-century realism (especially his commentary on Flaubert).

7. For a speculative discussion of Faulkner's infatuation with the poetics of failure, see my *Faulkner's Subject*, 156–62. Beckett and Faulkner both, in their different ways, partially escape Flaubert's sense of entrapment within stifling bourgeois norms—Beckett through the Irish vignettes and rhythms that increasingly punctuate his writings, Faulkner through an abiding affection for the tropes and vernacular meanderings of a native Southwest humor. Faulkner's priestly modernism oddly coexists with a traditional storyteller's delight in old tales. For a cogent discussion of his manner of operating both these literary "genres," see Bleikasten's essay in *The Companion to William Faulkner*. As Faulkner's work tends to exit (in the 1940s) from modernist convictions, it answers less to the generalizations here proposed.

8. The phrase is Faulkner's, uttered during an interview with Jean Stein and since then widely circulated (it served as the overarching topic for the 1980 Faulkner and Yoknapatawpha conference). My 1992 study of Faulkner, devoted to identifying his immersion within larger cultural practices, is subtitled "A Cosmos No One Owns."

9. Morrison's 1955 master's thesis, written at Cornell and titled "Virginia Woolf's and William Faulkner's Treatment of the Alienated," is a brief (thirty-nine pages) and strictly New Critical performance. Questions of race barely enter the discussion. Rather, arguing from an (implicit) stance in which alienation is a twentieth-century phenomenon to be resisted, Morrison finds in Woolf's work an endorsement of alienation as the source of honesty and self-knowledge (Morrison's twin values in the thesis). She sees Faulkner's work, by contrast, attaching those same values to a strenuous refusal of the appeal of egotistic isolation. (Quentin Compson, of both *The Sound and the Fury* and *Absalom, Absalom!*, serves as her major focus in the Faulkner discussion.)

10. It is not surprising that early praise of her work inserted her into a Eurocentric literary tradition and compared her to that tradition's canonical masters. Morrison was pleased but, at a deeper level, frustrated: "I am not *like* James Joyce; I am not *like* Thomas Hardy; I am not *like* Faulkner. I am not *like* in that sense. I do not have objections to being compared to such extraordinarily gifted and facile writers, but it does leave me sort of hanging there when I know that my effort is to be *like* something that has probably only been fully expressed perhaps in music" (*TM*, 408). The complaint in this 1983 interview with Nellie McKay has been widely addressed in the past several years. Recent Morrison scholarship focuses overwhelmingly upon her work's relation to the larger resources of African-American culture. (One of the most incisive discussions of Morrison's enabling relation to a range of traditions larger than Anglo-American practice is her own in "Unspeakable Things Unspoken.") For representative commentary on Morrison's work within a black cultural context, see the works by

Michael Awkward, Keith Byerman, Barbara Christian, Trudier Harris, Karla Holloway, Marilyn Mobley, Valerie Smith, and Hortense Spillers. I close this note by emphasizing that in this book-length comparison of Morrison with Faulkner, I do not propose that she is "like" him. The value I seek in placing them side by side requires, precisely, that we hear her own cultural "music."

11. So, too, does Faulkner's work require the active participation of the other, but Morrison requires it in a different way. Unlike Faulkner, who suffered from being (taken as) unreadable, Morrison suffers from being misread—usually by being immersed within a literary tradition that is only tangential to her practice. To be misread, one must first be readable; Morrison's prose, however dense, is more concerned than Faulkner's with not losing its reader.

12. For a shrewd reading of the social dimension coded in the formal dislocations of García Márquez's "magic realism," see Edna Aizenberg, Gerald Martin, and Kumkum Sangari. For a discussion of the presence of "magic realism" in Morrison's work, see Gabrielle Foreman.

13. Morrison recurs in her essays to the folkloric dimension of her practice: "If my work is to confront a reality unlike that received reality of the West, it must centralize and animate information discredited by the West—discredited not because it is not true or useful or even of some racial value, but because it is information described as 'lore' or 'gossip' or 'sentiment' " ("Memory, Creation, and Writing," cited in Otten, *Crime of Innocence*, 2).

14. Again, the generalization is too severe. *As I Lay Dying* and *Light in August* not only delight in the traditional rhythms and vocabulary of Southern vernacular, they recurrently infuse into that vernacular a quality of sheer wonder. Here is Byron Bunch in *Light in August*, suddenly contemplating the impossible:

> The mild red road goes on beneath the slanting and peaceful afternoon, mounting a hill. "Well, I can bear a hill," he thinks. "I can bear a hill, a man can." It is peaceful and still, familiar with seven years. "It seems like a man can just about bear anything. He can even bear what he never done. He can even bear the thinking how some things is just more than he can bear. He can even bear it that if he could just give down and cry, he wouldn't do it. He can even bear it to not look back, even when he knows that looking back or not looking back wont do him any good."   (712)

15. The fact that her work appeals powerfully to black and white, male and female, might seem to call into question the race and gender emphases of my entire argument. For one obvious implication is that differences posed by race and gender cease to matter when the writing is good enough. On the other hand, a covert counterimplication might be that such differences only seem to cease to matter: when white male readers—like myself—respond to and seek to assess her work, our own positioning leads us to mistake the deepest cultural bearings of that work. My book has sought, at first, to dissent from these opposed positions, in order to work out, at last, a way of coordinating and assenting to the insight lodging in them both.

Works Cited

Aizenberg, Edna. "Historical Subversion and Violence of Representation in García Márquez and Ouologuem." *PMLA* 107 (October 1992): 1235–52.

Althusser, Louis. "Ideology and Ideological State Apparatuses." In *Lenin and Philosophy, and Other Essays*, 127–86. London: New Left Books, 1971.

Appiah, Kwame Anthony. *In My Father's House: Africa in the Philosophy of Culture.* New York: Oxford University Press, 1992.

Awkward, Michael. *Inspiriting Influences: Tradition, Revision, and African-American Women's Novels.* New York: Columbia University Press, 1989.

——. "Negotiations of Power: White Critics, Black Texts, and the Self-Referential Impulse." *American Literary History* 2 (1990): 581–606.

——. " 'Unruly and Let Loose': Myth, Ideology, and Gender in *Song of Solomon*." *Callaloo* 13 (Summer 1990): 482–98.

Bailyn, Bernard. *The Ideological Origins of the American Revolution.* Cambridge: Harvard University Press, 1967.

Bakhtin, Mikhail. "Discourse in the Novel." In *The Dialogic Imagination*, translated by Caryl Emerson and Michael Holquist, 259–422. Austin: University of Texas Press, 1981.

Baldwin, James. *Notes of a Native Son.* 1955. Reprint, Boston: Beacon, 1984.

——. "Stranger in the Village." In *The Price of the Ticket: Collected Nonfiction, 1948–1985*, 79–90. New York: St. Martin's, 1985.

Benston, Kimberly. "Re-Weaving the 'Ulysses Scene': Enchantment, Post-Oedipal Identity, and the Buried Text of Blackness in Toni Morrison's *Song of Solomon*." In Hortense Spillers, ed., *Comparative American Identities: Race, Sex, and Nationality in the Modern Text*, 87–109. New York: Routledge.

The Black Book. Edited by Middleton Harris. New York: Random House, 1974.

Bleikasten, André. "Fathers in Faulkner." In Robert Con Davis, ed., *The Fictional Father: Lacanian Readings of the Text*, 115–45. Amherst: University of Massachusetts Press, 1981.

——. "Faulkner from a European Perspective." In Philip M. Weinstein, ed., *The Cambridge Companion to William Faulkner*, 75–95. New York: Cambridge University Press, 1995.

——. *The Ink of Melancholy: Faulkner's Novels from* The Sound and the Fury *to* Light in August. Bloomington: University of Indiana Press, 1990.

——. "*Light in August*: The Closed Society and Its Subjects." In Michael Millgate, ed., *New Essays on "Light in August,"* 81–102. New York: Cambridge University Press 1987.

Bloom, Harold, ed. *Modern Critical Views: Toni Morrison*. New York: Chelsea, 1990.

Blotner, Joseph. *Faulkner: A Biography*. 2 vols. New York: Random House, 1974.

Boone, Joseph A. "Creation by the Father's Fiat: Paternal Narrative, Sexual Anxiety, and the Deauthorizing Designs of *Absalom, Absalom!*" In Patricia Yaeger and Beth Kowaleski-Wallace, eds., *Refiguring the Father: New Feminist Readings of Patriarchy*, 209–35. Carbondale: University of Southern Illinois Press, 1989.

Bourdieu, Pierre. *The Field of Cultural Production: Essays on Art and Literature*. Edited by Randal Johnson. New York: Columbia University Press, 1993.

——. *Outline of a Theory of Practice*. Translated by Richard Nice. Cambridge: Cambridge University Press, 1977.

Bryant, Cedric Gael. "Mirroring the Racial 'Other': The Deacon and Quentin in William Faulkner's *The Sound and the Fury*." *Southern Review* 29 (1993): 30–40.

Byerman, Keith. *Fingering the Jagged Grain: Tradition and Form in Recent Black Fiction*. Athens: University of Georgia Press, 1985.

The Cambridge Companion to William Faulkner. Edited by Philip M. Weinstein. New York: Cambridge University Press, 1995.

Cash, W. J. *The Mind of the South*. New York: Knopf, 1941.

Christian, Barbara. *Black Feminist Criticism*. New York: Pergamon, 1985.

——. *Black Women Novelists: The Development of a Tradition, 1892–1976*. Westport, Conn.: Greenwood, 1980.

——. "Fixing Methodologies: *Beloved*." *Cultural Critique* 24 (1993): 5–15.

Clarke, Deborah. *Robbing the Mother: Women in Faulkner*. Jackson: University Press of Mississippi, 1994.

The Compact Edition of the Oxford English Dictionary. 2 vols. New York: Oxford University Press, 1971.

Cowart, David. "Faulkner and Joyce in Morrison's *Song of Solomon*." *American Literature* 62 (1990): 87–100.

Cox, Leland H., ed. *William Faulkner: A Critical Collection*. Detroit: Gale, 1982.

Danto, Arthur C. *The Philosophical Disenfranchisement of Art*. New York: Columbia University Press, 1986.

Davis, Christina. "Interview with Toni Morrison." In Henry Louis Gates and K. A. Appiah, eds., *Toni Morrison: Critical Perspectives, Past and Present*, 412–20. New York: Amistad, 1993.

Davis, Thadious. *Faulkner's "Negro": Art and the Southern Context*. Baton Rouge: Louisiana State University Press, 1983.

Demetrakopoulos, Stephanie A. "Maternal Bonds as Devourers of Individuation in Toni Morrison's *Beloved*." *African-American Review* 26 (1992): 51–60.

Dickerson, Vanessa. "The Naked Father in Toni Morrison's *The Bluest Eye*." In Patricia Yaeger and Beth Kowaleski-Wallace, eds., *Refiguring the Father: New Feminist Readings of Patriarchy*, 108–27. Carbondale: University of Southern Illinois Press.

Douglass, Frederick. *My Bondage and My Freedom*. In *Frederick Douglass: Autobiographies*. New York: Library of America, 1994.

Duvall, John. "Doe Hunting and Masculinity: *Song of Solomon* and *Go Down, Moses*." *Arizona Quarterly* 47, no. 1 (1991): 95–115.

Eagleton, Terry. *The Ideology of the Aesthetic*. Oxford: Blackwell, 1990.

——. *Ideology: An Introduction*. London: Verso, 1991.

Elkins, Stanley M. *Slavery: A Problem in American Institutional and Intellectual Life*. Chicago: University of Chicago Press, 1968.

Falkner, Murry. *The Falkners of Mississippi*. Baton Rouge: Louisiana State University Press, 1967.

Faulkner, John. *My Brother Bill*. New York: Trident, 1963.

Faulkner, William. *Absalom, Absalom!* In *Faulkner: Novels, 1936–1940*. New York: Library of America, 1990.

——. *As I Lay Dying*. In *Faulkner: Novels, 1930–1935*. New York: Library of America, 1985.

——. *Go Down, Moses*. In *Faulkner: Novels, 1942–1954*. New York: Library of America, 1994.

——. *Intruder in the Dust*. In *Faulkner: Novels, 1942–1954*. New York: Library of America, 1994.

——. *Light in August*. In *Faulkner: Novels, 1930–1935*. New York: Library of America, 1985.

——. *Requiem for a Nun*. In *Faulkner: Novels, 1942–1954*. New York: Library of America, 1994.

——. *The Sound and the Fury*. Edited by David Minter. Norton Critical Edition. 2d ed. New York: Norton, 1994.

——. "That Evening Sun." In *Collected Stories of William Faulkner*, 289–309. New York: Random House, 1950.

——. *The Unvanquished*. In *Faulkner: Novels, 1936–1940*. New York: Library of America, 1990.

Foreman, P. Gabrielle. "Past-On: History and the Magically Real: Morrison and Allende on Call." *Feminist Studies* 18 (1992): 369–88.

Fowler, Doreen, and Ann J. Abadie, eds. *Faulkner and Race: Faulkner and Yoknapatawpha, 1986*. Jackson: University Press of Mississippi, 1987.

——, eds. *Faulkner and Women: Faulkner and Yoknapatawpha, 1985*. Jackson: University Press of Mississippi, 1986.

Freud, Sigmund. *Group Psychology and Analysis of the Ego* (1921). In *The Standard Edition of the Complete Psychological Works of Sigmund Freud*, edited and translated by James Strachey, 18:65–143. London: Hogarth Press, 1953–74.

Gates, Henry Louis. *Colored People*. New York: Knopf, 1993.

——. "Dis and Dat: Dialect and the Descent." In Dexter Fisher and Henry Louis Gates, eds., *Afro-American Literature: The Reconstruction of Instruction*, 88–119. New York: MLA, 1979.

———. *Figures in Black: Words, Signs, and the "Racial" Self*. New York: Oxford University Press, 1987.

———. *Loose Canons: Notes on the Culture Wars*. New York: Oxford University Press, 1992.

———. *The Signifying Monkey: A Theory of African-American Literary Criticism*. New York: Oxford University Press, 1988.

———. "Writing 'Race' and the Difference It Makes." In Henry Louis Gates, ed., *"Race," Writing and Difference*, 1–20. Chicago: University of Chicago Press, 1986.

Gates, Henry Louis, and K. A. Appiah, eds. *Toni Morrison: Critical Perspectives, Past and Present*. New York: Amistad, 1993.

Genovese, Eugene. *Roll, Jordan, Roll: The World the Slaves Made*. New York: Random House, 1972.

Godden, Richard. "Iconic Narrative: Or, How Faulkner Fought the Second Civil War." In Lothar Honnighausen, ed., *Faulkner's Discourse: An International Symposium*, 68–76. Tubingen: Niemeyer, 1989.

Greenblatt, Stephen. *Shakespearean Negotiations: The Circulation of Social Energy in Renaissance England*. Berkeley: University of California Press, 1988.

Grimwood, Michael. *Heart in Conflict: Faulkner's Struggles with Vocation*. Athens: University of Georgia Press, 1987.

Guth, Deborah. "A Blessing and a Burden: The Relation to the Past in *Sula*, *Song of Solomon*, and *Beloved*." *Modern Fiction Studies* 39 (1993): 575–96.

Gutman, Herbert. *The Black Family in Slavery and Freedom, 1750–1925*. New York: Pantheon, 1976.

Gwin, Minrose. *The Feminine and Faulkner*. Knoxville: University of Tennessee Press, 1989.

Harris, Trudier. "Escaping Slavery But Not Its Images." In Henry Louis Gates and K. A. Appiah, eds., *Toni Morrison: Critical Perspectives, Past and Present*, 330–41. New York: Amistad, 1993.

———. *Fiction and Folklore: The Novels of Toni Morrison*. Knoxville: University of Tennessee Press, 1991.

———. *From Mammies to Militants: Domestics in Black American Literature*. Philadelphia: Temple University Press, 1982.

Hartz, Louis. *The Liberal Tradition in America: An Interpretation of American Political Thought Since the Revolution*. New York: Harcourt Brace, 1955.

Heinze, Denise. *The Dilemma of "Double-Consciousness": Toni Morrison's Novels*. Athens: University of Georgia Press, 1993.

Henderson, Mae G. "'Toni Morrison's *Beloved*: Re-Membering the Body as Historical Text." In Hortense Spillers, ed., *Comparative American Identities: Race, Sex, and Nationality in the Modern Text*, 62–88. New York: Routledge, 1991.

Hirsch, Marianne. "Knowing Their Names: Toni Morrison's *Song of Solomon*." In Valerie Smith, ed., *New Essays on "Song of Solomon,"* 69–92. New York: Cambridge University Press, 1995.

Hofstadter, Richard. *The American Political Tradition*. New York: Random House, 1948.

Holloway, Karla F. C. "*Beloved*: A Spiritual." *Callaloo* 13 (1990): 516–25.

Holloway, Karla F. C., and Stephanie Demetrakopoulos. *New Dimensions of Spirituality: A Biracial and Bicultural Reading of the Novels of Toni Morrison.* New York: Greenwood, 1987.

Horwitz, Deborah. "Nameless Ghosts: Possession and Dispossession in *Beloved*." *Studies in American Fiction* 17 (1989): 157–67.

House, Elizabeth. "Toni Morrison's Ghost: The Beloved Who Is Not Beloved." *Studies in American Fiction* 18, no. 1 (Spring 1990): 17–26.

I'll Take My Stand: The South and the Agrarian Tradition, by Twelve Southerners. Edited by Louis D. Rubin, Jr. Reprint, New York: Harper and Row, 1962.

Irwin, John. *Doubling and Incest, Repetition and Revenge: A Speculative Reading of Faulkner.* Baltimore: Johns Hopkins University Press, 1975.

———. "Horace Benbow and the Myth of Narcissa." In Donald M. Kartiganer and Ann J. Abadie, eds., *Faulkner and Psychology: Faulkner and Yoknapatawpha, 1991*, 242–71. Jackson: University Press of Mississippi, 1994.

Jacobs, Harriet (Linda Brent). *Incidents in the Life of a Slave Girl.* Edited by Valerie Smith. New York: Oxford University Press, 1988.

Jameson, Fredric. *The Political Unconscious: Narrative as a Socially Symbolic Act.* Ithaca: Cornell University Press, 1981.

Jehlen, Myra. *Class and Character in Faulkner's South.* New York: Columbia University Press, 1976.

Johnson, Barbara. " 'Aesthetic' and 'Rapport' in Toni Morrison's *Sula*." *Textual Practice* 7 (1993): 165–72.

Jones, Anne Goodwyn. "Male Fantasies? Faulkner's War Stories and the Construction of Gender." In Donald M. Kartiganer and Ann J. Abadie, eds., *Faulkner and Psychology: Faulkner and Yoknapatawpha, 1991*, 21–55. Jackson: University Press of Mississippi, 1994.

Jones, Jacqueline. *Labor of Love, Labor of Sorrow: Black Women, Work, and the Family from Slavery to the Present.* New York: Basic Books, 1985.

Jordan, Winthrop. *White Over Black: American Attitudes Toward the Negro, 1550–1812.* Chapel Hill: University of North Carolina Press, 1968.

Kant, Immanuel. *Critique of Judgment.* Translated by Werner S. Pluhar. Indianapolis: Hackett, 1987.

Kartiganer, Donald M. " 'What I Chose to Be': Freud, Faulkner, Joe Christmas, and the Abandonment of Design." In Donald M. Kartiganer and Ann J. Abadie, eds., *Faulkner and Psychology: Faulkner and Yoknapatawpha, 1991*, 288–314. Jackson: University Press of Mississippi, 1994.

Kovel, Joel. *White Racism: A Psychohistory.* New York: Random House, 1970.

Krieger, Murray. *Words About Words About Words: Theory, Criticism, and the Literary Text.* Baltimore: Johns Hopkins University Press, 1988.

Krumholz, Linda. "Dead Teachers: Rituals of Manhood and Rituals of Reading in *Song of Solomon*." *Modern Fiction Studies* 39 (1993): 551–74.

Kuyk, Dirk, Jr., Betty M. Kuyk, and James A. Miller. "Black Culture in 'That Evening Sun.' " *Journal of American Studies* 20 (1986): 33–50.

LaCapra, Dominick, ed. *The Bounds of Race: Perspectives on Hegemony and Resistance.* Ithaca: Cornell University Press, 1991.

Laplanche, Jean, and J.-B. Pontalis. *The Language of PsychoAnalysis*. Translated by Donald Nicholson Smith. New York: Norton, 1973.

Lawrence, David. "Fleshly Ghosts and Ghostly Flesh: The Word and the Body in *Beloved*." *Studies in American Fiction* 19 (1991): 189–201.

Leclair, Thomas. "'The Language Must Not Sweat': A Conversation with Toni Morrison." In Henry Louis Gates and K. A. Appiah, eds., *Toni Morrison: Critical Perspectives, Past and Present*, 369–77. New York: Amistad, 1993.

Lemann, Nicholas. *The Promised Land: The Great Black Migration and How It Changed America*. New York: Random House, 1991.

Levine, Lawrence. *Black Culture and Black Consciousness: Afro-American Folk Thought from Slavery to Freedom*. New York: Oxford University Press, 1977.

Liscio, Lorraine. "*Beloved*'s Narrative: Writing Mother's Milk." *Tulsa Studies in Women's Literature* 11 (1992): 31–46.

Locke, Alain Le Roy, ed. *The New Negro: An Interpretation*. New York: A & C Boni, 1925.

Locke, John. *An Essay Concerning the True Original, Extent, and End of Civil Government*. In Peter Laslett, ed., *John Locke, Two Treatises of Government*, 265–428. Cambridge: Cambridge University Press, 1988.

Lukács, Georg. "The Ideology of Modernism." In *Realism in Our Time: Literature and the Class Struggle*, 17–46. Translated by John and Necke Mander. New York: Harper and Row, 1971.

——. *Studies in European Realism*. New York: Grosset and Dunlap, 1964.

Macherey, Pierre. *Pour une Théorie de la production littéraire*. Paris: Maspero, 1966.

Martin, Gerald. "On 'Magical' and Social Realism in García Márquez." In Bernard McGuirk and Richard Cardwell, eds., *Gabriel García Márquez: New Readings*, 95–116. Cambridge: Cambridge University Press.

Martin, Jay. "Faulkner's 'Male Commedia': The Triumph of Manly Grief." In Donald M. Kartiganer and Ann J. Abadie, eds., *Faulkner and Psychology: Faulkner and Yoknapatawpha, 1991*, 123–64. Jackson: University Press of Mississippi, 1994.

Matthews, John. *The Play of Faulkner's Language*. Ithaca: Cornell University Press, 1982.

McDowell, Deborah. "Boundaries: On Distant Relations and Close Kin." In Houston A. Baker, ed., *Afro-American Literary Study in the 1990s*, 51–71. Chicago: University of Chicago Press, 1989.

McDowell, Deborah, and Arnold Rampersad, eds. *Slavery and the Literary Imagination*. Baltimore: Johns Hopkins University Press, 1989.

McKay, Nellie Y. "An Interview with Toni Morrison." In Henry Louis Gates and K. A. Appiah, eds., *Toni Morrison: Critical Perspectives, Past and Present*, 396–411. New York: Amistad, 1993.

——, ed. *Critical Essays on Toni Morrison*. Boston: G. K. Hall, 1988.

Middleton, Joyce Irene. "From Orality to Literacy: Oral Memory in Toni Morrison's *Song of Solomon*." In Valerie Smith, ed., *New Essays on Song of Solomon*, 19–39. New York: Cambridge University Press, 1995.

Mobley, Marilyn Sanders. *Folk Roots and Mythic Wings in Sarah Orne Jewett and Toni Morrison: The Cultural Function of Narrative*. Baton Rouge: Louisiana State University Press, 1991.

Modern Fiction Studies 39 (1993).

Mohanty, Satya. "The Epistemic Status of Cultural Identity: On *Beloved* and the Postcolonial Condition." *Cultural Critique* 24 (1993): 41–80.

Moreland, Richard. *Faulkner and Modernism: Rereading and Rewriting*. Madison: University of Wisconsin Press, 1990.

———. "Faulkner and Modernism." In Philip M. Weinstein, ed., *The Cambridge Companion to William Faulkner*, 17–30. New York: Cambridge University Press, 1995.

Morrison, Toni. *Beloved*. New York: NAL Penguin, Plume, 1987.

———. *The Bluest Eye*. New York: Penguin, Plume, 1994.

———. *Jazz*. New York: Penguin, Plume, 1993.

———. *Playing in the Dark: Whiteness and the Literary Imagination*. New York: Random House, 1993.

———. "Rootedness: The Ancestor as Foundation." In Mari Evans, ed., *Black Women Writers (1950–1980): A Critical Evaluation*, 339–45. Garden City, N.Y.: Anchor, 1984.

———. *Song of Solomon*. New York: Penguin, Plume, 1987.

———. *Sula*. New York: NAL Penguin, Plume, 1987.

———. *Tar Baby*. New York: Penguin, Plume, 1982.

———. "Unspeakable Things Unspoken: The Afro-American Presence in American Literature." *Michigan Quarterly Review* 28 (1989): 1–34.

———. "Virginia Woolf's and William Faulkner's Treatment of the Alienated." Master's thesis, Cornell University, 1955. Negative of microfilm held by Cornell University Libraries.

Nielsen, Aldon. *Writing Between the Lines: Race and Intertextuality*. Athens: University of Georgia Press, 1994.

Otten, Terry. *The Crime of Innocence in the Fiction of Toni Morrison*. Columbia: University of Missouri Press, 1989.

Pangle, Thomas L. *The Spirit of Modern Republicanism: The Moral Vision of the American Founders and the Philosophy of Locke*. Chicago: University of Chicago Press, 1988.

Patterson, Nancy J. "Introduction: Canonizing Toni Morrison." *Modern Fiction Studies* 39 (1993): 461–79.

Patterson, Orlando. *Slavery and Social Death*. Cambridge: Harvard University Press, 1982.

Peavy, Charles. *Go Slow Now: Faulkner and the Race Question*. Portland: University of Oregon Press, 1971.

Perrine, Laurence. " 'That Evening Sun': A Skein of Uncertainties." *Studies in Short Fiction* 22 (1985): 295–307.

Polk, Noel. *Faulkner's "Requiem for a Nun": A Critical Study*. Bloomington: University of Indiana Press, 1981.

Porter, Carolyn. "Symbolic Fathers and Dead Mothers: A Feminist Approach to Faulkner." In Donald M. Kartiganer and Ann J. Abadie, eds., *Faulkner and Psychology: Faulkner and Yoknapatawpha, 1991,* 78–122. Jackson: University Press of Mississippi, 1994.

———. "(Un)making the Father: *Absalom, Absalom!*" In Philip M. Weinstein, ed., *The Cambridge Companion to William Faulkner,* 168–96. New York: Cambridge University Press, 1995.

Putnam, Hilary. *Realism with a Human Face.* Cambridge: Harvard University Press, 1990.

Roberts, Diane. *Faulkner and Southern Womanhood.* Athens: University of Georgia Press, 1994.

Rodrigues, Eusebio L. "Experiencing *Jazz.*" *Modern Fiction Studies* 39 (1993): 733–54.

Ross, Stephen. *Fiction's Inexhaustible Voice: Speech and Writing in Faulkner.* Athens: University of Georgia Press, 1989.

Rushdy, Ashraf H. A. "Daughters Signifyin(g) History: The Example of Toni Morrison's *Beloved.*" *American Literature* 64 (September 1992): 567–95.

Said, Edward. *Orientalism.* New York: Pantheon, 1978.

Sale, Maggie. "Call and Response as Critical Method: African-American Oral Traditions and *Beloved.*" *African-American Review* 26 (1992): 41–50.

Samuels, Wilfred D., and Clenora Hudson-Weems. *Toni Morrison.* New York: Twayne, 1990.

Sangari, Kumkum. "The Politics of the Possible." *Cultural Critique* 17 (1987): 157–86.

Schapiro, Barbara. "The Bonds of Love and the Boundaries of Self in Toni Morrison's *Beloved.*" *Contemporary Literature* (1991): 194–210.

Schmudde, Carol E. "The Haunting of 124." *African-American Review* 26 (1992): 409–17.

Schopenhauer, Arthur. *Schopenhauer: Selections.* Edited by DeWitt Parker. New York: Scribner's, 1982.

Schultz, David A. *Property, Power, and American Democracy.* New Brunswick, N.J.: Transaction, 1992.

Schusterman, Richard. *Pragmatic Aesthetics.* Cambridge, Eng.: Blackwell, 1992.

Schwartz, Lawrence H. *Creating Faulkner's Reputation: The Politics of Modern Literary Criticism.* Knoxville: University of Tennessee Press, 1989.

Singal, Daniel J. *The War Within: From Victorian to Modernist Thought in the South, 1919–1945.* Chapel Hill: University of North Carolina Press, 1982.

Sitter, Deborah Ayer. "The Making of a Man: Dialogic Meaning in *Beloved.*" *African-American Review* 26 (1992): 17–29.

Smith, Valerie. " 'Circling the Subject': History and Narrative in *Beloved.*" In Henry Louis Gates and K. A. Appiah, eds., *Toni Morrison: Critical Perspectives, Past and Present,* 342–55. New York: Amistad, 1993.

———. "The Quest for and Discovery of Identity in Toni Morrison's *Song of Solomon.*" *Southern Review* 21 (1985): 721–32.

———. *Self-Discovery and Authority in African-American Narrative.* Cambridge: Harvard University Press, 1987.

Snead, James. *Figures of Division: William Faulkner's Major Novels.* New York: Methuen, 1986.

Sollors, Werner. *Beyond Ethnicity: Consent and Descent in American Culture.* New York: Oxford University Press, 1986.

Spillers, Hortense. "Mama's Baby, Papa's Maybe: An American Grammar Book." *diacritics* 17 (1987): 65–81.

——, ed. *Comparative American Identities: Race, Sex, and Nationality in the Modern Text.* New York: Routledge, 1991.

Steinberg, Stephen. "The Reconstruction of Black Servitude." In *The Ethnic Myth,* 173–200. Boston: Beacon, 1982.

Stepto, Robert B. " 'Intimate Things in Place': A Conversation with Toni Morrison." In Henry Louis Gates and K. A. Appiah, eds., *Toni Morrison: Critical Perspectives, Past and Present,* 378–95. New York: Amistad, 1993.

Stockton, Kathryn Bond. "Heaven's Bottom: Anal Economics and the Critical Debasement of Freud in Toni Morrison's *Sula.*" *Cultural Critique* 24 (1993): 81–118.

Stonum, Gary Lee. *Faulkner's Literary Career: An Internal History.* Ithaca: Cornell University Press, 1979.

Sundquist, Eric. *Faulkner: The House Divided.* Baltimore: Johns Hopkins University Press, 1983.

——. *To Wake the Nation: Race in the Making of American Literature.* Cambridge: Harvard University Press, 1993.

Swan, Jim. "Mater and Nanny: Freud's Two Mothers and the Discovery of the Oedipus Complex." *American Imago* 31 (1974): 1–64.

Tompkins, Jane. *Sensational Designs: The Cultural Work of American Fiction, 1790–1860.* New York: Oxford University Press, 1985.

Tully, James. *An Approach to Political Philosophy: Locke in Contexts.* Cambridge: Cambridge University Press, 1993.

Wadlington, Warwick. *Reading Faulknerian Tragedy.* Ithaca: Cornell University Press, 1987.

——. "The Stakes of Reading Faulkner: Discerning Reading." In Philip M. Weinstein, ed., *The Cambridge Companion to William Faulkner,* 197–220. New York: Cambridge University Press, 1995.

Webster, Noah. "A Citizen of America." In Bernard Bailyn, ed., *The Debate on the Constitution,* part 1, 129–63. New York: Library of America, 1993.

Weinstein, Arnold. "Dis-membering and Re-membering in Toni Morrison's *Beloved.*" In *Nobody's Home: Speech, Self, and Place in American Fiction from Hawthorne to DeLillo,* 265–87. New York: Oxford University Press, 1993.

Weinstein, Philip M. *Faulkner's Subject: A Cosmos No One Owns.* New York: Cambridge University Press, 1992.

——. "Mister: The Drama of Black Manhood in Faulkner and Morrison." In Donald M. Kartiganer and Ann J. Abadie, eds., *Faulkner and Gender: Faulkner and Yoknapatawpha, 1994.* Jackson: University Press of Mississippi, forthcoming.

Werner, Craig. "Tell Old Pharaoh: The Afro-American Response to Faulkner." *Southern Review* 19 (1983): 711–35.

West, Cornel. *Race Matters*. New York: Random House, 1993.

Wilentz, Gay. "Civilizations Underneath: African Heritage as Cultural Discourse in Toni Morrison's *Song of Solomon*." *African-American Review* 26 (1992): 61–76.

Williamson, Joel. *The Crucible of Race: Black and White Relations in the American South Since Emancipation*. New York: Oxford University Press, 1984.

——. *New People: Miscegenation and Mulattoes in the United States*. New York: Free Press, 1980.

——. *William Faulkner and Southern History*. New York: Oxford University Press, 1991.

Wills, Gary. *Inventing America: Jefferson's Declaration of Independence*. Garden City, N.Y.: Doubleday, 1978.

Wittenberg, Judith B. "Race in *Light in August*: Wordsymbols and Obverse Reflections." In Philip M. Weinstein, ed., *The Cambridge Companion to William Faulkner*, 146–67. New York: Cambridge University Press, 1995.

——. "Women in *Light in August*." In Michael Millgate, ed., *New Essays on "Light in August*," 103–22. New York: Cambridge University Press, 1987.

Wolff, Cynthia Griffin. " 'Margaret Garner': A Cincinnati Story." *Massachusetts Review* 32 (1991): 417–40.

Woodward, C. Vann. *The Strange Career of Jim Crow*. Rev. ed. New York: Oxford University Press, 1957.

Wyatt, Jean. "Giving Body to the Word: The Maternal Symbolic in Toni Morrison's *Beloved*." *PMLA* 108 (May 1993): 474–88.

Wyatt-Brown, Bertram. *Southern Honor: Ethics and Behavior in the Old South*. New York: Oxford University Press, 1982.

Yaeger, Patricia. "The Father's Breasts." In Patricia Yaeger and Beth Kowaleski-Wallace, eds., *Refiguring the Father: New Feminist Readings of Patriarchy*, 3–21. Carbondale: University of Southern Illinois Press, 1989.

——. "Faulkner's 'Greek Amphora Priestess': Verbena and Violence in *The Unvanquished*." In Donald M. Kartiganer and Ann J. Abadie, eds., *Faulkner and Gender: Faulkner and Yoknapatawpha, 1994*. Jackson: University Press of Mississippi, forthcoming.

Zeitlin, Michael. "Faulkner and Psychoanalysis: The Elmer Case." In Donald M. Kartiganer and Ann J. Abadie, eds., *Faulkner and Psychology: Faulkner and Yoknatawpha, 1991*, 219–41. Jackson: University Press of Mississippi, 1994.

Index

Italicized spans of page numbers refer to full-length discussions of texts cited in the main entry.